The Burden of Over-representation

GRANT FARRED

The Burden of Over-representation

Race, Sport, and Philosophy

TEMPLE UNIVERSITY PRESS
Philadelphia • *Rome* • *Tokyo*

TEMPLE UNIVERSITY PRESS
Philadelphia, Pennsylvania 19122
www.temple.edu/tempress

Library of Congress Cataloging-in-Publication Data

Names: Farred, Grant, author. | World Cup (Rugby football) (1995 : South
   Africa)
Title: The burden of over-representation : race, sport, and philosophy /
   Grant Farred.
Description: Philadelphia : Temple University Press, 2018. | Includes
   bibliographical references and index.
Identifiers: LCCN 2017053973 (print) | LCCN 2018007127 (ebook)
   | ISBN 9781439911440 (E-book) | ISBN 9781439911426 (hardback : alk. paper)
   | ISBN 9781439911433 (paper : alk. paper)
Subjects: LCSH: Sports—Philosophy. | Racism in sports. | Nationalism in
   sports. | Robinson, Jackie, 1919–1972. | World Cup (Soccer) (2010 :
   South Africa) | BISAC: SPORTS & RECREATION / General. | SPORTS &
   RECREATION / Baseball / History. | PHILOSOPHY / Essays.
Classification: LCC GV706 (ebook) | LCC GV706 .F36 2018 (print) | DDC
   796.01—dc23
LC record available at https://lccn.loc.gov/2017053973

♾ The paper used in this publication meets the requirements of the American National
Standard for Information Sciences—Permanence of Paper for Printed Library Materials,
ANSI Z39.48-1992

Printed in the United States of America

9 8 7 6 5 4 3 2 1

To Andrew Ross:

Intellectual

Contents

Acknowledgments

*T*he *Burden of Over-representation* began as a very different project, with a different name. I imagined writing a book on the notion of "conciliation." That first ambition was not so much abandoned as, first, channeled into the chapters on Jackie Robinson and François Pienaar (in reverse order, mind you) and, second, more or less overwhelmed by the figure of Jacques Derrida. Without recognizing it, the project insisted that everything, including the Pienaar (and Nelson Mandela) chapter, be thought through Derrida—not Derrida only, but all the thinkings that Derrida opened up as well. This incomplete list includes Judith Butler, Gilles Deleuze, Georg Wilhelm Friedrich Hegel, Martin Heidegger, Fredric Jameson, and Jean-Luc Nancy. Important as these "tributaries" (a truly impermissible term for which I apologize) were, however, Derrida remained the main source—so much so, in fact, that all my thanks must, perhaps, proceed from Derrida and especially the provocation that I found in two of his works: *Le Monolinguisme* and *Specters of Marx.*

I have, as regards the coming into being of the book, been fortunate in having two editors, Micah Kleit, who commissioned the book, and Ryan Mulligan, who saw it to completion, entirely sympathetic to and supportive of the process through which I came to write the book that unfolded rather than making me accountable to the project I proposed. Micah was, as he has been over our long years of working together, a fount of enthusiasm, affirmation, and enduring exchange. Ours is a relationship that I value increasingly. Ryan, who inherited the project, kept me (give or take a week or three) on schedule and showed himself to be assiduous in his editing and possessed of a keen eye for what *The Burden of Over-representation* needed and just where—that very articulation, that one, right there—it required attention. Most importantly, he was absolutely present as I rewrote the manuscript, again and again, offering the right advice at precisely the moment it was needed. *The Burden of Over-representation* could not have had a better editor to see it to publication. *It was a genuine pleasure to have walked the final miles with you, Mr. Mulligan.*

My friends Ian Balfour, David Faflik, and Ken Surin were, as they have always been, exceedingly generous with their time, thoughtful in their reflections, and sharp in their assessments. Ian was especially incisive in helping me to think the Derrida chapter, and his suggestions, as they have been over more than twenty-five years, were marked by his particular brilliance. David gave freely of his time and made it possible for me to present earlier iterations of this work with invitations to South Dakota and Rhode Island. Ken offered me, as he has from 1996, the benefit of his critical acumen and access to his fount of sports knowledge—all this, laced with his gentle assurance that I was on the right path; whenever and wherever a nudge was required, he did the necessary.

David Ellison's comments were, as they always are, unfailingly smart. They also came fully wrapped in his trademark wit. My thanks go to Nicole Anderson (London, 2010) and Katrina Schlunke (Sydney, 2009) for opportunities to present the Derrida chapter(s), in the various stages of incompletion. Dirk Uffelman made it possible for me to discuss the Pienaar chapter with his colleagues at the University of Passau, and he was wonderfully creative when confronted with my many—too many, I'm sorry—requests for assistance with German translations. Those terms, as offered here, would have been infinitely inferior were it not for Dirk. Dan Johns, now an emeritus professor at Duke University, invited me to present the first iteration of the Pienaar chapter in 2010. David Andrews was the best kind of critical reader I could have hoped for: unerring in his ability to spot exactly what needed to be addressed, self-effacing in his demeanor, and always happy to discuss the fate of Fulham FC, Liverpool FC, and cricket. The Jackie Robinson chapter owes its first articulation to his invitation to present at the University of Maryland in 2009.

I am grateful to my research assistant, N. Bragg, for being able to find, without fail, whatever the project needed. My thanks go to Sharon Powers, whose skills as a librarian are matched by only her irreverence. *Retirement, it is my hope, Ms. Powers, will not suit you at all.* As always, Reneé Milligan has shown herself to be a fount of administrative excellence.

I owe particular thanks to Ron and Peg Juffer. Ron, athlete extraordinaire, is a model of unfailingly gentle solicitousness; Peg makes the best rhubarb sauce and strawberry pretzel dessert.

In March 2010, a colleague gave François Pienaar a version of the draft I had presented at Duke University. François responded in a manner so generous as to be overwhelming. It is a moment that will live with me. *Ek is bly ons is nog in kontak. Dankie, vir daardie eerste ontmoeting.*

To WM, the mixed-monotheist, for offering, at key moments and over a period of more than two years, "reassurance" (his word, almost always his last word) and, no less important, access without hesitation: شكرية

Juanita retains, as she has for many a long year now, a steadfast indifference to my Derridean and Heideggerian pursuits. Questioning, with just the right dose of mockery, my appetite for abstraction remains her signal critique. *Gracias, mi amor.* Our children continue to constitute the core of our world: Bug, who could not make me prouder; Alex, who, no matter the obstacles, dedicates himself to writing; and Nip, whose inexhaustibility exhausts, whether it is his appetite for golf, swimming, or splitting wood.

My greatest intellectual debt is, as it properly should be, an unpayable one. I owe Jeff Nealon, and that debt is sure to increase with time and with extant and future projects. Jeff's strengths are many. Among those I have benefited from are his ability to effortlessly point me in the right direction, to suggest resources, and to identify those moments when my argument has to be torqued one more time—and then again. However, his greatest contribution to my thinking has been to allow me to understand—to "see," if you will—what it is I am trying to reach for, trying to achieve. *Once more, the pitchers are on me, as they have been since our earliest days—thank you.*

Finally, *The Burden of Over-representation* is dedicated to Andrew Ross. There is no doubt that Andrew will find it just a little amusing that my book, which derives from Derrida, is dedicated to him. In true Andrew fashion, Derrida is a thinker whom he admires but for whom he has no particular affection, in no small measure because he has (as yet) found no way to use his work. In a strange way, this gets at the heart of my relationship with Andrew. Since the autumn of 1990, he has taught me to pursue as many avenues of thought as I could, and to pursue them as assiduously as possible, and/but never to be stymied by the challenges a new project presented or to be overwhelmed by the amount of work it would require. Andrew taught me to be willing, despite my reservations, hesitations, or lack of competence, to walk down every intellectual avenue. Sometimes, he suggested, I should take those first steps with more trepidation than others. But, above all, he insisted on summoning up the courage to take those steps. Andrew has been, since our first encounter, now almost three decades ago, first and always my teacher. He was a remarkable dissertation advisor. I could not have imagined anyone more fitting. Andrew taught me to trust the idea and to value it. He guided me, in his inimitable way, toward a commitment to intellectual life, a life he models in the best possible way. Much of my work would not have been possible without him. And so, for his troubles, this most ironic dedication: I thank Andrew for allowing me to encounter Derrida and Heidegger; I thank him for demanding no fealty, for rejecting the guild system, and, most importantly, for offering only support, encouragement, and intellectual opportunity— all this with the most laconic of demeanors.

The Burden of
Over-representation

Introduction

The Algerian Philosopher and the Burden
of Over-representation

I love this country [Algeria] more and more, love it madly, which
does not contradict the aversion I have long stated for it.

—**JACQUES DERRIDA**, as quoted in Benoît Peeters, *Derrida: A Biography*

It is a bracing opening gambit. His argument, Jacques Derrida insists in
Le Monolinguisme de l'autres: Ou la prosthése d'origine, is not with the
Nazis. It is, rather, this existential crisis, provoked by this country,
France, that, Derrida says, he had heretofore called his own—this language, French, that he not only had inhabited but also preferred over the
"native tongue," the language, Arabic, that surrounded him (or, to phrase
this in colonial terms, Arabic, the language of the "other" that surrounded
him). And yet, one suspects from the silence around Arabic (because of its
otherness, no doubt) that it was a language that Derrida was not even, if
truth be told, fully aware of but that nevertheless haunted him, even
though, we might argue, he could not have begun to comprehend the power
of that haunting while growing up in El Biar, a neighborhood in the hills
above Algiers.

In El Biar Derrida lived at a remove from the language and culture that
is Arabic. In his biography of Derrida, Benoît Peeters, in comparing Derrida
to one of those other famous *pieds-noirs,* Albert Camus, insists that this
"French-Muslim Algeria, for which Camus had always striven, is what Derrida too wishes for" (*Derrida*).[1] Derrida was born, as it were, into French; it
was the language in which he learned to speak until he recognized that this
language, French, was not, despite all appearances to the contrary, his.

In *Le Monolinguisme* Derrida renders his condition in a wonderfully
succinct phrasing, one full of provocation for thinking the relation of the
self to language. "'I have only one language,' Derrida proclaims; "it is not
mine.'"[2]

It bears repeating: "I have only one language[;] it is not mine." How can the language that you "have," that is in your possession, as much, no doubt, as it possesses you (wherein may lie the rub), not be yours? It is to this conundrum, if "conundrum" is at all the proper term for what it is we are grappling with, that we return, repeatedly, in the course of this Introduction. We turn to it again and again in no small measure because bearing the burden of a "Derridean" language that is, that is not, yours, addresses directly the difficulty of the burden of over-representation. What does it mean to "present" yourself, to put yourself before the world, to have the world understand—and here the issue of translation must not, of course, be overlooked, though we do not linger over it here, important as it is—you in the "one language" that you have that is "not yours?"

As such, the Derridean condition provides the conceptual terms, broadly speaking, for thinking about the ways in which the logic (we might also name it an "il-logic" without detracting from it in the least) of the "language that is not mine" functions in relation to the other two figures in *The Burden of Over-representation*. For Jackie Robinson, where language must be understood as transgression (the expletive, the expletive as the event of race/racism), and for François Pienaar, where the (verbal) act of thanking—making of the pro forma "Thank you" a historical and historic moment—presents itself as the political displacement (and, the usurpation, in truth) of the other, the difficulty of speaking in excess of the self is raised, for each in his own particular way. But, for Robinson and Pienaar, language is nothing other—nothing less than—the articulation of record.

Distilled to its essence, the burden of over-representation turns on a relation to a sociopolitical phenomenon, in this language and/or race assumes primacy, where the self—Derrida, Robinson, Pienaar—is made to speak in such a way that makes its speech, its political intervention, at once exemplary, and, as such, excessive. (It is, as such, an excess that, leaving the self no choice, overdetermines the possibility of its responses to and in the world.) The self is at once distinct from and exceptional within its own political constituency. The overdetermined self is, precisely because of its exemplarity, required (indeed, expected) to exceed the normative expectations that are assigned its community. In the event of each of these three figures, their exceptionality is not, and never will be, in question. As such, because of their irreproachable and incontestable singularity, the burden of intervention, of speaking for, of speaking as, is intensified—making demands on them that are ceaseless and inescapable; they are always subject to the expectation of standing in for, standing as—and, because of this, each of them, in his turn, in the languages within and against which they struggle, in the language that they use in the process of making the event, makes evident the range of effects, politically inconsistent, linguistically unexpected, contextually incommensurate (with each other, as they should be) as they may be, that flow from the burden of over-representation, that particular burden that evokes at once, in Derrida's phrasing, "mad love" and determined "aversion." That is, in-consistency, infinite indeterminacy.

Through sport, the burden of over-representation, in the event of Robinson (baseball), Pienaar (rugby—and, it is, of course, acknowledged that Pienaar's singularity is unthinkable except in its relation to Nelson Mandela and the event of a post-apartheid South Africa), and Derrida, renders the political "visible" and thinkable in such a way as to understand over-representation as that which not only locates the exceptional individual disjunctively within his (or her) community but also, and this is a matter of some consequence, dis-locates him (or her) from that community. The effect of this dis-location, which is always subject to rearticulation, is to disrupt our—first, primary, deeply held—understanding of the figure in such a way as to make it imperative that we re-locate this exceptional individual, that we situate a Derrida or a Robinson differently, situate each, literally, in Derrida's case, "first" in an-other place, in the place of the other, that other place that is also theirs, sometimes unbeknownst to them. That is, over-representation is understood as, in different ways, "burdensome" to the figure under discussion and to the critic who undertakes the work of re-location because it demands its own specific responsibility; over-representation as such is the burden of responsibility that must be borne by the exceptional athlete (the out-of-place figure who is reaching for an-other place).

That is, having flung, say, Pienaar out (not so much into) from the world with which he is almost unfailingly associated (white, rugby-playing, intensely masculinized apartheid South Africa), the burden of responsibility imposes on the critic, without the possibility of (political) relief, the demand of accounting for this thinking, demands a thinking for and accounting of the effects of over-representation, demands an understanding, it is important to note, of the costs as well as the possibilities that emanate from the critique of over-representation. What happens in the process of such re-location? Such a re-assignment? And, as Derrida would insist, such a renaming?

It is in this way that Derrida's painful grappling with relation, a response hardly unfamiliar to the foreigner made citizen or the diasporic subject,[3] to the immigrant or the refugee, that oscillates between "love" ("mad" though it be—is "love" ever anything else?) and "aversion," delineates the terms for thinking the burden of over-representation. Not quite as, say, a poisoned chalice (tempting as such a conception might be, it is insufficient for the demand at hand), but rather as something more akin to a relentless,

restless (such are the effects of deracination) movement between attraction
to and loyalty for (this "country I love more and more") and a profound discomfiture with "that" place that can never be overcome. This is precisely
why one cannot negate the force of "mad love." As such, the burden of over-
representation almost always turns on the inability to not love, to render
the condition as a double negative, as much as it does to "consummate"
(with any enduring satisfaction) this "mad love," this self, this love, this love
of self, made "mad" by love, this love that cannot sustain the self in the only
language through which this "mad love" can be expressed. There is, then,
always the threat inaugural to the burden of over-representation: that it
will overwhelm those whom it subjects to the condition. To borrow, in this
regard, a phrase from Jacques Rancière, "Excess is the essence of the promise": The founding premise of the burden of over-representation is that it
must, it will, "exceed" the capacities of the self but, in so doing, in laying
bare the "limitations" of the self, it reveals the full extent (that is, its potentially massive debilitation of the self) of the hubris, so to speak, of this
burden. The effect of over-representation is to at once enfold the self within
it-self (the condition of over-representation) and then to almost submerge
that self beneath the weight of the attendant expectations.

In this way, the paradox is that (loosely speaking) the burden of over-
representation is indifferent to the fate of the self as much as it can articulate itself only through and because of that self; the very condition of
over-representation begins with and can happen only because of the (exceptional) self. This is not to locate the self as helpless. It is, rather, to locate the self fully within the workings and the imbrication of the burden
of over-representation, to begin a first delineation of what it means for
figures such as Derrida, Pienaar, and Robinson to bear this burden. It is
also to acknowledge, in advance, that even when the burden of over-representation is assumed "willingly" (though to imagine such an acceptance
is to veer, deliberately and without recourse, into the Christological, to
conjure up the specters of Jesus-the-Christ and the crucifixion or a St.
Christopher deciding to shoulder the sins of the other, again and again,
making of him a latter-day, "lesser" Jesus-the-Christ), it is impossible for
the self to ever understand the sheer scope, the extent of personal vulnerability (such responsibility always includes the possibility of fatality), and
the relentless demands that are constitutive of such an act. (Again, the
Christological can be invoked, if only as a counterpoint this time: "Lord,
let this cup pass me by," to render the event of Gethsemane in the vernacular. An object lesson in that it illuminates and crystallizes the refusal that knows itself as a futile political gesture. The crucifixion, then,
as the cup that must be drunk from, the crucifixion as the event that
turns on absolute responsibility, the responsibility to sacrifice the self in

the cause of the universal other.) As such, the burden of over-representation always operates—anything but mechanistically, which is to say it cannot be foretold or made to follow a script—on the order of the event. It is predictable (only) in its unpredictability; we anticipate it but are never truly prepared for it and it is, thus, punctual *only* on its own terms. The event adheres to its own "schedule" insofar as we can imagine the "timetable" of the event; the event arrives (only) in its own good time.

The event of dislocation, then, the relocation and rearticulation of Jacques Derrida "from" Europe, a Europe to which he has never fully committed himself and in which he could never fully immerse (or invest) himself, to Algeria (and, by extension, to the Maghreb, and, by further extension, to Africa, especially in Derrida's affinity for South Africa, both in his anti-apartheid stance and in his support for Nelson Mandela after the end of apartheid), positions Derrida as the "paradigmatic" figure for thinking the burden of over-representation. By delineating the terms under which Derrida might be understood as a philosopher of and from "French Muslim Algeria," from the Maghreb and Africa, I work here through *Le Monolinguisme* to suggest how the burden of over-representation might be thought in relation to Pienaar, Mandela, and Robinson, the three other figures who are the subjects of *The Burden of Over-representation*.

Thinking Derrida, first, here as the focal point of the Introduction, and then last, because he is the subject of Chapter 3, "I Think I Saw Jacques Derrida at the 2010 World Cup in South Africa," is of consequence because *The Burden of Over-representation* runs through Jacques Derrida insofar as it is his oeuvre that serves as the philosophical lynchpin, the point of departure (and, again, in the spirit of Friedrich Nietzsche, the point of endless if not "eternal" return) for how Pienaar, Mandela, and Robinson are considered— or, as Derrida would have it, "written." In purely chronological terms, which must not be understood as signaling a certain "terminality," *The Burden of Over-representation* also runs *to* Jacques Derrida in that Derrida bookends the project—this book works with and toward the thinking of Jacques Derrida. To that end, this book opens and, as it were, "closes," with Derrida: We are never very far from Derrida, as he haunts (in the terms of his notion of hauntology) the writing of Pienaar (who is "paired" with Mandela) and Robinson. Derrida's "voice," and what he enables us to give voice to, how his voice is brought into question (as a consequence of, as Chapter 3 makes evident, his own provocation), and what questions it allows *The Burden of Over-representation* to open up to, to open onto, resonates throughout this text.

However constitutive as it is of the project, Derrida's thinking by no means overwhelms the other figures. So much so that while the central category of this book's inquiry, the burden of over-representation, inflects, informs, and gives theoretical shape to all three chapters, different modalities of thinking obtain in "Stupid Bastards" (Chapter 1, on Robinson) and "Thank You, in (a) Sense" (Chapter 2, on Pienaar and Mandela). Modalities, it should be said, that do not always coincide exactly with how the burden of over-representation is thought. The politics of the expletive, inferred easily enough from the title of the chapter, and the ways in which the expletive concatenates race, sociopolitical expectation, and political repression (so that the burden of expectation cannot but limn the chapter's critical apparatus) are the dominant conceptual techniques in the Robinson chapter. In Chapter 2 the politics of refusal (Pienaar's insistence that "thanks" are not Mandela's to give but, to phrase this in Christological terms, to receive—"It is more blessed to give than to receive,"[4]—in its own way, of course, re-turns us to the burden of representation because both Pienaar and Mandela, at a pivotal moment in this newly democratized society, perform such important symbolic functions in and for their respective communities: rugby-mad Afrikaners and the oh-so-recently enfranchised black South African population), which, in a different context with some of the same resonances ("specters"), raises in its turn not only the issues of race, oppression, forgiveness, and the violence without which forgiveness is impossible (here again Derrida's work is crucial) but also how these several political dynamics are brought to life through sport, is the line of critique through which the chapter proceeds.

And it does so by making a signal claim on Derrida as thinker, as a thinker who brings, contrary to Stanley Cavell's critique, the "ordinary"— the "ordinary" language and thinking that surrounds and emanates from and through sport—into philosophical fullness. Or it is only through philosophy that we can understand the many layers of difficulty that adhere within, that constitute, sport. In his work *A Pitch of Philosophy: Autobiographical Exercises,* Cavell dedicates a chapter to Derrida's "famous encounter with Austin's work . . . [in] Jacques Derrida's 'Signature Event Context.'"[5] Cavell's Derrida chapter is preoccupied with "voice," Derrida's privileging of writing (which alone for Derrida can "authorize the seriousness or innerness of thought"), and, most importantly for Cavell, the distinction between "metaphysical and ordinary language . . . between what may be called the metaphysical and ordinary voice."[6] According to Cavell, Ludwig Wittgenstein and J. L. Austin argue against the preeminence of the metaphysical voice because it leads to the "suffocation of the ordinary voice."[7] The "irony of Derrida's work," Cavell asserts, "is that it contributes to this suffocation of the ordinary; I call it a continuation of philosophy's flight from the ordinary."[8] By thinking Pienaar (and Mandela) and Robinson through *Le Monolinguisme, The Burden of Over-representation* arrives at a very different conclusion. The "voice" of sport (the many voices that sport, and only sport, articulates, can articulate), a voice that is endemically "ordinary"[9] if it is anything at all, is liberated from the "suffocation" of philosophical indifference to which sport is routinely (if not always) subjected. It is Derrida's insistence on how one thinks, thinks sport, that makes his brand of philosophy—his mode of thinking about the world, in its peculiar, particular ordinariness—such a provocative, difficult (which is what the work of thinking must be), and generative fit for the event of sport, for the event in sport. After all, few other human activities apart from politics and the economy, as I have argued elsewhere,[10] turn so insistently on "the event," and the event is nothing if it is not the first condition for thinking, for thinking from, with, and because of the "ordinary."

The effect of Derrida's thinking is not, as Cavell claims, to deny voice to the "ordinary," but to liberate it into philosophy and, as such, to return philosophy, as it properly should, to the "ordinary." The effect of thinking sport through Derrida's philosophy is to refuse, without denying their different modes of apprehension, the distinction "between metaphysical and ordinary voice." It is, instead, to embrace without reservation what Cavell names "unlimited difference, strangeness, distance, and so on" (*A Pitch of Philosophy*).[11] The lure/allure of sport is that it grounds our love for football or baseball precisely in how "strange"—the event is full of, is nothing but, a series of, surprises—it can be, how through it the miraculous unfolds before our very eyes, how poetic beauty manifests itself in the "strangest," least-expected moments or encounters (read Eduardo Galeano's *Football in Sun and Shadow*[12] as a most stylistically inventive case in point), how it can situate us as fans at once in an intense proximity to the event and yet leave us inexplicably removed. No one sporting event, in either the banal or philosophical sense of the term, is ever like any other sporting event. "Unlimited difference" proliferates; it is the very stuff of sport; it is why athletes compete; it is why spectators watch; it is why partisans dedicate their very waking hours to following the fortunes of their club, patriots swear allegiance to a national team, or besotted fans proclaim—against all scientific evidence—that they "bleed blue" or "green" or "gold and black." No one result, whether that be defeat or victory, is ever like any other. Every sporting encounter contains within it the potential for the event sui generis.

The Burden of Over-representation, then, much as it leads through and to Derrida, does so in a way that seeks to "weave" Derrida's thinking into the critique, invoking his work at strategic moments but remaining as true as possible to thinking these three sports events in the spirit of the Derridean "ordinary."

Appropriately, given how much of the Derrida chapter is figured through the ghost of William Shakespeare's *Hamlet*, we might say that rather than being drawn on consistently, Derrida's work is the in-consistently spectral presence that gives *The Burden of Over-representation* its philosophical shape—as well as providing, relentlessly, as only the ghost can, the theoretical apparatus and impetus for thinking Derrida, Robinson, Pienaar, and Mandela through, and because of, needless to say, sport.

To this end, the remainder of the Introduction is an attempt to account, in the most provocative and in-complete way, for the ghost that constitutes, that brings to life, that gives philosophical shape to, and that stands as among the most important of Derrida's addresses to a (formative, so to speak) political issue, that of "origin," that of the site of the "first thinking," we might speculate, that—on the surface of it, his oeuvre, that is—for so long lies dormant, is for so long ignored. And/or, perhaps we should say "but," at the moment—and it is for this reason that *Le Monolinguisme* is the text of record, as it were—that it "finds" articulation in this "late-Derrida" text; the extent to which it has so long haunted Derrida reveals it as long present, long since constitutive of, his thinking, so much so that it seems, I would venture, "obvious." That "issue," as I have tentatively named it, is, of course, Algeria. And, this writing of Derrida is undertaken fully aware of Derrida's deep suspicions of "origins" as such.

In this way, *The Burden of Over-representation* is a struggle with, in struggle with, Derrida; it is, because of the argument, itself grounded in a massive speculation, the ghost of Jacques Derrida at the 2010 World Cup in South Africa (a speculation of the most precarious or perilous, Derrida might prefer, order), something of a "historical" argument, to phrase the project crudely, not so much with Derrida, as how to write (think) Derrida. And, importantly, the ghost that provoked the writing of *The Burden of Over-representation* is a ghost of the "geopolitical" variety, a ghost that haunts the writer writing Derrida here, which makes of this, to begin with (again) a most precarious and tentative engagement. That is, given how Algeria haunts Derrida, and given Derrida's preoccupation with South Africa, *The Burden of Over-representation* is—in a singular fashion—a text written between the African continent's two poles, north and south. (In truth, it is written from two Mediterranean locales in Africa, El Biar and Cape Town, which have hardly ever, to my mind, been put in conversation.) And, as such, following its own logic, it is a peculiarly "African thinking" of Derrida, an "African thinking" complicated, illuminated, and made possible by the experience of the diaspora, by the experience, appropriately, of dislocation—a dislocation, a rude deracination, that is, each in its own way, violent and yet provoking out of its violence a philosophical fecundity that might otherwise not have been imaginable.

In this way, the "long silence" (if such a conditional critique might be, for a moment, permitted) about Algeria that pervades Derrida's work finds echoes, resonances, and political as well as philosophical reverberations in Jackie Robinson's "sociopolitical" repression (the unspeakable, the mis-representation that forms Robinson's burden of over-representation; what Claude Lévesque names, in his roundtable discussion with Derrida, the unavoidable encounter with exemplarity, "exemplarization").[13] It is, then, the African American figure, in a quite unexpected way (such, of course, is the logic of the event), who bridges the three African figures, a concatenation, a linking among three continents (Africa, Europe, and North America), that enables this thinking to proceed from, through, and to Jacques Derrida by way of Jackie Robinson, the Brooklyn Dodgers, and U.S. racism—among the other pathways that *The Burden of Over-representation* follows, meanders along. It is ghostly enough, isn't it, that the Introduction and the opening chapter of this book feature two men, continents apart (continents triangulated), who share, one for his entire life, the other for only his youth, the name "Jacky/Jackie." "Jacky"—"Jackie"—"Jacques." (North) Africa—United States—Europe/United States. Concatenations, echoes, resonances, names repeating homonymically, without interruption, because of sport, because of figures otherwise entirely unrelated. (One hears "Jacky" as "Jackie"; there is, for the ear, no possibility of distinction. Maybe this is what it means for Derrida to hear his name, "Jacques Derrida," spoken in the "ear of the other," to borrow from Derrida's 1979 colloquium on "otobiography," "autobiography," and "translation."[14] How could "Jacky" not be heard as indistinguishable from "Jackie"? In the "ear of the other" fine distinctions in spelling mean nothing, nothing at all.)

It is only through sport, through the politics of sport, through the event that sport alone can make legible, that the ghosts of Vichy French anti-Semitism, the early civil rights struggle against racism, and the exchange of thanks between an iconic black and a white South African in the aftermath of apartheid (the ink on a promising nonracist democracy had barely dried), that Shakespeare's ghost can be mobilized to think the burden of over-representation.

Furthermore, in the Robinson and Derrida chapters, two of Shakespeare's major tragedies, *Othello* and *Hamlet,* are called into action, called to duty, in the explication of the burden of over-representation. The specter of the Moor haunts the writing of Robinson, not to the same extent that the ghost of King Hamlet is formative to the thinking of Derrida, the ghost of Derrida at the *Coupe du monde,* but present enough to provide the metaphorical language—"Rude art thou in speech" (*Othello*)[15] and "Speake to it" (*Hamlet*)[16]—critical to the writing of the groundbreaking baseball player and the one-time amateur footballer.

To borrow from, while simultaneously revoking, Duke Orsino's opening lines from *Twelfth Night:*

If music be the food of love, play on;
Give me excess of it, that, surfeiting,
The appetite may sicken, and so die.[17]

In this spirit, *The Burden of Over-representation* can be said to function on a principle more properly or, at least more playfully, understood as "If baseball/football be the food of love [as it is for countless millions], play on." The intent, unlike for the love-stricken duke, is to "quicken the appetite," and to think rigorously—with the utmost pleasure—so that such a thinking of sport, that conjuncture where sport, philosophy, race, diaspora, sociopolitical repression, et al. come into glorious contact and combat, may be made "healthy" for a thinking far in "excess" of the promise and potential contained individually in each of these concepts, in each of these modes of being. It is to indulge fully in "flights of fancy" so that, to again deliberately misread the duke, such a thinking "alone is high fantastical" (*Twelfth Night*).[18]

And so, this "flight of philosophical fancy," this dalliance with onerous political burdens, begins in a language, *le monolinguisme,* that, in Derrida's terms, refuses his right to "ownership" even as, without the right to any historical recourse, it claims him. It claims him, if not fully, then so nearly fully as to be indistinguishable from laying full and unapologetic claim to Derrida, to Derrida beyond this world but still a Derrida who is entirely of and beyond Paris, entirely of and beyond France, and entirely of and beyond Euro-American philosophy. A Derrida, in short, who makes impossible any kind of representation that is restrictive, territorial, sovereign, yet a Derrida who will not cede his right to be—to be-long, to be of—these places. As much as, that is, even though, these places can no longer be understood to stand—to function in their difference—at a remove from El Biar or, for that matter, South Africa. Representation, in short, as absolute entanglement, as the desire—the deepest desire—for an impossible sovereignty. The self as nothing less than that mode of being that is, at once, by turns, all the time, haunted by every place that touches it, that it has touched. The self as simultaneously in struggle with itself and reveling in the joys of its many entanglements. Derrida, then, as belonging in un-equal parts (a difference beyond measure, a difference whose distinctness must always be thought, counted, accounted for) to "Les Bleus" (the French team) and to the "Renards du Désert" (Desert Foxes) of Algeria. Derrida, to phrase the matter lightly and awkwardly, as *le tricolor renard*—the "three-colored fox." Chameleon-like, he can change his colors, and, like the fox, he is inveterately wily, beguiling us, bewitching us, seducing us into the most perilous certainty. That is, the unspoken promise—that promise that we would swear he made to us, made to us just yesterday—that he belongs, has always belonged, to only us. In short, in that presenting himself, he is, even though the promise is only an imagined one (it is, after all, the only way to inscribe our desire, to make our desire override his), representing us. It is, then, not only that Derrida is haunted by all places but also that the site of his most intense and enduring, and therefore most elusive, haunting is us. All the claims we make on him, every time we ask him to stand for something, for someone (us, of course, first, primarily), brings to life yet one more instance of his capacity to haunt us. In the spirit of *Hamlet,* we might take the liberty to paraphrase Marcellus and ask of Derrida, as Marcellus asks of Horatio, "Speake for us, Jacque, thou art," in no particular order, "an African/a philosopher, a French philosopher, the last colonial European who has no language but his own for living in Europe." The gift of the ghost is that, if we insist enough, we are liable to hear our own desires fulfilled, it echoes of our own mangled voice, our own voice distorted and made alien by the visor that shields the ghost from us. The gift of the ghost is that it refuses, in the final instance, to shield us from ourselves.

Colonial Derrida

> Thus as men with a vocation we may permit ourselves to be indifferent to everything else, and we have an eye only for this horizon of our world and for its own actualities and possibilities—those that exist in this "world." (Husserl, *Crisis of European Sciences*)[19]

Edmund Husserl warns against delimitation, he argues against the vocational impulse that causes men "to be indifferent to everything" but that which their vocation designates as important. It is possible to imagine Husserl's critique as an address between two Jewish intellectuals (or between, say, the Jewish-Lutheran Husserl[20] and Derrida's occasional naming of himself as a Jewish-Catholic), two intellectuals each in his own way significantly affected by the rise and consequences of National Socialism in such a way as to bind Husserl's post–World War I Germany (the founding and the dissolution of the Weimar Republic) to Derrida's Algeria. Most saliently, in this regard, Husserl is cautioning against the thinker who trains his "eye only" on the "horizon of his world and for its own actualities and possibilities." It is necessary, Husserl suggests, to always look beyond and to think in excess of the constraints of these self-same "actualities and possibilities."

Derrida writes the "actualities" as well as the "possibilities" of colonial Algeria long after the event of wartime disenfranchisement. (One of these "actualities," of course, was the desubjectivation that derived from his being Jewish—that act, emanating from Vichy Paris, that legally inscribed him as "Jew.") Derrida writes in his new (it is of course hardly new) guise as a diasporic thinker who understands himself as having been disenfranchised—as well as desubjectivated—before he was diasporized. And, we should add, before he became a postcolonial subject as such. Derrida reminds us of his overdetermined condition in *Le Monolinguisme*:

> Algeria has never been occupied. I mean that if it has ever been occupied, the German Occupation was never responsible for it. The withdrawal of French citizenship from the Jews of Algeria, with everything that followed, was the deed of the French alone. They decided that all by themselves, in their heads; they must have been dreaming about it all along; they implemented it all by themselves.[21]

It was not, Derrida is emphatic, the Nazis who disenfranchised him. No, it was Vichy France that enacted that law. The right of Jewish citizenship withdrawn not (if we might invoke Carl Schmitt here) by the enemy but by the "friend," the putative friend, the occupying colonial power—and, as such, a state, France, technically also (still) at war with the Nazis. The "friend," we should say, who is in effect not a friend because for Vichy France the Jewish schoolboy, expelled from Lycée Ben Aknoun in 1942 (at the age of twelve), for no reason other than being Jewish, is an enemy. If not an enemy, then he is certainly not a valued friend.

The blame for Jewish Algerian disenfranchisement lies, and here Derrida is unambiguous, not with Hitler. No, the blame rests squarely on the shoulders of Marshall Pétain and the anti-Semitic "dreams" that had long been resident in French "heads." If, as Julia Kristeva argues in her critique of Paris 1968, we can only achieve "salvation through desire, i.e., without desire no salvation,"[22] then what Derrida confronted in Vichy France—from afar, from the periphery that rearticulated his standing as political subject, or non-subject, his monolingualism notwithstanding, of the historic Jewish diaspora—was the exclusionary violence of the "desire for salvation."[23] The "desire" of the French state for "salvation" was overwhelmed, of course, by the Germans, but that "desire"—the expedient and historic (anti-Semitic) longing for "freedom"—was expressed at the expense of the colonized other. Appropriately, Vichy France's desire was an autoimmune one, to be sure, because there can be no staving off fascism, no matter who—the other, no doubt, first of all—is sacrificed in the unjust, unjustifiable cause of saving the self. The very determination to save the self from fascism—history is clear on this point—will only implicate the self more perilously in the very project from which it is trying to save itself. There can, on these terms, be no "salvation" for or of the self that does not begin and end in complicity, that does not sacrifice self as well as other.

Complicity in the death of the other produces the obeisance of the self and, finally, the making vulnerable, beyond measure, beyond time, of the self. That is, through trying to save itself, in trying to secure its own (inherently perilous) future, the self guarantees its own demise. Heinous as it was (the echoes of which remain audible in our day), in striving to "save" itself from further devastation by the Nazis, Vichy France crushed the "dream" of uninterrupted Jewish (colonial) citizenship, citizenship that had been acquired in 1870 through the Decree of Crémieux (*Decree Crémieux*), which gave French citizenship to some 35,000 Algerian Jews. The Vichy state, which was resisted vigorously and courageously from within, forever marked itself in that moment when France betrayed its own founding principles—*liberté, fraternité, égalité*. Consequently, in order for the French state to once again lay claim to those principles, the Vichy state and those who threw their lot in with Pétain and, by implication, Nazi Germany, would have to be confronted, judged, and denounced. And, lived with, forever thereafter.

Pétain's complicity with the Nazis provoked the unexpected "desire" in and for the Algerian child—of both Derrida's and subsequent generations, what preceded 1840 and succeeded 1942—to understand the ruptures already inscribed in his *le monolinguisme,* the language he speaks that is not his. In other words, to account for his speaking, or not speaking, as the case might be, Arabic. To not speak Arabic is, then, to be inaugurated very early into the difficulty of bearing responsibility—an undue burden, the kind of burden that perhaps only colonial history can impose, but a burden, the burden, that must, nevertheless, be born—for the language that is not ours.

Moreover, *Le Monolinguisme* seeks to create, for Abdelkebir Khatibi (Moroccan philosopher, author of *Love in Two Languages,* the text that provoked and therefore haunts *Le Monolinguisme*),[24] Derrida's interlocutor in *Le Monolinguisme,* a separation between self and colonial empire, to anticipate, perhaps unknowingly, the Front de Libération Nationale (FLN [National Liberation Front]), antipathy, violence, and gender-reinscribing resistance toward Gaullist France that was—that could be—glimpsed in the act of the young Jewish boy's disenfranchisement. Here, the historical Husserlian eye would insist, a thinker's sight needed to be trained, in this instance, on a moment just beyond the "horizon's edge," to see what existed before it came into being. The horizon, whose only name could be, simultaneously, dialectically (the best term, but an inadequate one, admittedly, to name this conflict that Derrida instigates, endures, lives, dies with), an "*independent* Algeria" and a postcolonial France. As Derrida says, "Let us understand 'relation' in the sense of narration, the narration of the genealogical narrative, but more generally as well, in the sense that Edouard Glissant imprints upon the impression when he speaks of *Poetics of Relation* [*Poétique de la Relation*], just as one could also speak of a politics of relation" (*Monolingualism of the Other*).[25]

A "relation" between/among languages—"French," "Arabic," the Algerian French spoken in a Jewish home in El Biar, a "relation" between figures, the Jewish boy and his family, the Jewish boy and his Arab neighbors (a fair number of them Muslim, no doubt), the Jewish boy and France in its pre- and post-Vichy incarnations, the Jewish boy and the French Resistance to Nazism and the politics of Pétain, the "relations" of anti- and post-colonized thinkers Derrida, Khatibi, and Glissant to, let us say, Franco-Maghrebian, African, and Franco-Caribbean anti-colonial thinkers—is established. This is a series of "relations" that is potentially sans end, that yields not comfort as such, but it does, signally, open onto an entire range of anti-colonial and anti-*mondialisation* thought that can be gathered under the sign of *le monolinguisme*. That is, the condition of thinking that we encounter as proper to us (it is our thought; thinking conducted in this language is/is not ours) and yet beyond us (all the while, it is the only language in which the work of thinking can be done), thought that is, as such, constitutively excessive so that it leads inexorably, as all thought worthy of the name must, in the direction of "more than one." It tends, as such, to point us toward the other.

The burden of language, *Le Monolinguisme* reminds us, if any such reminder is necessary, inscribes the burden of over-representation as a political and ethical responsibility to the other. A thinking of the self in relation to, unremittingly, wherever the imperative to think relation emanates from, it must account for the other. Thinking the relation to the other is as true of the work of Derrida and/or Glissant as it is of Michel Foucault or Jean-Luc Nancy, Kristeva, or V. Y. Mudimbe.

Conceived as such, relation in this book turns, as it properly must, on the other and responsibility, on responsibility to the other, on violence and forgiveness, on sociopolitical repression and the resistance it produces (/provokes) in (/through) the expletive, and the racially charged nature that is brought into relation through an exchange of thanks, an exchange that can be apprehended only through the politics of negation.[26]

Above all, however, the relation being invoked here through *Le Monolinguisme* is, of course, the act of prosopopoeia. Through this writing, Derrida is retroactively creating the presence—his own in Algeria, needless to say—of (the) one who is absent, the one who is absent in the land of his own birth. To phrase the matter more astringently, the one who is, who was, dead to his own "native land," to invoke the title of Aimé Césaire's poem "Cahier d'un Retour au Pays Natal Cahier" (Return to my native land). It is only through prosopopoeia, after his own departure can (now) bear the weight of his desire for reinscription back into his "abandoned" native land (no matter Derrida's famous argument against the desire "for origins"), that Derrida can address himself, can address himself to Algeria. That he can, as importantly, address and argue with Khatibi (with the spectral presence of Khatibi, who, it might be said, "embodies" the very presence of the Derridean "absence," itself, of course, a ghostly presence). Derrida addressing Khatibi in response to Khatibi's "love in two languages," Derrida writing (to) Khatibi after Khatibi had written him, written of his "un-speakable love," which enables Derrida to write the prosopopoeia of Jacques Derrida. A writing which, in the terms of *The Burden of Over-representation*, mobilizes (installs, acts through) the ghost of "Jacques Derrida" in such a way that its/his spectral presence haunts (shapes, informs) the project in its entirety. The effect of the ghost, as such, is never singular, extending from the event of anti-Semitism in the colonized Maghreb to the event of thanks in postapartheid South Africa, from the expletive uttered in the U.S. South to the esteemed halls of the French academy. The ghost proliferates, reproduces itself, again and again, so much so that, when all is said and done, the ghost is rendered unrecognizable to itself and, in turn, is made to confront itself as far more than itself. And, as such, the ghost comes to know itself fully as itself through its proliferation; its many figurations make the ghost more, never less, itself.

All this writing, one to another, one to the other, all emerges out of the writing of one Maghrebian philosopher to another. After the "death" of disenfranchisement comes the prosopopoeial writing of the self into Maghrebian life, the reclamation of a life of the un-/under-acknowledged Algerian thinker, the Algerian-born philosopher who comes late, again, to stake his claim to being of Algeria, the thinker whose thought was born in the event of (Jewish Algerian) disenfranchisement. We can say the event of the 1995 rugby World Cup in South Africa, won by Pienaar's Springbok team and "anointed" by the event of the "Thank you" exchange between Pienaar and Mandela, entirely "makes" of Pienaar a historic figure, a status bequeathed to him by virtue of the historic 1995 World Cup triumph. Pienaar is made a historic figure far in excess of sport, far in excess of the signal role that captaining the Springboks to victory in a World Cup assigns him; that is, the role of his "native" community, rugby-loving Afrikaners who had bristled against their exclusion, on the grounds of apartheid, from the international rugby community, is made minor—but not inconsequential—because of the event of the "Thank you."

As such, the event enables us to make historical claims. In the case of

Derrida, it is now, following the logic of the event (prosopopoeially understood), possible to argue that the deconstructive mind first came into its
own (it was, to phrase the matter poorly, "born") because of his expulsion
from the corridors of the Lycée Ben Aknoun, fully French in its syllabus
and functioning. That is, the deconstructive mind that is Jacques Derrida
arises out of the anti-Semitic exclusion of that not-yet-deconstructive
mind from that self-same French-Algerian institution. To pursue this line
of reasoning one step further, it can be asserted that the deconstructive
mind owes itself only secondarily to the postwar French university. Finally, following the argument presented in Le Monolinguisme, it is now
possible to claim that the first iterations, the first speaking, the initial
articulations of the condition of le monolinguisme are significantly indebted not to the language in which it is "written" as such, French, but to the
political haunting of the language not spoken. That is, we might speculate,
the Arabic that surrounded Derrida on the streets of Algiers, or the Berber
he might have encountered by accident in El Biar (not likely, but . . .) or . . .
some other language that some stranger spoke, a language Derrida might
have heard in passing, and, who knows, taken to heart. What language,
we might pause to wonder, would Marrano Jews (sometimes also called
"crypto-Jews") from Spain such as Derrida's family have come to Algeria
with? Ladino? How much of Ladino "survived," mutated into . . . Algerian
French? And, emerged as what, exactly? What traces did it leave over the
centuries after the expulsion triggered by the Inquisition? Is this the
language, one speculates, that Derrida seeks to discern in Cinders?[27] That
Derrida tries to discern from the cinders, this writing of the ashes of
death, the ashes that both materialize and deny death through their ethe-
real survival?

How different, we might reflect for a moment, is that arche ("prior,"
"origin," "beginning," or, in Aristotle's work, an "actuating principle"—an
event) in the intellectual formation of the African American scholar W.E.B.
Du Bois: "I sit with Shakespeare and he winces not,"[28] Du Bois proclaims in
The Souls of Black Folk. It is only in, unlike Du Bois, "wincing" at his non-us-
age of Arabic, of his coming late—but not, thankfully, too late—to the work
of Khatibi, that Derrida can, in accounting for the difficulty of living "mono-
lingually," imagine thought in another language. That he can "dis-own," or
"own" without ever "owning," French, that he can begin to imagine thinking, that he can proffer thought, in what might have been, what might constitutively be, his "first" if not his "native" language, the language that will
not, even now, live only prosopopoeially.

The prosopopoeia constitutes, in Le Monolinguisme, a means of subject
formation, a means of political self-authoring. (It does so in much the same
way, surely, as Pienaar's negation of Mandela's "Thank you," the very articu-

lation on which the event turns, must be understood as the "archetypal," in Aristotle's sense, moment in the formation of a postapartheid white South African political self. A self that refuses, no matter that it cannot fully grasp, in the moment of refusal, the effects of the event, or the political costs, immediate and medium term. In much the same way, U.S. racism and the unjust treatment of blacks is the prosopopoeial facticity of black life, no matter the event of Robinson's historic ascension into Major League Baseball.) In this way the exchange, Derrida addressing Khatibi, between thinkers, Derrida "and" Khatibi, Derrida in relation to Khatibi, names an encounter haunted by death, enables a making of the self after the moment of "disenfranchised" death. Talking with Khatibi allows for the making of the (colonial, postcolonial: a sovereign Algeria and so a potentially "sovereign" Algerian who can only with the greatest difficulty stake his claim to such a name) self, the prosopopoeial inscription of the other who is also, if we were to think of Emmanuel Levinas's work on the political effects and affects of the face-to-face encounter for a moment, the self—the self that could not, even in the event of extreme political violence, be acknowledged. What prosopopoeia reveals is how any narrative of the self is always borne out of the need, only occasionally articulated, to mark, however tentatively, that place, that imprecise time, named "beginning"—the *arche*. At once more categorically and more tentatively, that place that has to (/must decidedly not) be understood as "*the* beginning."

Salvaging the Language That Is Not Yours

However, what if the "politics of relation" yields, ultimately, (as Giorgio Agamben[29] would have it) the "ban" that is nothing but the politics of "non relation"—"to ask if the political fact is not perhaps thinkable beyond relation and, thus, no longer in the form of a connection"?[30] Derrida, in his delineation of self, recognizes that the threat of an Agambenian non-relationality produces, not always as an accidental (or, one must concede, as an inevitable) consequence, other, potentially more destructive forms of disenfranchisement and alienation. (And, in so doing, making of the very process of this delineation a deconstructive undertaking.) In his turn, Derrida argues precisely for a consciousness of the cost of non-relationality:

> Today . . . certain people must yield to the homo-hegemony of dominant languages. They must learn the language of the masters, of capital and machines; they must lose their idiom in order to survive or live better. A tragic economy, an impossible counsel. I do not know whether salvation for the other presupposes the salvation of the idiom. (*Monolingualism of the Other*)[31]

How do you, and why would you, "save" the language that you speak that is not yours? The idiom must be "salvaged" because, while it is not your language, it is the only language that you do (not) have. Nothing can be salvaged without language, the only language that inhabits us, that language which, out of sheer historical force, refuses our proprietary claims, that language that through our *monolinguisme* defines our lack of a proprietary relationship with it. This is the lesson, no matter that Derrida does not say so; he had to learn as his founding existential crisis—his first encounter with colonialist France, the object lesson of being an Algerian, an Algerian Jew, disenfranchised by Europe, by and because Europe is at war with itself over, narrowly (but not overly so) conceived, the very subjectivity that is his: Jewishness. The condition, the experience of deracination, of the Marrano, is once more at the core of the conflict of what Europe is, who might be said to constitute it, and who is allowed to, through the rights of *Blut und Grund,* stake a claim to belonging in and to it. A claim that finds articulation in the dictates of Vichy France (disenfranchisement of the Jews), that declares itself on the matter clearly so that it is heard by a young Jewish schoolboy in the outlying colonial hinterland that is the Maghreb. No one who does not belong, whose *Blut* denies them the right to the *Grund* that is Europe, can be deaf to this decree issued in Europe, implicitly issued by Europeans of ostensibly differing ideological stripes. But, as we well know, the effect of which achieved the same devastating political end. That effect was death on a massive scale, disenfranchisement, deracination, all emerging out of the same political conjunction, all flowing from the political confluence that was Nazi Germany's occupation of France.

It is for this reason that Derrida reminds us about the importance of the "idiom." If we cannot "save" the "idiom" which is, in truth, nothing other the right to a certain mode of life, the ability to maintain what is valuable, precious, and articulable within a culture (and as such in the self, what is at stake for the self), then we have to recognize that the diaspora and the postcolonial are, above all else, the inscription of a code of political conduct. A code in which mourning, loss, and the desire to confront and, if at all possible, to overcome these conditions are all deeply embedded. As such, the postcolonial and the diaspora house within them a fragile collection of things that could as easily be lost as salvaged. "Beyond memory and time lost," before Vichy France and Marshall Pétain, before being cut off from the Arabic (and/or the Ladino) he did not learn, that is Derrida's winsome hope (*Monolingualism of the Other*).[32] As a code of political conduct, the diaspora operates perpetually as a movement against: against the time about to be "vacated," against the threat presented by the "masters, capital and the machines." The diaspora marks, as much as it marks anything (and everything), the recognition of the imperative to leave, to vacate the here and now (this place and time, this *Grund und Zeit*), and it knows the impossible task of protecting "beyond memory and time lost." How does one preserve that because, surely, there is no *salut* (salvation) to be found in the diaspora? And, yet, one must, for without those the "idiom"—which is, we assume, nothing but the disenfranchising language of the self (Pienaar, speaking not in his native Afrikaans but in English, a second language for both him and Mandela, since Mandela's first language is Xhosa)—would assuredly be lost. (Is *salut* only to be found in language? This language that is not "ours"?) It is for this reason that the diaspora is deliberately charged with serving as a bulwark against the *l'avenir*, the fearful uncertainty of the "end" of movement, not necessarily a prospect to be welcomed, in favor of a linguistic facility that exceeds Derrida's life-long inhabitation of the language that, as he so poetically phrases it, "will never be mine, this language, the only one that I am thus destined to speak, as long as speech is possible for me in life and death; you see, never will this language be mine" (*Monolingualism of the Other*).[33] And so, *salut* is left, as it properly should be, to language. No wonder so much depends upon what Derrida names "that strange French word *salut* ['salvation']" (*Monolingualism of the Other*).[34]

It is only in "death," perhaps, that the fullness of what it means to speak this "language" that will "never be" Derrida's, speaks itself, delineates the contours of how this "language" will "never be" his. Every "idiom," then, serves as a hedge against "death," even as it severs the dead from the living. (For Derrida, the first such "idiom" would be Ladino. The death of the idiom, the specter of its death, as such, is all too familiar to him.) The dead can come alive, again and again, in and through the "idiom," no matter that the "idiom" that is *le monolinguisme* reminds us that the constitutive core of every "idiom" is a contradiction. Every "idiom" is, at once (in the spirit of Heidegger), both toward and against "death." It is all that stands in the way of death even as the "idiom" knows, as a certainty, the prospect of its own death. The "idiom" as such speaks death as much as it gives language, as Derrida asserts, to the dead in "death" so that the "idiom" is destined to outlive the self—as much, that is, as it promises to speak that self, for or against, in "death." "The Thing," as Derrida phrases it so memorably in *Specters of Marx: The State of the Debt, the Work of Mourning, and the New International* (and resonantly for the purposes of our discussion here), "is neither dead nor alive, it is dead and alive at the same time."[35] As much as this is true as it pertains to our understanding of the "idiom," we are also free to propose that, like the "idiom," "Algeria," Derrida's Jewishness, his Maghrebianness, his (North) Africanness too, is both "dead and alive at the same time."[36]

Because of how Derrida figures the role of the "idiom" in "death," it is not surprising that the matter of the language that is not his preoccupies Derrida profoundly in his "final years." In *Learning to Live Finally: The Last Interview,* he reiterates, with a minor recalibration: "I have only one language, and, at the same time, in an at once singular and exemplary fashion, this language does not belong to me."[37] Still, as we well know from the culture (the literature, the music, the art, the life-sustaining practices) of the diasporized, there is in the movement against the determination to make life—to make a language—in that precarious moment between the irrepressible past and the indeterminable future. A contentious place to be, as Derrida recognizes in *Learning to Live:* "I am at war with myself, it's true, you couldn't possibly know to what extent . . . and I say contradictory things that are, we might say, in real tension" (*Learning to Live Finally*).[38] In her introduction to *Learning to Live,* entitled "Bearing Loss: Derrida as a Child," under the rubric of Derrida as "'lost child' of Judaism," a "non-/relation" that complicated his identification with the state of Israel, Jean Birnbaum reiterates this notion of Derrida "being at war" with himself ("Bearing Loss").[39] Birnbaum writes, "Derrida often recalled the double movement of acquiescence and identity, of love and revolt, that characterized his relationship to the tradition of Israel. Evoking in this regard 'the obscure and uncertain experience of inheritance,' he underscored the violence of an assignation of identity inscribed from the outset" ("Bearing Loss").[40]

What is this "double movement," so overwrought with the affect that attends to the politics of relation ("acquiescence and anxiety, love and revolt"), but the difficulty of learning to live with, to live against, to live despite, the "violence" that is the imposition ("assignation" seems not to do the "violence" justice) of "identity"? That is, to learn to live in the face of what is most autoimmune: the affirmation that derives from the "certainty" of who it is the self is (is supposed to be) that exists in constant struggle with what it is, with who it is, the self is—what is supposed to be is in "real tension" with what, for better or worse, is. Here Robinson's struggle, his refusal to conform to the terms of the burden of over-representation that was imposed on him as the historic black baseball player, reverberates. It is in his preference for the expletive, "Stupid bastards," that we see—that we "hear"; ours is the "other ear," in Derrida's terms—Robinson straining against, contravening, at the level of language (and ontology, dare one say?), the constraints he was made to endure. In speaking out of turn, in turning to the expletive rather than a more decorous phrasing, Robinson "releases" himself into himself—the expletive is the political equivalent of carpe diem, Robinson seizing the right to be done, for the moment, with decorum and linguistic protocols. (An inoffensive phrasing, in any case, would not produce the event; only the expletive, we might speculate, can raise language to that politico-philosophical order.) However, as we later see, Robinson's is an act of linguistic-political liberation that, while performed—or uttered—in public, is not publicly available and, as such, must be made public. In itself, then, an act of "double movement," between the putatively private and the stridently public, between what is permissible and expected, and what is proscribed. The expletive signals, moreover, a form of speech, a mode of speaking, a political address, that Robinson must claim as his because it is not, in and of itself, before itself, available to him. A different kind of circumscription, but one that nevertheless finds resonances—of the explicitly political kind, unavoidably, and a good thing too, I hasten to add—with Derrida's Vichy experience.

Notwithstanding Birnbaum's analysis, Derrida remains quite correct in his assertion that he is "at war with himself." What is more, he is locked into this battle to such an "extent" that it is not only beyond us but also beyond his capacity to "possibly know." However, where we can identify with him is in his recognition that the diaspora is that moment of "being at war," that mode of life that must be lived, always, contingently, fraught with contradictions and "real tensions." As Derrida expresses it in *Specters of Marx*, "one must sort out several different possibles that inhabit around the same injunction. And inhabit it in a contradictory fashion around a secret" (*Specters of Marx*).[41] The secret, *Geheimnis,* that is, of course, not a secret[42] precisely because what is known about diasporic life is repeatedly revealed. The diaspora is a demanding mode of being that, however, constitutes a response to the "same injunction"—that act of being against that also recognizes the imperative of departure, that contradiction that, always unsuccessfully, pits the constitutive here against the unimaginable, hopeful there.

In the eloquent last line of *Le Monolinguisme,* Derrida offers a cryptic description of this condition. The force of the contradiction is such that, as he says, "I finally know how not to have to distinguish any longer between promise and terror" (*Monolingualism of the Other*).[43] As the various scholars of *mondialisation,* and African "globalization" in particular, to which have been appended names such as "diaspora," "postcoloniality," and "migration" and to which are seemingly inexorably linked those twin conditions "promise" (Why else would one leave "home"? Why else would the subject struggle against colonial exploitation and oppression? Except that it is sustained by the imagining of better prospects) and "terror" (that unspeakable fear of the unknown, the barely known, that foreboding that "here" and "there" might not always be distinguishable, that today's "freedom fighter" might become tomorrow's brutal dictator), we are too familiar with the hopes of a promise (and, of course, its brutal failures, its bloody conflicts) and the terror that has befallen the African continent, in iterations that apply to here as well as to there, wherever those places might be—and where, we might ask, are those places not?

It is through this intimacy with both "promise and terror" that it becomes possible to critique the conditions of diasporic and postcolonial life—to not only, in the case of the latter, denounce it as a political, in Carl Schmitt's sense, that bears too closely, too often, in too many articulations, as death—as the reconfiguration of black life. It becomes possible, that is, to denounce it as a set of political circumstances that iterates the question of life, that makes explicable another thinking of friend and enemy so that a philosopher such as Schmitt, who supported the very project that disenfranchised Derrida—who, after all, in the postcolonial landscape, is the enemy who was also not, until, it seems, just yesterday, the friend, the comrade—might be usefully engaged. Robert Mugabe, after all, was once Joshua Nkomo's comrade in arms in the Patriotic Front's military struggle against Ian Smith's Rhodesia, and then, after Zimbabwean independence, his most ferocious enemy.[44] In this regard the Agambenian conceptions of *zoē* and *bios* do not have much to offer. After all, what distinguishes bare life from political life in the postcolonial state? Is there any distinction worth holding on to at all? How often is bare life the limit of the political horizon for the diasporic subject? And yet, there is in the unrepresentability of the diaspora the recognition of that crucial encounter with the limits of political life, that limit at which the diaspora—or the postcolonial— might be spoken, must be inscribed, demands its own, repeated, contradictory writing. A writing for, toward, a political project, a project seeking articulation under the conditions of late capitalism, seems always *l'avenir*. There is Derridean insight aplenty (of the Trotskyist persuasion, the "revolution" must always be approached as though it were "permanent") in *l'avenir*, but there remains inscribed in that insight a real limit: the exhaustibility of living the political project as infinite postponement. Derrida's is a wise caution, a perpetual call to arms, but it can be sustained only if it operates on the logic of succession. Every succeeding generation must be willing to pick up the cudgels where the "exhausted" generation it follows has left off. As such, we are reminded that politics is an incessant business and that it is always likely to demand more than it rewards. *A luta continua*. The struggle continues, and it continues only because it retains an ethical core that inspires generation after generation with the logic of *l'avenir*, a logic that demands eternal replenishment because it poses politics as that project that must be taken up, generation after generation, father to daughter, grandmother to grandson (there is no reason as such for it not to skip a generation; politics always lies in wait, punctual in only its own terms) again. And then, yet again. This is a logic to which we return very shortly.

The Diaspora

There is no articulation of the diaspora that does not require the invocation of difference, the assiduous naming—identification—of what is different. How are the conditions of life not the same? Or, for that matter, all too familiar? What is the point, the precise political juncture, at which difference emerges? These are questions that obtain with the same vehemence, urgency, and veracity for both the postcolonial and the diasporic subject. Is difference simply restricted, as Derrida seems suspicious of, to the force of narrative? Does difference emerge only in the articulation—or, for that matter, the espousal—of the other's narrative? Or the lack of the other's narrative? Because, most disturbingly, of the other's narrative and political unrepresentability? To think a politics without representation or a politics that speaks, directly and forcefully, to a politics that recognizes the impossibility of representation?

The other's experience of its own history of resistance is, paradoxically, what finally demands of the postcolonial and the diasporic subject a careful thinking of transgression. On its own, the acting against, the deliberate act of resistance, the taking on of, the confrontation with the state has to, because of history, be reevaluated. The state, in its apartheid and postapartheid incarnation, and the ghost of the former that hangs (that will always hang) over the latter, is especially crucial to the ways in which the "exchange" of thanks is transformed into (an) event, as we see in Chapter 2, through the unexpected negation of one offering of (formulaic) gratitude. Transgression, in whatever form it takes (such as a "solitary" string of expletives or the repetition of the same expletive, "bastards"), contains within it the always dangerous possibility of the reinstatement of the limit. To wit, most obviously, the failed, or failing, or nonfunctioning state, postcolonial or otherwise.

Transgression constitutes, without the Agambenian act of "non-relationality," the act of going beyond, the political practice of marking, erasing, and then inscribing again—without a necessarily clear sense of where the difference resides, exactly—the limits of subjectivity. We are, as it were, left to argue again with, against, *arche,* that first, founding act of inscription. But, as always, politics must begin, must begin in the spirit of *l'avenir,* following a logic true to only its own dictates. Begin again, as if for the first time, and so it is not that we militate against political transgression but that we reiterate that any displacement, any forced, un-intended movement, always demands, always frames itself as a question—not only of origin but also of movement: Where are you going to? What are you going toward? What, do you imagine since you can't know, will happen there? Motion, we recognize, is by its very nature provocative. Residing within motion, we might say, is the time of displacement: the time it takes to get from here to there, the time of resistance, the time of the diaspora, the time to which the postcolonial once aspired. The time, we might now improperly say, now lost. Love, we are reminded, requires not one but "two" languages: Arabic and French, the "here" and the "there," the "now" and *l'avenir,* the "to come," what is to come—what, and no doubt who too, is desired in and of the time to come.

Because of the trace,[45] the trace of love in time, the time of love that can be "recovered" only through the trace, any act of subject making, of becoming ("postcolonial" in Derrida's case; "postapartheid" in Pienaar and Mandela's, with the different resonances that such a political designation has for them; "coming into Civil Rights," "coming into enfranchisement" in Robinson's, almost a century after Reconstruction) can never be an act unto itself. Such an act of "becoming" (born as it is through the burden of over-representation), always arches, backward or forward, toward something else, toward another time, a different mode of political being: Derrida, in *Le Monolinguisme,* toward Khatibi. The diaspora and the postcolonial must, per force, preclude any foreclosure: neither the irreducible past nor the inarticulable future can be excluded. They must be thought in the same gesture. French, the language that is not, and Arabic, the language that, as it were, followed Derrida, came after him now, could we not say, arrondissement after arrondissement, in Paris, in Montpellier, in Bordeaux, in Marseille. The language Derrida did not speak in Algiers, as a child, became the language, inhabited, fully—dare one suggest?—all over France. Colonialism, that "other" act of historic disenfranchisement, forced Derrida, long after he had left, back to Khatibi's (and his own, might we say?) tongue, back to Algiers (and, as such, back to El Biar, where, one presumes, Arabic was—if only marginally—not so substantial a presence), but never, it would seem, out of *le monolinguisme.* Derrida acknowledges as much: "I love what made me what I am, the very element of which is language, this French language that is the only language I was ever taught to cultivate, the only one also for which I can say I am responsible" (*Learning to Live Finally*).[46]

It is for this reason that the diaspora, and postcoloniality, is not only a conscious straining against coloniality, hegemony, exclusion, conformity, racism, or *doxa* but also a strain within itself, the strain of learning, again, to speak a language that is not yours. The political costs and imaginings of the diaspora and the postcolonial, the movement against and the struggle within, ensure that both these articulations of global African life always have a future. The name of that future is the epistemological or, even, the ontological crisis to come. That moment when the founding myth of *le monolinguisme* is undone, when the language of the self, or any language for that matter, cannot be singularly inhabited. That is the crisis of language: It encodes nothing so much as the crisis at the very core of language. Let us, for the sake of crude translation, name it *la crise à venir*: "the crisis" that is, for now and always, "to come." That crisis, we might say, that always seems to impose itself on the de-colonized/postcolonial (but never, it would seem, "sovereign")/racialized subject, with a rare and lasting political force. For this subject, therefore, re-subjectivation presents itself as an always necessary (and, yes, potentially exhausting onto-logical) and impossible political undertaking. In the grim terms of the diasporic South African poet Arthur Nortje, "Bitter though the taste be, it is life somehow."[47] A life that must be lived, a life whose very terms of existence must be struggled against. As solace, we have Nietzsche's "Was mich nicht umbringt macht mich stärker" ("What doesn't kill you makes you stronger").[48]

Invoking W.E.B. Du Bois's famous declaration about the Negro "being a problem,"[49] we can safely say that the black subject—in its diasporized or postcolonial or neocolonial or desubjectivated form—is never simply, can never simply be, a problem for "itself." The condition of black life is that it has, historically, refused to be a problem for only itself because, as Derrida recognizes from his location in colonized, "at war" (if only by virtue of colo-nial "intimacy" and "proximity") Algeria, there is the persistent issue of the relationship to the other—the problem that, Agamben's argument notwith-standing, seems to deny any possibility of the nonrelational. (This, of course, echoes Du Bois's sentiment exactly. He names it a "history of strife,"[50] a "history" that we must understand as always implicating all those who surround, have power over, or come into contact with the "Negro." For the Negro, of course, the internal effects of this strife are precisely what produces in her or him that most famous Du Boisian condition, "double consciousness.") Whether in economically and politically ravaged Zimba-bwe or in the act of wearing the head scarf in France (a "problem" we might suggest, that properly can be traced back to Algeria or, more generally, France's colonial presence in the Maghreb), the problem of the diaspora, with every passing political event, threatens to become more urgent, more pressing, and, in so doing, to present itself as irresolvable and therefore precisely the question that must be thought. The problem, we might say, of language, of speaking that which is not ours, that speaking of the self with-out which the self would not be able to rise to the level of speaking. The problem, so understood, of love: "I love what made me what I am, the very element-al of which is language."

Today the Maghreb, the Algerian who has long since simultaneously ceased and continued to be Maghrebian (and here Derrida is our paradig-matic figure) still haunts France. Much like the Nigerian or Indian or Jamaican haunts Britain, and the indigenous communities and the Mexican deracinated and impoverished by American capitalism and geopolitical adventurism in centuries past and present continue to hang over the body politic of the United States, the Aboriginal presence, daily, reminds Australia (or Canada or Paraguay) of another origin. There is little doubt that there is, of course, more than one ghostly presence at work in that subsidiary, easy to overlook, Derridean clause invoked in the opening paragraph of this Introduction. Let us recall that all too readily (easily?) forgotten clause, the one in which Derrida offers his narrative of disenfranchisement. It reads, "with everything that followed." The backdrop to Derrida's thinking was, of course, the event of the Holocaust, which Husserl did not live to experience. More evocative, however, is that other ghost, literally, in the anti-prosopopoeial mode, to come—narrative of a death foretold: the Algerian war of independence, to which the French responded brutally and, we now know, unsuccessfully, against the FLN.

Resident ghost of the historic "what followed" was, if you will, the "Hamlet" of existential philosophy and anticolonial violence that rudely disrupted the condition of monolingualism. Anti- and postcolonialists have long known that rupture as Frantz Fanon, the Martinique-born, French-trained psychologist who struggled, philosophically we might say, on behalf of the Algerians and the Martinicans and the Kenyans and the Indians against the French and the British.

Fanon, the Negro who at once recognized and could not quite find himself in that haunting phrase uttered by a Parisian child, "Look, a Negro" (*Regarder, un Négre*). A phrase unutterable, in such a formulation, to Derrida in the moment of Vichy, and, yet, of course, a condition that he might have, approximately (what proximity, exactly, might the Jewish schoolboy have experienced in relation to the "Negro" who was being identified and not, as such, addressed), grasped. Would Derrida have recognized Fanon's own act of living with the violence of *le monolinguisme* after having been exposed to the "language that is not mine" in a different colony, Martinique, but, with the same intense sense of having to undo, to work with and against, in spite of, this language? Fanon, unarguably the most renowned existentialist philosopher of anticolonial blackness; Fanon, anticolonial theorist who surely knew rather than simply anticipated, in his reading of the *damnes de la terres,* the failures of the postcolonial to come; Fanon, who struggled against the "actualities and possibilities" of his world, who came to know how unhomely Paris was as the place that gave him this monolinguistic language. This condition of *le monolinguisme* that empowered a language (his, not his) to act against him—to act against him in its own name, in his name, claiming him for itself, unutterably deaf to the incommensurate cadences of his and Derrida's speaking. Their conjoined, sovereign speaking against Vichy France, against postwar France, war-battered and yet still resolutely imperialist, and violently so in its Gaullist formation. Fanon, who came to Algeria to fight years after Derrida had left. Fanon, who came, like a revolutionary lover, and knew Algeria (could be sovereign) before Derrida. This place, at once El Biar and Algiers, the neighborhood on the hill and the city down below, this place that was not Derrida's, not his and not even Khatibi's, the place of the monolinguistic heart. Could, we are moved to wonder, Derrida ever have called Algiers "home?" It is only, properly speaking, in *Le Monolinguisme,* his conversation—his strangely arresting struggle that produces echoes so disparate that we can think Derrida with Jackie Robinson and François Pienaar, and less jarringly we can think Pienaar through Nelson Mandela "because" of Derrida—with Khatibi, that Derrida can be said to think the politics, and the impossibility, of return. That we can subject Derrida to the sustaining, Nortjean "bitterness" of such a life, a diasporic life, a deracinated life, and yet, we must always remember, a life lived with an unyielding commitment to the politico-philosophical.

It is, of course, important to recognize—and here, much work has already been and continues to be done—Fanon's standing alongside Paulo Freire, Amilcar Cabral, arguably even the work of the Croatian Catholic Ivan Illich, and, of course, Karl Marx, the philosopher of the oppressed. However, this argument for Derrida as, first, Maghrebian and then a Franco-European and then an African philosopher seeks to think the condition of race and philosophy, possibly even the movement that is African globalism, proceeds, as it were (and this calls for an elastic sense of linearity and chronology, a call that perhaps stretches credulity to breaking point), "backward." *The Burden of Over-representation* thinks Derrida "in reverse," thinks him "back to" as much as that which is *l'avenir.* The project here is to think *l'avenir* as the first condition of and for what it means "to become," what such a "becoming," posited as at once—if such a crude phrasing might be indulged—a prospective and a retrospective entails, how such a "becoming" must be thought as nothing other than an event. As nothing other than the event that is, like most of what is signal in philosophy, made by haunting, the event that only haunting can make—we can be made only through that which haunts us. Without haunting—dare one say it?—we are not, we are no-thing, we are nothing.

As Derrida acknowledges in *Specters,* it is haunting alone that addresses us as it has called thinkers across the ages to account. "If Marx, like Freud, like Heidegger, like everybody, did not begin where he ought have 'been able to begin' (*beginnen können*), namely with haunting, before life *as such,* before death *as such,* it is doubtless not his fault. The fault, in any case, by definition, is repeated, we inherit it, we must watch over it" (*Specters of Marx*).[51] The event of Jacques Derrida, of Jacky Derrida, is a determined—not forced, to be absolutely clear—writing of a historic, philosophical, and political haunting. It is the writing of that which is accountable to, responsible for, we might even say, what Derrida has bequeathed us, and, in order to "watch over" Derrida, it is necessary to think, at once and by turns, first one and then the other, only one at a time, all simultaneously, "life" and "death," "life-in-death" (Derrida taking his distance from Heidegger), "being toward death" (Heidegger, as such), and the life of a historically haunted deracination. If we are indeed destined to "repeat" Marx, Sigmund Freud, and Heidegger's "fault," then we must do so in a redistributive sense: the "fault" must be lessened, reduced, rearticulated, and invested with new calibrations. It is not enough to take solace that the "fault" is historic or unavoidable.

Instead, "we must watch over it" in order to minimize its effects. Anything other than that amounts to our having failed the "fault." And, even as Derrida inoculates Marx et al. against criticism, it is impossible to read his injunction to think haunting as anything less than absolute responsibility. It is for this reason, above all others, that haunting must be written, that the writing of haunting, the writing of the haunting that haunts Derrida's writing, must be written here. We must not submit to the terms of the "fault"; we must not submit, because, in his writing, in his direct address to the "specter of communism," in his taking up the deconstruction (the act of making Marx useful, again, as he always is, this time in the *le monolinguisme* of deconstruction),[52] Derrida issues what is both an invitation to think the specter and a caution. The specter, Derrida warns us, must be treated with philosophico-political respect. The specter must be thought on the multivalenced, variegated, literary-political (Shakespeare's *Hamlet* being prime among them), and intensely philosophical terms that *Specters* draws together in order to obviate and undermine the immunization against criticism that any inability to "begin" from the specter is "doubtless not our fault." It is necessary not only to "watch over" the specter but also to watch how it is that we apprehend, that we write, the specter, what kind of politics arises out of and because of the specter. Through the specter, Derrida calls himself, before all others, to account, as he calls us to account. The specter must be reckoned with because it antedates ("before . . . before") both life and death. There is no thinking, to repeat Derrida's litany of historic names, without the specter.

We are haunted into thought. And that is why we must not only follow the haunting but also seek it out as that place where, that moment when, our thinking is inaugurated. We are, then, permitted to whisper, in whatever register we so choose, that for our thinking of Derrida we are at once guided by, guided in the direction of, and guided out of the event that is El Biar. Everything, we can claim both boldly and with real reservation, begins with that house on the hill. All Derrida's language, his *le monolinguisme,* is haunted by that house, by that place, by, we might say, that place that is/is not his. "I have only one place, and yet it is not mine." But, it is ours, yours and mine, it is given to the Maghreb and to Africa, to the Maghreb and to Europe, to the Maghreb and to Euro-America. It is given to Marx, Freud, and Heidegger. *Specters* is Derrida's political, philosophical, postcolonial, anti-/Semitic, antiracist bequest to us, one and all, the living and the dead, the dead as they are recuperated and claimed again through the life of the specter. Through *Specters* Derrida has given life to all, the specter and the specter of the (/that haunts the) philosopher and to the Maghreb of his youth and the Europe that survives in his passing. To Nelson Mandela and to Jackie Robinson, to François Pienaar and to "Jacky Derrida" he makes the bequest of the troubled but intensely provocative inheritance that is *le monolinguisme.*

Talking Is Not Conversation

As such, as Derrida makes clear in the concluding paragraph, *Specters* is dedicated to the work of thinking. More precisely, to the future of the work of thinking that the intellectual *l'avenir*—if such a term might be permitted—must take up, must recognize as a responsibility that "begins" with Marx, Freud, Heidegger, and, of course, Derrida himself. Phrased as a Shakespearean injunction (borrowing the voice of *Hamlet*'s Marcellus), Derrida commits himself to thinking through and because of the specter:

> If he loves justice at least, the "scholar" of the future, the "intellectual" of tomorrow should learn from the ghost. He should learn to live by learning not how to make conversation with the ghost but how to talk to him, with her, how to let them speak or how to give them back speech, even if it is in oneself, in the other, in the other in oneself: they are always *there,* specters, even if they do not exist, even if they are no longer, even if they are not yet. They give us to rethink "there" as soon as we open our mouth, even at a colloquium and especially when one speaks in a foreign language. (*Specters of Marx*)[53]

The work of the intellectual, of today and "tomorrow," is to think for "justice," a commitment to "justice" that can only be "learned from the ghost." The ghost, then, as political pedagogue, teacher of "justice," like Socrates, the ghost asks questions of us, difficult questions. The ghost who is, importantly, already extant: the "specter" is "always" with us, already with us, already within us. However, in order to "learn from the ghost" we must first distinguish between "conversation" and "talking" with the ghost. That is, to "converse" is, following *Webster's,*[54] to engage "informally" or "casually" with another; it is to engage on the level of, because of, familiarity with the other. That is, to "make conversation" is to engage the ghost as though we already know how to have this exchange, as though the terms to hand are language sufficient for the difficult work of engaging the ghost. It is patently not because we must endeavor to "talk to the ghost," a mode of exchange that, again according to *Webster's,* operates on a higher plane.[55] To "talk" is to engage in a mode of communication where "ideas" are exchanged; to "talk" is to, at least at one level (the one privileged here, in any case),[56] speak about, say, poetry or philosophy, rather than to prattle on about inanities—say, to talk about the state of a community's roads or, in the most prosaic sense, to "talk about the weather."

In order to "learn to talk" to the ghosts, a certain seriousness of (philosophical) purpose is required. The stakes, as it were, are considerably higher because what the ghosts have to teach us is how the specter, how the politics of haunting (as we have already noted), are instrumental (not in the usurious sense) and instructive for the work of thinking, of thinking "justice." "Talking" with the ghost does nothing less than, as Derrida says, teach us how to "live," a project of no small significance to Derrida. And, in order to learn how to "talk to the ghost," it may well be required of us develop an extraordinary auditory capacity—we learn how to listen as if we knew nothing of listening, as mundane an everyday practice as one could imagine; we have to develop an "ear for the other"—and an almost otherworldly ability to "give speech" to the ghost. Not to give it to the ghost for the first time, but to, on this point Derrida is clear, "give them back speech." That is, the ghost already knows how to "talk." It is up to us to, as it were, simply "remind" them of their already existing capacity for engaging us philosophically; we simply, no easy task, of course, need to "draw" their (innate) capacity for "talking" out of them. Doing so would, in all likelihood, require us to—no pun intended—"re-animate" the ghost, bring the ghost back to life, as it were. Even if, in the most "extreme" case, the ghost has, as it were, passed on or, in Derrida's phrasing, is "no longer."

In many ways, however, "talking" with the ghost, "learning from the ghost," is an autodidactic political exercise. The ghost, Derrida insists, is already "in oneself." At worst or at farthest remove, it is "in the other, in the other in oneself." That is, we are, to phrase the matter in terms of Derrida's distinctions, already on speaking terms with the ghost. We need only, no mean feat but one that is certainly not beyond us, learn—again, as if for the first time—how to "talk" with the ghost, the ghost that is already in us, of us, the ghost whom we can recognize in (or even as) the other. Phrased as a political demand, we might say that in order to "talk" with the ghost we must (re-)acquaint ourselves with the Heideggerian dictates of philosophy: "Only philosophy thinks." Learning to "talk" is nothing less than learning to think, to think with the ghost, to think because of the ghost. To learn to live with the ghost is to make of every encounter an exercise in learning to think. The specter of the ghost, that specter that haunts us, is the most necessary political provocation: it is a reminder of the imperative to, again and again, learn how to think. To learn, at the risk of repetition, to think as if we had no idea as to what thinking is. To learn to think is to take on the task of learning how to live, how to live in thought, how to live because only thinking and thinking alone can give us life. In this regard, it matters not what language the ghost speaks. Every language, we can assert with confidence, is "foreign" unless it is made to, it makes us, think, unless it serves as an invitation to thinking. Above all, we must learn to speak to the ghost. Our lives depend on it. Most apropos then, that Derrida concludes *Specters* with that famous injunction on "talking" from *Hamlet*: "*Thou art a scholar, speake to it, Horatio.*"[57]

To learn how to talk with the ghost is not to make possible the impossible. Rather, it is to draw out of us what is already in us—in us and keeping us alive. To learn how to talk is to understand, if such a phrasing might be permitted, that which is most life sustaining and sacred within us—our capacity for thinking: philosophy. Heidegger, once more.

Writing the Self Back . . . Into . . .

Derrida, as a French-speaking, Algerian-born philosopher, in his contemplations on *le monolinguisme* undertakes the project of writing himself back into the place that is, and, of course, is not, and could never have been, his. And yet, of course, it is that place which still, and always will, haunt him, so that we can understand as it is the "there" that he designates at the end of *Specters*. All the while, of course, Derrida is, with the ghost of Husserl all too discernible, drawing the very act of writing into question. Saliently, however, Derrida is compelling us, against our expectations, into the condition of coloniality so that his subsequent thinking can, with the benefit of *Le Monolinguisme*, be opened into the larger issue.

Jacques Derrida becomes the Franco-Maghrebian philosopher who will never allow himself to eschew the force of the (philosophically and politically constitutive) "there." Derrida becomes, at the very least, the Maghrebian intellectual writing the complexities of the politics of turning to, of re-turning to the Maghreb, to the un-learned, phantasmagoric Arabic that is Khatibi's, after the irresolvable, nonrepressible history of disenfranchisement: in *Le Monolinguisme*, no less than an extended essay on the crypto-Jewish Derrida's relationship—hence the signality of "narration" and the invocation of Glissant—with the Moroccan philosopher Abdelkebir Khatibi, on their relationship to the Maghreb, on their place in that world, on how their writings speak to or do not "talk" to each other, on, as it were, how they see their own "poetics of relation" to this now postcolonial place. (On the specter of Ladino in this haunted place.)

As such, *The Burden of Over-representation* offers a thinking of Derrida that at once recognizes his standing as a, some might even say "the," definitive European philosopher of the late twentieth century and argues for the complication of that prevailing perception. The politicization of Derrida's standing as "European"/"Euro-American" philosopher into a precarious, and therefore provocative, thought-inducing Maghrebian Africanity. The writing, the invocation, of the Maghreb and sub-Saharan Africa is a presence that haunts Derrida's thinking in, as we have seen, works from *Specters of Marx* to *On Friendship*, both texts that provide some form of ghostly engagement with that foundational moment of disenfranchisement. (And surely this mode of thinking the politics of "there" will, by pure interrogative force, extend to works such as *De la Grammatologie* and *Dissemination* and *Rogues* and others. "There" is, as it were, always somewhere in the "there" that is, say, *De la Grammatologie*.) The Maghreb fled, the North African "there" never left behind; it will not allow itself to be abandoned, and so, we might say, it returns in and as the question, in and as the difficulty of *le monolinguisme*.

Who, we might rightly ask, among diasporic intellectuals, from St. Paul and St. Augustine to Bob Marley, from Josephine Baker to Grace Jones, among others, has not had to write her- or himself out of it, sought to write so as to make sense of being displaced out of the self's political language? In this regard, Heidegger's demands seem especially timely. "Higher than actuality stands *possibility*," Heidegger writes. "We can understand phenomenology solely by seizing upon it as a possibility."[58] Derrida's difficult act of locating himself in Algeria constitutes, for the condition of the other, of all others, we might go so far as to say, a "possibility" for thinking the diaspora, disenfranchisement, deracination, and violence against the other that must be seized upon. In situating himself as, at the very least, a Franco-Maghrebian Derrida, he has confronted himself, and us, with possibilities for thinking qua thinking.

At the very least, he has presented possibilities for thinking deconstruction, for thinking deconstruction's North African roots, for thinking as indistinguishable from philosophy as such (situating Derrida in a Maghrebian lineage that runs from St. Augustine to Albert Camus to Louis Althusser to . . .), this time from some other "there," and, in the process, for compelling ourselves to account for the *Specters*' "there." That is, to recognize how much of his work, such as the interviews in *Positions*, for example (which, among other things, demonstrates his long engagement with Husserl), allows us to "trace" the circuitous, unexpected roots of phenomenology and existentialism (to give proper regard to Camus, a *pied-noir,* and to Sartre, who took up the political struggle against French colonialism in his inimitable way) in the Franco-Maghrebian thinker.

Derrida, is then presented as a Franco-Maghrebian of sorts, a Franco-Maghrebian sui generis, and, to extend the "possibility" even further, an African of sorts, a diasporic thinker who inclined toward Mandela, who understands, in the name of "justice," why it is a matter of responsibility for the intellectual of today to critique the violence and injustice that is visited on black African bodies on the continent's farthest southern tip. And injustice visited on black bodies is, even if in very different registers, what binds Mandela to Robinson, the memory of which binds—as the refutation of the "Thank you"—Pienaar to Mandela, and, finally, what draws Derrida to all these other bodies, black and white. Derrida's struggle with the "there" that we have named "El Biar," that place that constituted out of enfranchisement-disenfranchisement-alienation-memory-forgetting-re-turn and so on, is, of course, not Pienaar's "talk" with the history of apartheid.

However, Pienaar's is a "talk" that comes fully into its own only if it is thought, only if it is understood as in need of a philosophical speaking to, a philosophical speaking to an especially lively constituency of specters. Alive with historical hate, bristling with Afrikaner resentment and black euphoria; the specters that speak of deracination, disenfranchisement, injustice, legal inequality, *différance,* are, if you will, the specters of apartheid gone mad. As it turns out, there is no thinker of the "there" more attuned to thinking it than Derrida. As such, Derrida's oeuvre is replete with a language in which to "talk" to Pienaar, Mandela, and Robinson. To each his own *le monolinguisme.* To each a specific *le monolinguisme* that draws its language for "talk" from the same Derridean source.

The "actuality" that is sport, that is the event in sport, has raised the "possibility" of a Derridean critique, a philosophical thinking (to risk a redundancy, at least in Heidegger's terms), that allows for thinking a "there" (let us name it "the event") that is only incipiently there in Derrida's work. It is, however, the "possibilities" presented by apprehending that "there" that, because of Derrida's thinking and his love of football, *The Burden of Over-representation* seeks to "actualize," philosophically. Sport as pure philosophical "possibility." A "possibility" that, in all probability, only Derrida invites us to "actualize," to think as something other than itself, as something that can be grasped as fully itself only through philosophy.

1 "Stupid Bastards"

Conciliation, the Act of First Encounter

Rude am I in speech,
And little blessed with the soft phrase of peace.
—**WILLIAM SHAKESPEARE**, *Othello*

The Burden of Over-representation

Problems are the price you pay for progress.
—**WESLEY BRANCH RICKEY**

Sometimes conciliation can begin only with or as an address to the self. That is certainly the case in the salient Jackie Robinson moment on which this chapter turns. Sometimes conciliation can begin only as an address to the self, an address best understood as a Socratic moment. As we well know, in Socrates's terms we are never alone because we are always in our own company. We are, Socrates insists, always dialogically present with, to, and for ourselves. As Michel Foucault phrases it in his work on the history of sexuality, the "relationship of self with self" is critical to "the form-

---

ing of oneself as subject."[1] The presence of the "self to self" means that any such conversation between the self and it-self constitutes, inveterately, by its very nature, a public speaking. It may be a public speaking of the most intimate variety, but it remains unfailingly a public mode of address—the self, in this speaking, always exceeds it-self. Whenever we say anything audible, even if it is only murmured or muttered (spoken, in the colloquial, "under our breath"), we are addressing the world. The world, as such, "hears" us (we are always in the "ear of the other"), whether or not we intend to be heard or whether or not the world is listening; it does not matter whether or not the world actually processes what is said.

What is more, when a figure such as Jackie Robinson speaks in the early years of the integration of Major League Baseball (MLB), even when he thinks he is only grumbling to himself, he does so from the position of precedence. That is, his every speaking is a matter of consequence, a speaking that belongs to the world, in the world, a speaking that is almost denied any possibility of or right to privacy. As the black player who broke the game's "color line," Robinson immediately becomes historic, and as a figure of history his words stand, as they necessarily must, as a first speaking. Because of who he is, because of how history works through him, through his words, we might say, every syllable he utters is of consequence—disproportionately so, of course, but that is what it means to speak as the "force" of history, as the force through which history speaks, a history, furthermore, that has up to the point of Robinson's entry into MLB been denied such a speaking.

Jackie Robinson is, of course, inscribed as a historic figure in American and, obviously, African American, culture. Robinson authored the event of April 15, 1947, when he became the first black player to participate in an MLB game. After careful scouting by Brooklyn Dodgers part owner and president Wesley Branch Rickey to find exactly the "right" Negro ball player, Robinson was recruited by the Dodgers, also known affectionately as "Da Bums" because of their reputation for being such "lovable losers." A lawyer by trade (but he preferred baseball), the cigar-smoking Rickey ranks among baseball's great innovators. Among Rickey's greatest accomplishments was establishing the Minor League Baseball system, a system that was soon adopted by other major league clubs, the Dodgers included, while he was in the front office of the St. Louis Cardinals. After leaving the Dodgers, Rickey became president of the Pittsburgh Pirates, and it was there, in 1953, that he introduced helmets, which he insisted be worn both while at bat and in the field.[2] And it was Rickey who oversaw the construction of the Dodgers' spring training facility in Vero Beach, Florida. Although Rickey retired from the Pirates in 1955 because of ill health, it was he who drafted Roberto Clemente, the first Hispanic baseball star. The Puerto Rican–born

Clemente would go on to become a legend with the Pittsburgh Pirates, winning two World Series rings (1960, 1971), a Most Valuable Player (MVP) award (1966), a World Series MVP award (1971), and multiple All-Star appearances. Clemente was inducted into the Hall of Fame in 1973,[3] the same year that the Pirates retired 21, his number.[4]

Rickey was a shrewd and by all accounts a parsimonious executive, refusing to compensate either the Kansas City Monarchs (the Negro League team for which Robinson was then playing) for Robinson or their fellow Negro League team the Newark Eagles[5] for starting pitcher Don "Newk" Newcombe.[6] In Roger Kahn's sardonic phrasing, Rickey was a "man of principle. He had a Puritan distaste for money in someone else's hands."[7] No wonder, then, that the ever-strategic Rickey had Robinson thoroughly vetted before signing the Monarch shortstop to a contract that saw Robinson assigned to the Dodgers' International League (Triple A Minor League) affiliate, the Montreal Royals, for the 1946 season. Robinson would end up the International League batting champion that season, his only award in Minor League Baseball, as well as leading the Royals to the league championship that year.[8] Rickey understood that he was signing Robinson not only because of his baseball prowess. There were other players in the Negro Leagues who were arguably better baseball players than Robinson, such as pitcher Leroy "Satchel" Paige[9] (who was Robinson's teammate on the Monarchs and later became the second African American player to join the Cleveland Indians, after Larry Doby), catcher Josh Gibson (Homestead Grays), outfielder Monte Irvin (Newark Eagles), pitcher Don Newcombe (Newark Eagles, later Robinson's teammate on the Dodgers), and second baseman Larry Doby (Newark Eagles).[10] (Three months after Robinson broke baseball's color line, Doby became the first black player in the American League.) Still, as Clay Hopper, Robinson's manager with the Montreal Royals, so succinctly summed it up when asked about the prospects of other African American baseball players, "'There's only one Jackie Robinson.'"[11]

In August 1945, Rickey signed Robinson from the Monarchs, for whom Robinson was an exceptional shortstop. (Robinson finished out the season with the Monarchs. He reported for spring training with the Dodgers in 1946.) In addition to his baseball talents, Robinson had been a four-sport athlete at the University of California at Los Angeles, "lettering" in baseball, American football, basketball, and track. Rickey wanted Robinson over any other player from the Negro Leagues in part because of his education (although Robinson never graduated from UCLA, he was still, formally speaking, very well educated relative to his peers in both the Negro Leagues and MLB) but also because of his "temperament."[12] In Robinson's first seasons, 1947–1949, "Branch Rickey counseled him to 'turn the other cheek.'"[13] He would require forbearance of the Christological

variety because, as Kahn recalls, "Robinson was thrown at almost daily.
. . . [H]e was assaulted with terminology proceeding from 'nigger.' . . . In
the face of this Robinson was sworn to passivity and silence. He had promised Rickey that he would encase his natural volatility in lead" (*The Boys
of Summer*).[14] Robinson was not, by any means, either "passive" or "silent,"
but, in the main, Rickey knew that Robinson was the "Negro" player to
integrate because he could be trusted to keep, as Rudyard Kipling says,
"his head about him"—while everyone else around him, of course, was
allowed to lose "theirs." Rickey knew, because of what the stakes were
(nothing less than the future of baseball's great "experiment"), that he
could rely on Robinson to demonstrate poise, to maintain equanimity,
and to show restraint, perhaps restraint above all, in the face of the inevitable racism that he would have to endure from all quarters: opponents
out to hurt him (infielders or runners spiking him on the base pads, pitchers throwing at him), fans set on taunting him with racist epithets, and
officials resentful of his "intrusion" into their lily-white game. In Montreal Robinson thrived, as he would in MLB (the "Majors") when he was
promoted to the Dodgers club the following season, in no small measure
because, as Hopper reflected, "There's only one Jackie Robinson."

In his "passivity," Robinson, in Derrida's terms, "bears witness, mani-
festing already, as question, the response that testifies to a sufferance, a
passion, a not-being-able."[15] ("Passivity" and "not-being-able" is an issue
that we turn to again, using this same Derrida passage, in the chapter on
Pienaar; in that instance there is also a focus on Jeremy Bentham, from
whom Derrida takes the question "Can they suffer?," a question that obtains with especial resonance for Mandela [*The Animal That Therefore I
Am*].)[16] The "question," as such, for Robinson is not so much "Why?"—as
in "Why is he not able?"—because the answer to that line of inquiry is,
baldly phrased, entirely historical. That is, it is rooted completely in the
politics of race—American racism. The "question," rather, is a Foucaultian
one: What is the cost of "not-being-able?" Or, to refine the inquiry even
more precisely, what kind of articulation emerges out of "not-being-able"?
How must the politics of "not-being-able" (American racism) manifest itself? What kind of thinking does it demand? It might be better to cast this
situation in base psychoanalytic terms: How does the effect of "not-being-
able" "already manifest" itself? That is, how is "not-being-able" displaced?
Or where does it manifest itself? How is it encountered? What effects does
it produce?

Understood as such, "passivity" should be rendered not as the refusal
"to do," to act, because "something," an act, a response, will derive from
"passivity," but rather as the exploration of what happens because of "not-
being-able." What does "not-being-able" cause? What does it make im-pos-

sible? The Robinson event demonstrates clearly that while he is capable of "sufferance," of enduring in MLB in the face of racism, hatred, and the prospect of violence (including the possibility of being made the victim of a career-threatening or -ending injury), his capacity for enduring has its limits. That is, there is a point beyond which Robinson will not, will refuse, to "suffer"; that point is, as is discussed later at some length, the expletive, so that for Robinson the expletive must be understood as the limit; for him the expletive must be understood as the limit of endurance even if, or, especially because, of its "private" (a misnomer if there ever was one) nature. Moreover, what emerges at the limit is, cast in Derrida's terms, the "sufferance," that moment, that historical conjuncture where "not-being-able," gives way, cedes to, is overwhelmed by, "passion." The "passion" for, be it justice or enfranchisement (full membership, the right to fight back, the right to initiate a conflict, the right to swear), be it against something as consequential as systemic racism or as mundane as the right to dispute an umpire's call, is what will finally out; it is that which must, when everything has been said and done, out, make itself felt, and, as importantly, in the Robinson event, make itself heard. That is the path of history, the result of history's inexorable winding toward the refutation of the limit, and, of course, it also writes itself as the inscription of a new limit. The event establishes the (very) limit it intends to undo.

Not A . . .

There is, then, nothing of the martyr about Jackie Robinson. Or, at best, he is only a reluctant one, a subject assigned a role by history that he both accepts and chafes against, in both instances for the same reason: He detests the restraints imposed by history. Even as he is historic (the discourse of "first-ness"), makes history, it is not a history that sits well or easily with him. The burden of over-representation is not a mantle worn with great comfort; it is frequently borne entirely, we might surmise, with no joy at all. But this is, as Derrida grasps, where the contradiction comes into its own. It occurs on the fault line between a "*dynamis* or *hexis,* this having or manner of being, this *habitus* one calls a faculty or 'capability,' this can-have or the power one possesses (as in the power to reason, to speak, and everything that that implies). This question is disturbed by a certain *passivity*" (*The Animal That Therefore I Am*).[17] "Power" and "passivity" abut one another, complicate one another, mutually inform, restrict, and reinscribe each other. That is, the kind of enfranchisement that derives from Enlightenment thinking—"the power to reason, to speak, and everything that that implies" (the rights of the human)—is thrown into (political) relief by "passivity," by the knowledge, or should we call it the "sense," that the "power" of rationality (Jackie Robinson as, first and fore-most, before all else, a thinking being, a figure of thought, a figure imag-ined, fought for, in blood, and achieved in, through, and because of the Revolution that realized, in some incomplete measure, the Enlightenment project, the Enlightenment's political goals) and "voice" (in Derrida's ful-some rendering) can be damped down, can be clamped down on. That is, "passivity" as a politics, and here Derrida addresses ("directly") Branch Rickey's injunction (his "clamp down"), throws all other "power" (/powers) into not only question but also silence. "Passivity," then, as possessed—as it properly must be (Mahatma Gandhi, after all, made of Satyagraha, the "insistence on truth," a successful anticolonial weapon, as Martin Luther King Jr. made of it the preeminent strategy of the civil rights move-ment)—of many iterations, many of them not consistent or consonant with each other. In fact, the "power of passivity" must be understood not as a contradiction or an oxymoron (although substantial "power" resides in the contradiction) but as a struggle, conducted with uneven degrees of success, over how to best articulate a mode of political intervention that is ostensibly based in "not-doing," that rises out of "not-being-able."

"Passivity," as such, is indeed a mode that does, in fact, require "doing something," even if, or especially because, what is being done is nothing, when what must be done is nothing, when the situation can tolerate noth-ing else except the determination to do nothing—that is, the discipline not to do, not to act[18]—the "power," as it were, of acting through with-holding, of holding the self in check, of holding the self to itself, despite having to put up with physical (the threat of injury on the base pads, for example) or verbal provocations (racist taunts, inter alia), with remark-able discipline. Enforced self-containment, enforced over the course of a long season—more than 150 games, in the friendlier confines of the Brooklyn Dodgers' home park, Ebbets Field, or on the road, where the crowds were invariably more hostile, especially in cities such as Philadel-phia and St. Louis where the opponents (especially the Phillies' manager, Ben Chapman) and players (such as Enos Slaughter of the Cardinals, most notoriously) were unrepentant racists.

Robinson's "habitus," his entrée into MLB, playing with white team-mates who were not all enamored of his arrival in their ranks, the burden of over-representation, all of these demanded that he understand exactly the tensions inherent to and constitutive of "passivity." This meant, per-haps above all, that he must grasp unfailingly what was apropos of the moment, that he must respond to, act in the terms of, that which most fitted the moment. That is, Robinson had to be able to distinguish be-tween, categorically conceived, enduring ("sufferance") and assertion (act-ing in terms felicitous to the power of the self). Here Marx's injunction from the "Eighteenth Brumaire of Louis Bonaparte" is useful, in no small measure because it reinforces our understanding of—and the political need for—"passivity." "Men make their own history," Marx writes, "but they do not make it just as they please, they do not make it under circumstances chosen by themselves, but under circumstances directly found, given, and transmitted from the past. The tradition of all the dead generations weighs like a nightmare on the brain of the living."[19] The ability to act, to change "circumstances," to bend history to human will is, at best, a complicated business because, as Marx reminds us, we are not in a position to "choose" the very "circumstances" against which we (ostensibly) struggle. From the very beginning of any political struggle, the conditions are determined by history, by the very facticity of "what is." This does not mean that there should be no struggle, of course; on the contrary, if the conditions call for the overthrow or destruction of an unjust or racist state, then this struggle must be commenced with the utmost vigor and commitment. However, in order to conduct this struggle Marx calls for an awareness of the limitations that are imposed, a priori, by what is. It is, as we well know, entirely possible to make history. It is, however, nigh on impossible to do so under conditions of our own choosing. It is to struggle to make history within the conditions that history "allows," to struggle for history always aware of the "traditions" that "weigh on the brain of the living." The first condition of struggle may very well be, in light of Marx's warning, to understand what is and then to struggle determinedly against it, all the while making allowances for contingency, circumscription, and, yes, the possibility of political opportunity. In other words, any political struggle is a struggle for the event that can be achieved only through responsibility to history.

However, even as he "knows" the conditions under which he is integrating MLB, Robinson is all the while reaching for what he believes he "can-have," those rights to which he, as American citizen and as MLB baseball player, understands himself to be entitled to, even if, and especially because, those rights were historically denied to blacks in the United States. Robinson seeks to unleash the "power" that he "possesses," that "power" that is at once within and publicly on display on a daily basis. Robinson, we might say, wants nothing so much as to be burdened by nothing more (a considerable enough set of demands) than his everyday MLB ordinariness, his inning-by-inning effort to make plays, routine and exceptional, routine and spectacular, an undertaking that is real enough for every baseball player, regardless (needless to say) of race. The burden of over-representation, understood as articulated through Robinson, works most determinedly in the direction of its own undoing. The subject who bears the burden of over-representation seeks nothing so much as the accomplishment of his own un-exceptionality. As figured in Robinson, the burden of over-representation intends its own liquidation so that it (the Negro-integrating MLB) too can be judged, rendered, critiqued on the terms of universality. Or, phrased in the affirmative, the burden of over-representation works for its own nullification so that its exceptionality is thought as exceptional only in terms of universal criteria. "Jackie Robinson is a great player"; "Willie Mays is the greatest center fielder of his generation"; and so on. All difference, then, is articulable as exceptional only in terms of the democratic norm.

More than anything, what "passivity" reinforces is the subjection of the other to a set of (deviant) terms that severely delimits the other's capacity to fully "possess" itself, to "possess" itself as self, and not, before all else, as other. The only difference the other desires is that which distinguishes it from the universal through its exceeding the expectations of the universal (not the exceptional terms it is burdened with), not that which arises out of the discourse and the restriction (the intense politicization of difference—along the fault lines of race, gender, ethnic identity, and so on) that is the burden of over-representation, and not that which is grounded in the political soil that is the history of racism or misogyny or homophobia. That is, as Marx might have it, the "nightmare that weighs on the brain of the living," the "nightmare" that is the lived political reality of a Jackie Robinson or an Arthur Ashe or a Serena Williams.

The burden of over-representation is that inhabitation of otherness that works diligently to not be other, to be same, in the most substantive, subversive, and democratic fashion imaginable. It is the commitment to "making history" that, first, rejects and makes nothing of the extant history, and then, second, comes to make itself history, or historic, in its having superseded that "which was." It is the desire to superannuate one "what is" with another "what is" that is entirely disjunctive with the original "what is." It is to, once and for all, consign the original "what is" to history; it is the commitment to making possible an entirely new set of historical conditions. It is to open history to possibilities foreclosed by that "which once was." "What is" must, on these terms, always provide the ground for "what is not yet" and is only "not" because of the restrictions imposed on the extant history.

Because Jackie Robinson was both endemically opposed to "what was" and aware of what needed "to be," he was the ideal subject for the "great experiment" precisely because he was committed to being "just" another—not an-other—Dodger baseball player, albeit one with an extraordinary desire for victory. The echoes of Robinson's appetite for "sameness" can be heard in an apocryphal story that the Dodger captain and shortstop Pee Wee Reese tells about Robinson. (With Robinson at second base and Reese at short, the Dodgers boasted a formidable middle infield combination.) Listening to Robinson complain about how journalists were treating him, some of which Robinson attributed to his race, Reese responded: "Jackie, have you ever thought that they don't like you not because you're black, but because they just don't like you." Robinson pondered what Reese had said for a moment, and then gently acknowledged that his captain might have a point. Robinson, we might conclude, was fine with simply not being liked. In fact, in a nutshell, that might have been all he really wanted. To not be liked simply because he was Jackie Robinson.

Such is the force of negation. This is, Derrida might suggest, the "gift" of democratic ordinariness—to be like every other MLB player, a "gift" that derives from Derrida's critique of the Holocaust. For Derrida the *"gift can only be a sacrifice, that is the axiom of speculative reason. Even if it upsurges 'before' philosophy and religion, the gift has for its destination or determination, for its* Bestimmung, *a return to self in philosophy, religion's truth"* (Cinders).[20] In order for the "gift" to be made, there must be, for Derrida, some notion—an inkling, at the very least—of something that is being "given up," "given up" to the other. It is because of this exchange that Derrida turns to a formulaic logic, "axiom of speculative reason." There can be no precision, no exact accounting, for the relation between the "gift" and the requisite (the prerequisite, we are free to say) "sacrifice"—that which must, with advance knowledge, be "given up." The self must "sacrifice" in order to give to the other—something, and only something of value to the self rises to the level of "gift." In order to be worthy of the name "gift" it must, this "thing" that is being given, be—before itself—outside the logic of fair exchange. It must, in truth, serve as nothing so much as the complete refutation of the logic of exchange.

This is the "truth" of "*Bestimmung*"; this is its "destination or determination," insofar as the "sacrifice" articulates itself in relation to Robinson's "sacrifice," his un-willingness to cede to his exceptionality in order to arrive, as it were, at a very different "destination," the intensely ordinary. (Every "destination" marks the "determination" of its own truth; every "destination" seeks its own truth. Every "destination" knows that it cannot, by itself, despite its best and most concerted efforts, "determine" its own path to that "truth." It is for this reason that every "destination" must be thought, because the yearning, and desire, for every intention to arrive at or achieve said destination belongs, by way of its thinking, to Marx and, as such, to "philosophy.") Because of the auto-intensity of the Robinson exchange (Robinson gives himself the "gift" of his own "sacrifice"; what could be more costly, more difficult, yet for all that, so absolutely necessary) that is simultaneously not limited to the self (Robinson is also "sacrificing" himself, not quite Christ-like but evocative enough of that ultimate sacrifice), Robinson's "gift" adds the complexity of internality to the ways in which Derrida accounts for the logic of the "sacrifice." Robinson does this most obviously in that his dual exchanges reveal an element of "giving/giving up-receiving" that is not, certainly not at first glance, "axiomatic."

There is nothing self-evident about how, or even whether, there can be such a calculus; Robinson accounts for how the "sacrifice" that he is making might be rendered in the economy of the "gift," and the absolute conditionality of that exchange. Derrida, after all, phrases this economy in the declarative—the "gift can only be a sacrifice"—so that amending or rethinking this logic must begin not so much by arguing against or with, of all things, the difficulty of *Bestimmung* but by endeavoring to engage fully with the constitutive elements (philosophy itself) that make the logic of *Bestimmung* possible. What struggles, we might ask as a preliminary inquiry, take place under the sign of "destiny or determination"? What is neither inevitable nor solely achievable by dint of intense labor in making it possible to arrive at, say, the Robinsonian *Bestimmung* that is at once open to and demanding (more, more is needed in thinking the Robinsonian articulation) of a "truth" that expects nothing other than a "religious truth"? How does this logic cast Robinson in a different light, if at all?

Robinson's Natural Disposition

As Robinson remarks in *I Never Had It Made,* his autobiography, Rickey's injunction was fundamentally at odds with his natural disposition. At his core Robinson possessed a fierceness of being (borne of racial pride, as we later see, from his time in the U.S. Army and a native athletic competitiveness), which meant that Rickey's injunction was, (again) as we later see, fundamentally at odds with Robinson's natural disposition. "Not being able to fight back is a form of severe punishment," Robinson writes. "I was relieved when Mr. Rickey finally called me into his office and said, 'Jackie, you're on your own now. You can be yourself now.'"[21] In truth, of course, Robinson had, in an existential sense (the friendship and support of teammates such as Pee Wee Reese, the Dodgers' captain, notwithstanding), been effectively on his own from the moment that Rickey signed him. He was "on his own" in Montreal, and it would be a while before he was not "on his own" in the Dodger clubhouse. Like Jack Johnson and Joe Louis (in their different ways) before him, Robinson would have to bear the burden of over-representation[22] alone. That he spoke with the "easy fluency of an educated man"[23] was to his advantage, but—no matter that after Larry Doby began playing for the Cleveland Indians soon after he made his Dodgers debut and that within a few "short" years there would be African American baseball players on most ball clubs (Cubs: Ernie Banks, 1953; Yankees: Elston Howard, 1955; Tigers: Ozzie Virgil, 1958; Red Sox [last team to integrate]: Elijah Jerry "Pumpsie" Green, 1959;[24] and Dodgers [after Robinson]: Roy Campanella, Joe Black, Junior Gilliam)— the responsibility of representing, in and because of his exceptionality, his entire race ("'Maybe I'm doing something for my race,'"[25] Robinson remarked, clearly conscious of his role in history) remained singularly his. (That he would seem here to accept this role in no way, as we see momentarily, when we turn to Friedrich Nietzsche's work on "morality," ameliorates the relationship between sacrifice as such and its costs. Nietzsche, above all else, is clear about the costs to the self that attends to sacrifice.) The arrival of Doby, Paige, Banks, Campanella, and others in no way diminished Robinson's burden. He was, as he remains in history, the exceptional individual who is assigned, whether he wants to or not is of no consequence, the role of speaking for, speaking as, his "race."

Robinson, we can assert, was given the role of "doing something for his race," and everything he did would be judged in terms of the "plural." The burden of over-representation can never be understood to be singular. In this regard Judith Butler's work in *Giving an Account of Oneself* offers, contiguously, a way to think the condition of the over-burdened o/One. Wending her way through a counter-posing of Nietzsche and Foucault's construction of the subject (broadly phrased, "bad conscience" and "subjectivation—*assujettisement*," respectively), Butler argues for the sociality of all relations that the "I" forms. "The 'I' has no story of its own that is not also the story of a relation—or set of relations—to a norm."[26] There can, of course, be no gainsaying the veracity and political accuracy of Butler's description. However, what is specific to the burden of over-representation is, paradoxically, the non- or anti-particularity of its particular politics. The burden of over-representation designates the "exceptional" individual (think, say, W.E.B. Du Bois's notion, in all its problematics, of the "talented tenth") of a marginal or minority community as being responsible, standing in as, standing (in) for, her or his entire community—Martin Luther King Jr. or Althea Gibson, Muhammad Ali or Josephine Baker, say, "representing" all African Americans. Every act, of word or deed, of the "exceptional" individual is inscribed—over-burdened, over-determined—by its (particular) "universality" which is, of course, not a "universal" at all, at least not in any etymological sense. The "exceptional" individual, in this way, is allowed no exceptionality. It is denied the exceptional individual because any transgression, of even the most insignificant variety, assumes a disproportionate importance. Failure, as such, is not an option for the exceptional individual—too exceptional to fail, we might say. (There are, of course, exceptional figures from minority or marginalized communities who refuse these constraints. Jack Johnson and Muhammad Ali, in their different ways, come immediately to mind, allowing for their different modes of transgression, of course, or Serena Williams, as a more contemporary heir to the Johnson-Ali legacy of outspoken opposition to the forces that be. However, such figures are, not to put too fine a point on it, themselves exceptions within the logic of the burden of over-representation and the ways in which that responsibility is borne by exceptional figures more generally. And these exceptions, as we know and as I have written about elsewhere,[27] are more often than not made to pay a high price for their transgressions, for their refusal to submit to the terms of the burden of over-representation.)

No exceptions can be brooked, so that the "exceptional" individual is always expected to conform to, to act in accordance with, the dominant norms; every "failure," real or imagined, substantial or putative, opens the (public-dominant) door to a condemnation of the entire community. And, in his or her very "exceptionality," the "exceptional" individual is, simultaneously, proposed as (absolutely) different to and representative of its community. In this way, the exceptional individual is the very iteration of potentiality, both as a singular being and as that figure who embodies, metonymically, the potentiality of the marginalized collectivity. The condition of the exceptional individual is, finally, explicable only as negation. In the first sense, negation follows the logic of inexorability, inflected with a Darwinian twist: "failure" is always held up as nothing but the "natural" (expected) aptitude for recidivism that dominates the marginal community; in the second sense, the "exceptional" individual stands as a judgment on her or his entire community and their "collective" (that is, the collectivity of historically failed, and failing, individuals) "failure" to meet the standards of the "exceptional" individual. This logic of "exceptionality" institutes a vicious political cycle.

When the "exceptional" individual "fails," he affirms the a priori negation that his accomplishments stand counter to; when she "succeeds," she condemns her own community in the harshest possible terms. In this way, the "exceptional" individual also performs, in and through its exceptionality, a disciplinary function in its standing as the exemplary subject from the margins—of marginality. The "exceptional" individual becomes the discursive mechanism for keeping the other, or, more precisely, others like her or him, in line; the exemplary subject can be invoked, because of its exemplarity, to keep order among the others, to keep the other in her or his "proper" place. Cast in Michel Foucault's terms (especially in *The History of Sexuality*, vol. 1),[28] this is the logic of neoliberal efficiency—the marginalized can be made to police themselves, can be made to conform to dominant expectations simply by singling out, and thereby reifying, the exceptional individual. The burden of over-representation, rendered as a Foucaultian enterprise, is ruthlessly efficient, in no small measure because of its ability to "outsource" (through the subject's "internalization") the work of "self-discipline." The other is made responsible for "otherness," for the other, for all others. The exemplary subject serves as a visceral (intimate, proximate, and "mimetic") reminder to the other in its "ability" to stage "appropriate behavior." Biopolitically speaking, the exemplary subject can be understood as the minimalism of the discursive: The other is introduced to, reminded of, held to the same standards as, the exemplary subject. The exemplary subject is who—what—all others must aspire to.

"Failure," as such, awaits the "exceptional" individual at every turn. At best, it is postponed; at worst, a postponement does nothing but delay the (historical) inevitable. "Failure," as such, is inveterately temporal. It is always *l'avenir;* it is always only a matter of time. No wonder, then, that Butler insists that all and every relation is, before itself, ethically constituted. An ethics that obtains with an especial force, and virulence (we might as easily designate it "racism" or "homophobia" or "ethnocentrism" or . . .) for the "exceptional" individual of the over-burdened variety. For such an individual, and here Jackie Robinson stands as both a "routine" and a historic instance, the burden of over-representation allows for no division, no fissure or aporia, between the "universal" and the particular. The particular or the singular (if these might be permitted, for a moment, as interchangeable) is, without question, the "universal," indistinguishable from the whole; the part is the whole, and the singular is relentlessly pluralized at once into and against its own singularity.

So conceived, Robinson is subject to, is the exemplary subject of, the force of symptomaticity. As the first player from the Negro Leagues to play in MLB, Robinson can be said to constitute, for all political intents and purposes, his "race." He thus stands "on his own" in the singular plural— the "universalized," against his will, singular. As in, Jackie Roosevelt Robinson, the son of a single mother (effectively) from Cairo, Georgia, transplanted to Pasadena, California, *is* blackness, *is* black America. He is one, he is the One, he is All. Jackie Robinson is, in Butler's term, subject/ed to an act that is "radically unwilled" (*Giving an Account of Oneself*).[29] (The blatant lack of choice inscribed in or as the force of the "radically unwilled" evokes the Christological that Kahn raises with his allusion to Christian "passivity"—Robinson operating under the Methodist Rickey's injunction to "turn the other cheek." The high moment in the Christian discourse of the "radically unwilled" is, of course, the Crucifixion; rendered colloquially, it is Jesus-the-Christ "accepting" his fate, the fate that he would prefer not to endure but submits himself to per his Father's command. We know this as the submission that is "Let not my will but Thy will be done," so that we are always, with a figure such as Robinson and whenever the burden of over-representation is present, aware of the language and the demand of the sacrificial—the self made vulnerable or, worse, the self made vulnerable against its own will, as in the case of Jesus-the-Christ on the eve of his being put to death or, in the logic of the martyr, the self un-willingly sacrificing itself.)

The burden of over-representation endured, no less, not only externally—Robinson, ensconced within the Dodgers organization, not safe there, against the racist predations of the world—but also internally. As history shows, there were Dodger teammates who shared the antipathy of America's white majority. Kahn writes that the "most extreme of Dodger racists turned out be Dixie Walker."[30] (Appropriate, one might say, as if to make the "aptly" named "Dixie Walker" stand as the overdetermined bearer of the defeated South: Walker, the "Dixie Dodger," Walker, the Dodger against the kind of integration still, in 1947, prohibited south of the Mason-Dixon line and elsewhere in the United States, of course.) In *Jackie Robinson: A Biography,* Arnold Rampersad provides a fuller list of the Dodger players opposed to Robinson's promotion from Montreal to the Brooklyn club: "At the center was a core of Southern veterans: the pitchers Hugh Casey of Georgia and Kirby Higbe of South Carolina; a backup catcher, Bobby Bragan of Alabama; and Dixie Walker, also of Alabama, not only an explosive hitter and outfielder but also the most popular player in Brooklyn—'the People's Cherce,' in the local lingo. The outfielder Carl Furillo of Reading, Pennsylvania, also backed the revolt."[31] In the face of this, Robinson was duty bound by his promise to Rickey to "encase his natural volatility in lead."

Such were the "problems" that Robinson faced, these "problems" that he confronted were the "price of progress" that Rickey could, at best, only ever have imagined but that constituted the everyday experience that was Robinson's professional life as a baseball player. The "problem" with Rickey's delineation of the "problem," as it were, was that—again—it required the payment of a "price" that was inordinately borne by the exemplary subject, by the black subject he, Rickey, the white man from Ohio, determined to be "exemplary," exceptional within the ranks of "his people." The burden of over-representation, we might suggest, assumes, simultaneously, several forms. This exacts its costs in many currencies; it speaks itself in a range of political registers, including what Shakespeare calls, in *Othello,* as we see shortly, the "curse of service."

Before There Was Rosa Parks, There Was Second Lieutenant Robinson[32]

Jackie Robinson came into MLB in 1947 as a figure who had a history of opposition to institutional American racism. Robinson's propensity for resisting American racism goes back to his army days. More precisely, it can be traced to that day, July 6, 1944, when Second Lieutenant Robinson refused, in historically prescient terms, to go to the back of the military bus while he was serving at Camp Hood, Texas, the "headquarters of the 761st Tank Battalion," a military station where Jim Crow obtained with a force (Rampersad).[33] Robinson had been transferred from the Fort Riley, Kansas, army base, "home . . . to the only all-black cavalry regiment in the military," where life for black servicemen was, if not exactly free from racial incident, then certainly easier than Camp Hood (Rampersad).[34] (Fort Riley was the same army location where both Joe Louis and Robinson did their basic training. Robinson and Louis became friends, playing golf and riding together, among other things. Robinson had been drafted in 1942, as was Louis.)[35] The event of July 1944 therefore situates Robinson's resistance to Jim Crow legislation as one of the first instances of defiance in the movement that would become, in the 1950s, the full-fledged campaign for civil rights. As a historic figure in the civil rights movement, Robinson can be said to be the (heir of the nineteenth-century Elizabeth Jennings and the) progenitor of Rosa Parks, whose December 1955 refusal to give up her seat to a white person inaugurated the thirteen-month-long bus boycott in Montgomery, Alabama. This led to the Supreme Court decision in December 1956 finding the Montgomery and Alabama laws upholding segregation unconstitutional.

The boycott by African Americans of the Montgomery Bus Line stands in many ways as the inaugural event of the civil rights movement, supported as it was by prominent figures such as Martin Luther King Jr., Ralph Abernathy, and other key black leaders in the struggle against statutory racism. Parks herself was the secretary of the Montgomery chapter of the National Association for the Advancement of Colored People (NAACP) and as such was practiced in the art of politics. As a member of the NAACP she was assigned to investigate cases of sexual assault, including the 1945 one where she oversaw the inquiry into the gang rape of Recy Taylor in Abbeville, Alabama. (In September 1944, Taylor was on her way home from church when she was kidnapped and raped by six white men. The men admitted guilt, but two grand juries refused to indict them, meaning that the case never went to trial.) All this a full decade before the event that bus driver James F. Blake set in motion. All this, we might say, following Foucault, as Parks is "discovering" the "truth of her being," the intensity of her "desire" for justice, equality, and the rights of citizenship in a southern state dedicated to the practice of Jim Crow. We can say of Parks, as we can of Robinson (allowing for the specifics of their experiences), that every encounter with the bus driver Blake (there were two, more than a decade apart), every encounter with discrimination on the Montgomery Bus Line or elsewhere in her work as a respected seamstress or in her activism as an NAACP member brought Parks ever more intensely "into play" with her political desire.

Robinson's refusal to give up his seat on a military bus, of course, had nothing like the impact that Parks's decision to remain in hers did. (Parks, we should recall, refused because she was in the black section when a white passenger got on, and the white bus driver, Blake, told her to move.[36] Parks, insisting on her right to sit in the "Negro" section, refused, and the boycott was born.)[37] However, the Fort Riley event provides both access to and the history of the "truth" of Robinson's political "being." In the same period, 1944–1945, that Parks was investigating sexual assault, Robinson was enacting resistance in much the same way that would make Parks a national figure in the discourse and history of modern American race and (resistance to) racism. Across a decade of institutional racism in America, Robinson and Parks are concatenated by the same political desires, by the shared desire to "discover," before the world, the "truth of their beings": to show that "truth," and to present that "truth" on the order of a Rickeyean "problem" for America.

By June 1944, the army "forbade segregation on its military bases," a fact of which Robinson was well aware (Rampersad).[38] When the driver of the military bus, Milton N. Renegar, told Robinson to move from his seat—in the middle of the bus, sitting next to Virginia Jones, wife of First Lieutenant Gordon H. Jones Jr., who was serving in the same battalion as Robinson—to the back, Robinson refused. (In Alabama, Joe Louis and another great boxer, Sugar Ray Robinson, encountered similar experiences and invoked the same regulations that Jackie Robinson did.) Renegar contacted the Military Police (MP) ahead of getting to the bus station, who summarily escorted Robinson into their facility. While being held there, Robinson got into a series of verbal altercations with a number of white MP and military personnel (at least a couple of whom, in Robinson's account, used the N-word, an issue that Robinson would address when he appeared before the nine-member tribunal), insisting on his right to seating as consistent with army regulations. The upshot of the incident, which lasted for a good few hours, saw Robinson transferred to the 758th Tank Battalion and, on the very same day of his transfer, July 24, 1944, arrested by the MP. (Twenty years later, to the day, the great baseball slugger Barry Bonds, one of the last players in the "Majors" to actively keep Robinson's memory alive, would be born.)

Robinson was court-martialed, and the case, which lasted more than four hours, was heard on August 2, 1944. The charges included "insubordination, disturbing the peace, drunkenness, conduct unbecoming an officer, insulting a civilian woman, and refusing to obey the lawful orders of a superior officer."[39] The panel, which needed six votes to acquit, found Robinson, who spoke eloquently in his defense, "not guilty." However, a month after the court-martial, after being nominally reassigned to the 761st, he was transferred from Camp Hood to Camp Breckenridge, Kentucky, where he joined the 372nd Infantry Regiment; after that he was reassigned yet one more time, in this case to Camp Wheeler, Georgia. But, for all intents and purposes, Robinson's time in the U.S. military was a thing of the past.

"The Curse of Service"

In November 1944, Second Lieutenant Jackie Robinson was honorably discharged from the U.S. Army. However, what Shakespeare's Iago calls the "curse of service," historically speaking, was, in truth, only beginning for Robinson. While Robinson's capacity to confront power—or injustice, in the Camp Hood instance—led, in the wake of the court-martial and the situation that provoked it, to Robinson's acquiring a reputation as a confrontational figure,[40] *that* Jackie Robinson has been rendered largely incommensurate with the historic figure of the "Negro" who integrated baseball. In short, the Jackie Robinson of the Camp Hood court-martial, an event that is either too easily glossed or parsed (etymologically: that his anger or "violence" belongs to an earlier Robinsonian "grammar," if you will), is too often disarticulated from and overwhelmed by a necessarily fictive Jackie Robinson—that is, Robinson not so much as a figure "made up" by history, a history of the present that was pre–civil rights America as well as all the succeeding presents but as the "Negro" baseball player who facilitated the transition to integration in the "smoothest" possible way. That is, Robinson figured as the least racially contentious and politically fractious "Negro" and, as such, the black body most "amenable" to effecting the change that was actually a massive upheaval in not only the racial composition of MLB but also the national psyche—Jackie Robinson, then, as a figure of quiescence.

Of course, this representation has been challenged by several authors (a number of whom are invoked here), but the Jackie Robinson of the popular imaginary, if you will, persists. After all, such a Robinson serves American self-narration very well. And so, because of his historic role in desegregating baseball, Robinson has been overdetermined as the de-racialized figure of tolerance and integration par excellence. That is, Jackie

Robinson as simultaneously the exemplary integrationist, as the re-
strained, disciplined Negro who made black players tolerable to white
America and Jackie Robinson as the (now) eviscerated political cipher who
"transcends" race by making it, in the face of the (receding, denuded) history he made, a matter of "history"—that political configuration that belongs, incontrovertibly, to a moment that is past.

In this regard Robinson, as a man who is made to do his historical duty,
evokes Shakespeare's Iago. A man anachronistic to his time (as Robinson
has been rendered a man for all postracial times, a time which may now, if
one is not scrupulous about the actual conditions and faithful to Robinson
himself, be traced all the way to April 15, 1947), relying on a model of political ascent that the Moor Othello dispenses with, at, of course, his cost.
Iago reflects:

> I follow him to serve my turn upon him.
> We cannot all be masters, nor all masters
> Cannot be truly followed.
> (Othello)[41]

At the very least, it seems that we should agree that "now" (Robinson's,
ours, and every contemporary in-between) is always the moment, always a
good moment, to reinstitute Robinson as a figure who was, in some moder-
ate measure if not entirely (none of us are, after all, completely in control
of ours), the "master" of his own fate. However, such a recognition must
begin with the plethora of demands that Robinson confronted. After all,
to phrase it as a matter of pure arithmetic (or, more precisely, as a matter
of addition), how many "masters" is it exactly that Robinson was called on
to "serve"? Such a query must, of historical necessity, proceed from the
demands placed on Robinson by his own community. For other "Negroes"
in that era, Robinson incarnated the pride and aspirations of black America reaching for the moment that would become the civil rights movement.
All this, of course, while still having to endure the political violence extant
in an age when Jim Crow was still very much a thriving enterprise, in the
North as well as the South. (An enterprise that, in light of police brutality
against black bodies in Baltimore, Minneapolis, Ferguson, inter alia, and
the event of white supremacy/KKK/Nazism in Charlottesville, continues
to thrive well into the twenty-first century.) And what of the ambitions of
Branch Rickey, a baseball man with as keen a sense of history as of the
pocketbook? For Rickey Robinson was, among other things, the passport
to a more competitive Brooklyn club, as well as a more financially lucrative
one. And, as his fellow Negro Leaguers knew, every Robinson success (that
is, every hit, every brilliant play in the field, every stolen base, every game-

winning home run) was inscribed with an import that extended far beyond the field of play: If Robinson succeeded, their chances of "diversifying"—to use an ugly term—MLB increased significantly; should he fail, of course, the same logic applied, only negatively.

It is in this regard that Kahn's *Boys of Summer,* part homage to the "Jackie Robinson Dodgers," part bildungsroman (the coming-of-age of the young Jewish boy in Brooklyn, a tale of love, literature, and loss), and part commentary on an America at war with itself over its racism, offers an insight that throws just about everything into question. Robinson's sense of propriety, his (acquired, who knows at what cost) aptitude for suffering, as Shakespeare might have put it in that other famous tragedy (the most famous, many might say), the "slings and arrows of outrageous" American racism, is—if not undone then—certainly thrown into stark relief by a little-regarded incident in Kahn's book. In this situation, as described by Kahn, we find Robinson, for once (within the confines of the baseball field), not temperate but "rude," like the Moor Othello, "in speech," refusing the "soft phase of peace." Here, in this "small" moment in *The Boys of Summer,* we have the opportunity to come face to face with Jackie Robinson being "rude." And, what is more, a Robinson apparently in no mood for "peace."

Let us make our acquaintance with this Jackie Robinson, uncast, liberated for a moment, from Rickey's shackles. Let us listen to Robinson, as it were, in his own words. And this is what, to wrest the moment entirely out of its context for a moment, in order to better grasp the context(s) later on (there are two such situations), we witness. We are privy to Robinson in full political flow, emphatically denunciatory. Jackie Robinson declaring: "Stupid bastards. . . . You got it coming. You're only getting what's coming. Don't cheer those bastards, you stupid bastards. Take what you got coming. Don't cheer" (Kahn).[42] Confusion is allowed here, but let us follow Jackie Robinson's imperative and agree on at least this: "Stupid bastards" should "not cheer" for "what they have coming."

"Stupid Bastards"

It is a little difficult to figure who exactly the object of Jackie Robinson's scorn and ire is in his "stupid bastards" declamation. As a matter of grammatical distinction we are, therefore, left to wonder how we tell one group of "bastards" from that other group. Indeed, what makes "those bastards" different from other ones, the "stupid bastards"? "Stupid bastards," apparently, are everywhere, as, apparently, are your run-of-the-mill, garden-variety "bastards." However, such is the intensity with which the expletive "bastard" is uttered by Robinson that we cannot but suspect that this address cannot but contain within itself, located within it, there where its articulation and application might be most powerful and, possibly, corrosive, a painful address to the self.

This scene might constitute the moment, an instance of unmitigated rage, when Robinson achieves the patina of a tragic Shakespearean figure. Jackie Robinson as Othello, saying after the Moor: "As if there were some monster in [my] thought / Too hideous to be shown" (*Othello*).[43] Speaking here to Iago, whom Othello still at this stage believes to be an "honest man," Shakespeare's Moor affords us a glimpse of the internality of Robinson's anger. That is, the anger that can find no public enunciation because of Robinson's "moral contract" with Rickey, a contract based on the impossible, the repression of the self, the repression of the "truth of being." What Rickey's contract sought was to insist that Robinson's anger, which, as we know, has an anti-institutional history, be retained into the self, that it be, as it were, kept inside the self. Like Othello, then, there can be little wonder that, because it is institutionally imposed, because it intends to secure Robinson's public silence, these two historic black figures cannot but assume the visage of the "monster," an anger, a "truth of being" that is "too hideous to be shown."

However, the "hideousness" of the "monster," we are well aware, derives from without: Its origin, as a political symptom and cause, lies outside of Robinson; the racism to which Robinson is responding is the cause of Robinson's anger; the terms of Rickey's "moral contract" are, as such, unjust to Robinson and constitute yet one more racist iteration of what Foucault names the *"mode of subjection (mode d'assujettissement)"* (*The Use of Pleasure*).[44] If the contract, as proposed by Rickey and agreed to, however reluctantly or wholesomely, by Robinson, is founded on "subjection" in any form, then, we can assert, the contract, from its very inscription, from its very first speaking (when Rickey proposed this to Robinson), can make no claim on the status of "morality."[45] Such a claim is *verboten* because, as Nietzsche reminds us in the "Second Essay: 'Guilt,' 'Bad Conscience' and the Like" of *On the Genealogy of Morals,* any relation that is grounded in the "will to self-maltreatment" amounts to nothing other than, when all is said and done, "bad conscience."[46] The "will to self-maltreatment," as Nietzsche elaborates, resides at the perverse core of the "enigma" that is *"selflessness, self-denial, self-sacrifice"*: It is the "nature the *delight* that the selfless man, the self-denier, the self-sacrificer feels from the first: this delight is tied to cruelty" (*On the Genealogy of Morals*).[47] This is a Faustian bargain, one agreed to in perverse knowledge (self-knowledge): The price the "selfless man" must pay for his "delight" is an exacting "cruelty." A "cruelty" imposed on the self, but not entirely by the self on itself. It receives help from elsewhere, in this regard. This cost constitutes part of the inaugural "agreement"—"from the first"—to which the "selfless man" appends his name.

The price of pleasure or "delight" is pain or "cruelty." The "delight" of playing in the "Majors," the historic "delight" of being the first player from the Negro Leagues to be signed by an MLB club, cannot, "from the first," be thought apart from the "cruelty" that is "from the first" present in the agreement. This is, in the blues lore of Robert Johnson, the deal that "delight" (Robinson) makes with "cruelty" (Robinson) at the crossroads that is the integration of MLB (Rickey, as architect of the deal). "Selflessness" in no way inoculates the "man" against the inherent "cruelty." No good deed, especially not one that is conceived out of the amalgam that is "delight-cruelty" (a perversity, in truth), goes unpunished. This Jackie Robinson found out what, even if he could not, no matter that he could not, at the moment of his signing, have known in advance. In fact, we might propose Robinson as the "self-sacrificer" (giving himself up for the "greater good"—more opportunities for other black players, accelerating the nascent historical process that was the incipient civil rights movement, intensifying the move toward more social integration in the United States) who once signs his name to the agreement ("delight") but who also, in the same political gesture, countersigns his name ("cruelty"), thereby obviating and renouncing his claims to the former. Robinson, in other words, both signs for and against himself. In this way, Robinson's is nothing other than a historic signing, a signature that makes history at the very moment that Robinson puts pen to paper.

Robinson's self-negating signatures, there is no other way to understand his "dual" signing, write for us the "enigmatic nature" of "cruelty." In that most enigmatic of his works, *Glas* (in the "section"/"autonomous text," if either of these is the correct term, that is, let us agree for the sake of economy, ostensibly on Jean Genet),[48] Derrida extends our thinking of the contract as a "cruelty" into a more fatal obligation. Once a signature has been appended to the contract, there can be only one outcome. The contract, Derrida writes, "does not have the burial (place) as its object. Burial is not an event to come, foreseen by a contractual act. Burial is the signature of the contract."[49] The contract is, by its very nature, overdetermined and, as such, guarantees nothing more than a morbid end-ing. (An end, we might speculate, that is signed by the signature.) Death, from the moment the hand inclines toward "inking" its name, tying itself to the other, is all—is the very most?—that can be expected. What begins as the promise of self-negation (the act of signing), is precisely what is delivered. Writing the self, as scrawl, a squiggle, the clear, simple rendition of the name in cursive, the indecipherable penmanship that flows naturally from a life of practice, is nothing but the act of writing, in a single palimpsestic act, the death of MLB as it knew itself, the death of the "gentlemen's agreement" as much as it constituted the death of the self, the sacred act of writing the self toward death. (The "gentlemen's agreement" was the pact that white MLB owners made to never sign a player from the Negro Leagues. That is, the pact was to keep America's pastime white for all time. It was an agreement that was at once discriminatory and fragile because, as MLB found out, once Rickey signed Robinson, the agreement was nullified. Even, that is, if it took teams such as the Boston Red Sox longer to sign black players.) And here, we must recognize, the Heideggerian "inflection" that all being is being toward death cannot be avoided. In light of Heidegger's assertion, we can say that the "gentlemen's agreement" was always destined for the dustbin of history, it was always going to end up with an unceremonious "burial." Jackie Robinson's role, his responsibility, was to hammer the first nail in the coffin of an immoral agreement. His signature marked, ceremoniously, a political death of a high order.

But, the grave "stake of the signature," as Derrida puts it, also allows, contra Heidegger, for the possibility of constituting—of making, of living—life in death (*Glas*).[50] In this way the signature(s)—Robinson's and Rickey's—also recognize, in Nietzsche's terms, life as the intervention into the life afforded by the (fatality of the) contract. We can *setzen* (posit, locate, put; the term will be discussed more fully shortly) Robinson, then, as a man of, at the very least, insight, or, as is equally likely, a figure possessed of a historic foreknowledge born out of, as Nietzsche puts it, a commitment to the "ideal"—a man born determined to ring a full life from the time before the "burial" (*On the Genealogy of Morals*).[51] Reductively phrased, Robinson *knew* (as much as it is possible to know under any given set of circumstances, which is why Nietzsche insists on concatenating self-sacrifice to self-denial) that selflessness and sacrifice, Nietzsche's moral architecture, are bridged—inveterately connected—by denial. As such, we can argue that for a figure like Robinson it is not advisable or wise to contemplate too much the "cruelty" that awaits, to linger too long on what it was he was signing on for (as in the case of Jesus-the-Christ); instead, it is more historic, and poetic, to posit him as possessed of an exceptional insight, since he knew "it all," since he knew it as only the man who can uphold both the terms of selflessness/self-sacrifice and self-denial can. No wonder, then, that Nietzsche, echoing Shakespeare's key adjective, concludes that such an agreement is founded on a "rude kind of logic" (*On the Genealogy of Morals*).[52] It is the kind of "rude logic" that ensures the ubiquity of "cruelty." It is the "kind of logic" that causes Nietzsche to, parenthetically, of course, indict a philosophical predecessor in terms that are at once gentle and sardonic (it stands as one of the many funny moments in *On the Genealogy of Morals*), with the former serving only to ameliorate but never to obfuscate the latter: "Not even in good old Kant: the categorical imperative smells of cruelty."[53]

Out of this "rude logic," however, Derrida—in the spirit of Robinson, or Robinson, true to the *l'avenir* spirit of Derrida—offers the possibility of the signature, in all its ephemerality, inked under the sign of fatality, as the repository for a future, a future that must, in the case of Robinson, begin with an eye toward potentiality, toward that fullness of life that seeks to ensure life beyond itself. In these terms, Derrida writes in undiminished hope of and for the signature, "At the limit, of the text, of the world, there would remain nothing more than an enormous signature, big with everything it will have engulfed in advance, but pregnant with itself alone" (*Glas*).[54] "At the limit," that very "limit" that Rickey's and Robinson's signatures first tested, then erased, then consigned to the "eternal future" that is history, there comes into being "Jackie Robinson" writ large, "big with everything." And, in its having been written, in the inking of the signature that inscribes an "enormous" name (a list which may or may not include God, g-d, and, say, utopia)—the name that belongs to a future that it is impatient to write for, a future that takes its very lexicon from that which it intends to extinguish, to write "out," the black man's hand "blacking out" in anticipation of "engulfing" the entirety of *l'avenir*—there is to be found a new itinerary of names, boldly pronounced, names that "engulf" and overwhelm through the elision (and the shaming) of the "gentlemen's agreement," "names" that "engulf," before their arrival, and announce themselves.

Let us permit ourselves a short roll call of these games. We can begin with Moses Walker (in May 1884, the first black player in MLB), Charlie Grant (a "light-skinned" black player who tried to pass as a native American), and proceed through "Cool Papa" Bell (St. Louis Stars, Monarchs, Chicago American Giants, Homestead Grays), "Satchel" Paige, Willie Mays, Hank Aaron (Braves), Minnie Minoso (Chicago White Sox), all the way to Roberto Clemente. Along a striated surface, interspersed with the cruel cuts of racism, from one century through another, these names "engulf." And yet, the name, *the* name, "Jackie Robinson," remains singular. Robinson's signature gave these names, all of them, new life, or a life, so that they can all be said to emerge out of his (name). His name, however, retains to itself that singular force. The name "Robinson" is "pregnant with itself alone." It birthed these, and many other, names, and as such it has given birth to legions of other names (Rod Carew, Barry Bonds, Ken Griffey Jr., David Ortiz), but it is a name, "Robinson," that will remain "fertile" and flush with possibility for as long there is MLB. As such, the name "Jackie Robinson" means.

An "Immoral Contract"

> The *fear* of the ancestor and his power, the consciousness of
> indebtedness to him, increases, according to this kind of logic, in
> exactly the same measure as the power of the tribe itself increases,
> as the tribe itself grows ever more victorious, independent,
> honored, and feared.
>
> —FRIEDRICH NIETZSCHE, *On the Genealogy of Morals*

The effect of Rickey's "moral contract" is, understood in Nietzsche's terms,
a profoundly "immoral" imposition, notwithstanding its (too late, too
slow) liquidation of the extant (unsigned because it needed no signature; it
could stand, until it could not, by itself) "gentlemen's agreement." It is "immoral" even if, as has been argued earlier, one allows for the historical
context, a context that is, as we well know, overdetermined by the burden
of over-representation. There can be no "moral contract," no matter that we
ascribe only an etymological understanding to "moral," if it begins from
the premise of the "will to self-maltreatment." We cannot, as Nietzsche
points out, but think the "im-moral" contract as an agreement, as the conciling of one individual to another (the legal contract as the [first] act of
political encounter, the legal contract as conciliation, in the case of Rickey
and Robinson) that is haunted by the specter of violence, which is especially true of and for black players from the Negro Leagues because they
were all subject—that is, vulnerable to—the effects of the (white) "gentlemen's agreement" among all the owners of MLB franchises not to sign
black players. In signing Robinson, Rickey was "violating" that "agreement"
(immoral, we can agree) and, as such (an issue to which we turn later in this
section), ensuring not the undoing of that agreement but (to think it in
Derrida's terms) its "burial."

All "moral contracts" of the Rickey-Robinson variety, Nietzsche reminds us, consist in the "sphere of legal obligations" (*On the Genealogy of
Morals*).[55] It is in this "moral conceptual world" that "'guilt,' 'conscience,'
'duty,' 'sacredness of duty' had its origin: its beginnings were, like the beginnings of everything great on earth, soaked in blood thoroughly and for
a long time" (*On the Genealogy of Morals*).[56] In the "Second Essay," Nietzsche
ranges over a wide variety of rights and contracts. He begins with animals, stating "To breed an animal *with the right to make promises*"; invokes
the Greeks; muses about the "original tribal community"; critiques civil
law; historicizes *Don Quixote*; reflects on his compatriots, the Germans,
and their history of punishment; and returns ever so often to the ways of
the "Christian God" (*On the Genealogy of Morals*).[57] All the while Nietzsche,
a little disdainful of our modern sensitivities, a little mocking about our

inability to endure our cruelty, at once funny and disconcerting in his (perverse?) critiques of distaste for cruelty, insists on the ways in which, before "us moderns," pain (punishment, cruelty) was constitutive of human pleasure, a fact of life that was preeminently present in "pre-modern" festivals, and he is wistful for the "days when mankind was not yet ashamed of its cruelty" (*On the Genealogy of Morals*).[58]

Everywhere, as he ranges, Nietzsche brings to light some form, some inscription, of violence, violence and inequity. In figuring the case of Robinson's integration into MLB, we cannot but invoke the specter of violence. The history of violence against black bodies in the United States that marked the "Robinson era" (symptomatic of this period, the mid-1940s to the mid-1950s, might be, epigrammatically, Recy Taylor and Emmett Till), of course, is a centuries-old endeavor, and so if one thinks Robinson's willingness to accept, as his "duty" to his race (in a tone that is no way free from the discourse of "self-sacrifice"), the Nietzschean specter of historical experience "soaked in blood thoroughly and for a long time" rises before us. (Such a specter, we can insist, is true of every historical experience.) In presenting Robinson as an exemplary subject there is nothing to do but calculate the costs that attach to the "sacredness of duty." What Nietzsche also makes imperative in our thinking of "baseball's great experiment" is to recognize the unbreakable link between the "great beginning" that Rickey seeks to inaugurate through and with Robinson's conscription into history and the "bloodiness" that preceded (and succeeded) it. It is possible, furthermore, to understand Nietzsche's motif (which echoes white southern violence), "soaked in blood," not only in terms of the black bodies against whom violence was enacted, a real enough history, but also in reflecting on the careers of players—stalwarts, stars, up-and-coming young players, journeymen—in the Negro Leagues who were denied "great-er" (economic and athletic) opportunities.

The deliberate (racist) circumscription of professional prospects constituted an act of economic violence against talented black players in the Negro Leagues. This was one of the intended effects of the gentlemen's agreement. Violence, then, understood as more striated in its operation, was more wide ranging in its effects. Damaged bodies, destroyed hopes, racial economy, and, arguably most important of all, devastated psyches and historically unfulfillable athletic and professional ambition. We see a glimpse of the last mentioned in the bitterness that "Satchel" Paige barely represses—in public, at least—at Jackie Robinson's ascension. Paige understands Robinson's "first-ness," his historicity, as having been achieved at his, Paige's, expense. Thwarted ambition, in Paige's case, was almost indistinguishable from perceived injustice and (intraracial) *ressen-*

timent. Violence here (white on black), violence there (black on black, although, it must be said, of an altogether different variety and order), bloody violence everywhere.

However, at the core of Nietzsche's concern with the "sphere of legal obligations" is the question of who has the *"right to make promises"* (*On the Genealogy of Morals*).[59] Rickey and Robinson operate, from the very beginning, in precisely this "sphere" so that the question of "right" applies to the "contract" between Rickey (a lawyer by training) and Robinson, between white and black, MLB owner and the architect of the "great experiment," and constitutes both a legal and a moral agreement. Nietzsche is careful about this matter, going so far as to provide us with the political profile of the constitution of the subject who possesses the "right to make promises." Nietzsche's is a profile that Jackie Robinson will challenge, in no small measure because of what Nietzsche's language evokes. But for the moment, let us familiarize ourselves with Nietzsche's profile, a politically dense portrait, to be sure. According to Nietzsche, only the "emancipated individual, with the actual *right* to make promises, this master of a *free* will, this sovereign man. . . . [this man whose] mastery over himself also necessarily gives him mastery over circumstances, over nature, and over all more short-willed and unreliable creatures . . . [t]he 'free' man, the possessor of a protracted and unbreakable will, also possesses his *measure of value*" (*On the Genealogy of Morals*).[60]

Following Nietzsche's argument, it would be entirely plausible to *setzen*[61] (posit) Rickey (the white man, the white man who stands unquestionably as the—enfranchised—"emancipated individual") as the only party to the contract who possesses the "actual right to make promises." On the face of it, Robinson, conceived within an American legal and political context that had, just to begin with, denied him the right to sit where he chose on a military bus on a military base as a conscripted military officer, denied all Negroes before him the play in the "Majors," allowed Jim Crow legislation to disenfranchise large numbers of its black citizenry, can hardly be posited as a "sovereign man." On these legally unequal (immoral, il-legal) terms, which lead inexorably to the question of political (and, possibly, ethical) record, how could Robinson and Rickey be "equal partners" to their "moral contract"?

In the terms of extant U.S. law (pre–civil rights legislation), Rickey was transgressing—as we see in the Dixie Walker et al. response to Robinson's promotion to the Dodgers MLB club—the nation's "immoral contract" and breaking irrevocably with the "gentlemen's agreement" that his co-owners were (largely) intent on upholding. Until Rickey contracted Robinson, the official unofficial prohibition on signing black players to the "Majors" obtained, and it promised to do so for the foreseeable future—

this despite what can be described only as minimal "moral" pressure on MLB franchises, leading to sham tryouts such as the one that the Red Sox staged for Robinson.[62] While granting that "legal" equality between Rickey and Robinson could not be actualized at the moment of their "moral" agreement, it can, however, not be denied that, in all crucial aspects, it is Robinson, the de facto disenfranchised Negro, who, paradoxically and yet not, conforms more than any other figure in the "great experiment" to Nietzsche's profile of the "emancipated man." And, in so doing, Robinson issues a constitutive challenge to Nietzsche's conception but, more importantly, he presents an instance of ethical rebuke as well as a political threat to the American status quo.

To begin, poetically, at the end of Nietzsche's profile. There can no doubt that as an individual Robinson possessed an acute estimation of the "measure of his value." To render Robinson in the most base/basic ontological terms, Jackie Robinson knew himself—everything in his life up the moment that he signs for and then historically (April 15, 1947) takes the field for the Dodgers. He knew, as several biographers and baseball historians have noted, who he was, and he had a very clear sense of his own self-worth: "This was the man Branch Rickey hired, proud, as his mother had wanted him to be, fierce in his own nature, scarred because white America wounds its fierce proud blacks" (Kahn).[63] This does not mean, however, that he ever fully grasped how much the success of the "great experiment" he was undertaking depended on him.

Rather, it was precisely his acute and intense sense of that "pride" that derived from maternal demand, his innate "fierceness" that enabled him, in the clubhouse, on the field, in press conferences, to stand in the face of opposition, hostility, and, of course, violence. In order to do so, Robinson was able to call on, to rely on, not only that which was his and that which he had been given but also on how those qualities had consolidated into his "protracted and unbreakable will." (In addition to which, as we have since come to learn, Robinson was able to lean heavily on his wife, Rachel Robinson.) Nothing less than an "unbreakable will" could have sustained the black player in his singularity, in his exceptionality, in his exemplarity, confronted as he was with the political obstacles ranged against him, and the paucity of resources (his wife, of course; Rickey, in his peculiar own way; and a few teammates, most notably Pee Wee Reese) at his disposal.

In a distinctly Nietzschean register, then, we can *setzen* Robinson as a "'free' man" because it was demanded of him (and here the terms, as we have seen, are determinedly Rickey's—"encase your natural volatility in lead") not only that he demonstrate on a daily basis (some 150 regular season games, to say nothing of the added intensity of postseason baseball) that he possessed "mastery over himself" but also that he bring his self-mastery to bear "over the circumstances" in which he found himself, into which he had cast himself—into which history had cast him. Crucial to his self-mastery, of course, was his ability to show restraint in the face of those—again, opponents, and here Ben Chapman's Phillies and the St. Louis Cardinals, with the notable exception of their star, Stan Musial, were especially notorious but by no means exceptional—who had, so to speak, the benefit of the right to be "short-willed and unreliable creatures." Robinson's self-possession, self-discipline, and his remarkable (if strategic) restraint can never, it goes without saying, be argued as a "true" "sovereignty." These qualities do, however, rise to the level of a mode of being very proximate to Nietzsche's ideal. So much so, we could say, that it is Robinson, for all the circumscription to which he was subject, rather than Rickey, who emerges as the figure of Nietzschean ethicality and integrity. This is not to diminish Rickey. It is, rather, to give Nietzschean articulation to the distinctly different demands made on the two signatories to their "moral contract." It is also to insist, to recognize, Robinson as, critically, philosophically, equal partner to the agreement. Robinson's ontology, as it were, is what transforms the facticity of legal inequality into something on the order of "moral" equality.

Indeed, it is possible that Robinson hews to Nietzsche's profile precisely because of the circumstances in which he found himself and the unprecedented challenges that he had no choice but to confront. (To paraphrase Marx as we encountered him in the "Eighteenth Brumaire of Louis Bonaparte," human beings do not make history under conditions of their own choosing.) It is possible to imagine that Robinson possessed, as Nietzsche frames it (in his delineation of "conscience"), a "proud awareness of the extraordinary of *responsibility*, the consciousness of this rare freedom, the power over oneself and over fate" (*On the Genealogy of Morals*).[64] Robinson, as we well know, was acutely aware of his political—his racial—"responsibility" ("Maybe I can do something for my race"), a responsibility "extraordinary" and historic in its scope, in its demand, and in its political effect. However, Robinson also possessed the "consciousness" of a historical subject who managed, within the strictures of the moment and the institutions (the American political and MLB, with its history of systematic, racist exclusion), to secure for himself a "rare freedom." Robinson, as Kahn reminded us earlier, played the game hard, without apology, and, above all, every day, he played to win. Under the circumstances that he was performing, from the day of his entry into the "Majors" until his retirement in 1956, Robinson's can, we are well within our rights to allow it, be conceived of as the "rarest freedom." That is the only proper name we can append to "freedom" claimed, secured, acted on, in the face of structural racism.

"Self-Mastery"

You can have no dominion greater or less than that over yourself.
—LEONARDO DA VINCI, *Notebooks*

It may be, in this regard, Robinson's singular courage that, more than any of the other Dodgers whom Kahn profiles in *The Boys of Summer*, accounts for the ways in which Robinson moves the former *Herald Tribune* sports journalist to poetry. Kahn is especially lyrical as it regards Robinson's desire for freedom, a freedom secured at the cost of the several "wounds" America had inflicted on this "fierce proud black" man. He writes about Robinson in epic terms, as the figure who must be properly remembered and understood as a political survivor and a champion for freedom, as the figure who emerges out of a "brave, fatherless boyhood" into a "free man who walked with swift and certain strides" (*The Boys of Summer*).[65]

While Robinson did not, as none of us do, have the "power of his fate," he demonstrated time and again his "power over" himself. (A power at once sovereign and not, a power over the self that emerges out of the very condition it so determinedly opposes: U.S. racism.) In sport, especially, the power to know the moment, to understand it fully, in a fraction of a second, to grasp what that moment demands, what precise act is required, constitutes the very definition of discipline, the very incarnation of the player on whom the team—the Dodgers—could always depend, as Pee Wee Reese was apt to encourage (plea?) from the dugout: "'Come on, Jack. We're counting on you'" (Kahn).[66] As Reese and all those legendary Dodgers (Billy Cox, Duke Snider, Gil Hodges, Preacher Roe, Roy Campanella) knew (a fact of Dodger life on which they counted), there are few athletes who possessed discipline of the da Vincian order—he exercised "dominion over himself." Robinson understood that he could "do something" for his race only if he exercised absolute power over himself. In this way, Rickey's proscriptions were an aid, not an impediment, to the "great experiment." Rickey's "rules," let us call them for the sake of assonance (an assonance that is not only rhetorically convenient but also possessed of an evocative truth) a set of demarcations of the possible and the permissible that Robinson could "observe" or subject to the Robinsonian "stress test," as he thought fit, he thought the moment demanded. As such, we recognize that Robinson, in every encounter, sought to "inspect" the limits of what he might accomplish, of what he might be able to "get away with"; itself an experiment, of course, that was as likely to produce failure as success.

However, if it is out of Nietzsche's thinking that we are able to propose a "moral" and political equality between Robinson and Rickey, then it is as important to understand that, as a "free" man, Robinson was also implicated in the process of his "self-maltreatment." That is, those moments in which he "silently" (because it will, as we later see, always find its voice) endured humiliations (segregated hotels, when the white players had the best accommodations the Dodgers had to offer and Robinson could not accompany them; racist epithets hurled at him on the field; violence directed toward him at the plate; and so on) and had no choice but to "encase his natural volatility in lead." As such, we gain some sense of the cost of what it means, under arduous, hostile political conditions, to claim the right to stand security for oneself and to do so with pride, thus to possess also the *"right to affirm oneself"* (Nietzsche).[67] The "right to affirm oneself" always takes place in the face of political forces working precisely to "deny" the self's right to "self-affirmation," and, because of this, that right is always subject to circumscription or, worse, outright denial. In asserting his (his and, by extension, his people's) rights, Robinson's claim inserts itself fully into the political, the consequence of which is both to allow for the possibility of the articulation of sovereignty and to anticipate its denial. Politically rendered, by staking his rightful claim to rights, Robinson made himself fully vulnerable to a kind of realpolitik of the pre–civil rights America variety.

As such, the terms of the political subject (and the process of its formation, which is always susceptible to undoing and violence) are fully operative for Robinson. There would, then, be moments for full assertion as well as the need for moments of self-censure or, worse, humiliation, or a series of humiliations that could, in turn, lead to rationalizations or dissembling. (All of these acts, in one way or another, in resisting or "acquiescing," required—and this is the contradiction of record—that he exhibit "dominion." "Sovereignty," we might suggest, as intimate knowledge of the im-permissible.) In the graceful, if terse, terms that Rachel Robinson prefers, "'My husband underplays things. That's his style. Don't let him fool you. What he came up against, and what we all came up against, was very, very rough'" (Kahn).[68] In other words, Robinson is at once the unexceptional subject, recognizable to any political anywhere, and entirely exceptional in his determination to secure what he understands to be rightfully his and yet proscribed by (U.S.) law. Out of this cauldron, where there is no political will (on the part of the *état voyou*, the "rogue state," that is, the United States,[69] which is both the cause and the effect of the history of American racism) to enforce rights, a subject such as Jackie Robinson emerges (here it is worth invoking the more forceful concept, "upsurge,"[70] which Jean-Luc Nancy prefers, a term that lends the process of "emergence" a violent urgency). It is not, however, that the figure of Robinson simply "surges up" out of, and into, history.

It is, rather, as Nietzsche insists, that it is precisely history that produces, that births, in all likelihood violently, such a figure. In Nietzsche's horticultural metaphor, a metaphor that must be thought of as nothing less than the event, history has long since undertaken the work of preparing the world for this figure of historical inevitability. It might not be, in our terms, punctual, which is why Nietzsche describes it as a "ripe fruit, but also a *late* fruit," but then, as we well know, the event is always only punctual to itself (*On the Genealogy of Morals*).[71] The event operates, if such a mechanistic (and Taylorist) phrasing might be permitted, and is true to only its own schedule. The event always operates on its own time, according to its own clock. Nevertheless, we are left to wonder, "How long must this fruit have hung on the tree, unripe and sour! And for a much longer time nothing whatever was to be seen of any such fruit: no one could have promised its appearance, although everything in the tree was preparing for and growing toward it!" (*On the Genealogy of Morals*).[72] This is the event, this is the timetable of the event. The fruit, "unripe and sour," promises its "ripening," its "fruition," and when that moment arrives, it appears inconceivable that no one had, until its very happening, expected it. The event is inevitable, Nietzsche promises, because everything—in the analogical "tree"— was doing nothing but "preparing for and growing toward it." And yet the world was entirely unprepared, not even remotely ready, for the event of MLB integration. The world is never ever ready for the "dominion" of the other.

The "Majors" would be integrated; the "burial" of MLB racism was inevitable. A black player—from the Negro Leagues, most likely but not as a precondition—would break the "color barrier" and take his place in history. However, the nature of the event is such that it is inevitable (it is always, no matter what, guaranteed; the event, which underwrites itself, is its own guarantor) and it will require, nay, demand, that the figure who "surges up" into—and out of history—is fitted to the task before her or him. History, we can say, makes the event, but the subject of that history is, as history would insist, fit for the work of the event. In this instance the event is the integration of the "Majors." There is no absolute commensurability, no neat synchronization between moment and man, no perfect symmetry between the demands of the moment and the fitness of the subject, but there is enough (in common) between them, they share enough, so that the figure who "surges up" is adequate, and then some, to the task—to the exigencies—of the event. No matter how "rough" things got, and they got "very, very rough," as Rachel Robinson reminds Kahn, Jackie Robinson was, as both Rickey and Robinson himself knew, up to the task. The event, as Nietzsche prescribes it, promised a Jackie Robinson. In his turn, Robinson was prepared—the flight of his single mother, Mallie McGriff Robinson, from Cairo, Georgia; surviving abandonment by his father; negotiating his way through what was a potentially self-destructive Pasadena boyhood and youth; the athletic excellence of his UCLA years; the political "will" that sustained him during the Camp Hood trial; his brief time with the Monarchs—for all that the event would ask of him.

And more, some would say.

Because it is only through the event that Robinson came fully into himself. It is in the event that he is most fully himself, that his "dominion over himself" is most evident. In uttering, issuing (as a multivalenced and multidirected indictment), the expletive, the event makes of Robinson what he truly is, what he has long since been: a man capable of a glorious self-mastery that is never without the patina of (potential) violence.

No wonder then that as Robinson grew more, in Nietzsche's terms, "victorious, independent, honored, and feared" ("feared," especially, because opponents did not like playing against him), he expected those who belonged to his (racial) "tribe" to walk in lockstep with him. When they did not, Robinson gave voice to his displeasure. He crafted, in bitter response to the "acquiescence" of his "tribe," the language of "bastardization." A language, we can only imagine, that must have reverberated with the force of the autobiographical for Robinson because the black player from the Negro Leagues who integrated the "Majors" was, etymologically (and, it must be said, psychologically), intimate with the condition of bastardization. He was, as we well know, the son of a man who had abandoned him by the time the boy was a year old. When we align, therefore, Robinson with the Shakespearean "monster" in *Othello,* we do so in the knowledge that the several "monsters" who combined to make Robinson's entry into and stay in the "Majors" "very rough" will, whether Robinson wants it or not, find their voices in him, because of him, and sometimes despite his best efforts to still them. These voices will speak as Robinson, as, that is, themselves. The Dodger might, in popular parlance, be artful or elusive, but the Dodger cannot escape himself or the event that has "surged up" in and through him. "Stupid bastards" is only one of the "monster's" names, although it might be among the more important ones; for the purposes of this discussion, it is a central one.

"Bastardization"

"Bastardization" requires, even if it possesses such a potent internality and an inevitable self-confrontation, an external scene. In this regard, for the event of Robinsonian "bastardization" there are at least two venues. In the initial instance, there is Hartwell Field in Mobile, Alabama, an exhibition game in the spring of 1952. In Mobile, Alabama, on the way to the game, the white taxi driver taking Kahn and a colleague, Bill Roeder (New York *World-Telegram*), was full of racist invective: "'Say, you guys goin' to see the coal?' . . . 'We're coming to where I grew up.' . . . 'Coal now. The coal is taking over. How do you like that? Where I grew up there's all these fucking cannibals'" (Kahn).[73] Roeder and Kahn protest the cab driver "through nontipping," repulsed at the white Alabama native and his reference to those "fucking cannibals" who had usurped his old neighborhood (*The Boys of Summer*).[74] It is, however, the geological metaphor "coal" that lingers, that resonates in disturbing timbres, as though the driver were marking the deep earthiness of Robinson's blackness, as though Robinson, the very apogee of appropriative black "coal-ness," marked an unvarnished, almost morphological blackness. Kahn remarks on Robinson's salience: "Both teams used other blacks. But to the crowd, Sam Jethroe and Roy Campanella were ball players who happened to be colored. Then there was Robinson, the threatening, glorious black" (Kahn).[75] Robinson is the "coal" who stands out, who will never be mistaken for a "ball player who happens to be black." He is, in his "threatening, glorious blackness," the very incarnation of the "coal taking over." Once more, Robinson, as exemplary, the black player burdened with a representation beyond, in excess of, himself, a black that is ontologically of the soil—"*Schwarz und Boden*," as it were, to render this in poor Heideggerian.

This event, in which "coal" played with and against whites in an exhibition baseball game, both explicitly and implicitly threatened the precarious racial peace in the Deep South, what some in the United States then called the "American hookworm belt." This was an early name, not exactly for what we know today as the "Bible Belt"; their geographical parameters do not coincide exactly. In Alabama a historic number of blacks got on line early and then crowded into Hartwell Field: "The black humanity of Mobile stood and squatted and bent and sat wedged two to a seat," in what Kahn describes as a "cattle car of a stand" (*The Boys of Summer*).[76] The "black mass" who "diffused and became individual men and women . . . who wore bright red and yellow and green" were there to watch Robinson, and when he was out on a "short fly to left," the whites and black spectators, respectively, voiced their "enthusiasm and disappointment" (*The Boys of Summer*).[77]

The expectation that he bore, the antipathy that he was asked (in the name of black Alabama or wherever else in the "hookworm belt" the Dodgers preseason took the team) to endure (or chose to or had to make himself willfully ignorant of), was part of the responsibility assigned to Robinson. He had, as it were, signed on to this, whether or not he imagined that such a responsibility was what he was "inking." However, if Hartwell Field was, as such, representative and not in the least exceptional, then there is indeed a salient iteration that disturbs and disarticulates the "routineness" of an occasion such as Alabama. This event took place in Pelican Field in New Orleans.

Since there were vacancies in the white section of Pelican Field, the white police opened the traditionally white area for—to mark this exceptional moment—their black clientele.

Along the third-base line stood the Dodgers captain, the Louisville native Pee Wee Reese, tossing lightly with his teammate. Playing catch with Reese was our master speaker of the all-purpose expletive "bastard": Jackie Robinson. We do not, much as we might or might not be aware of the army bus incident, conceive of Jackie Robinson this way, as given to the violent expletive. Nor is the first public recollection of him as a man prone to unleashing so violent a stream of expletives or letting loose such a torrent of expletives with such violence. Through Kahn we make the acquaintance of a politically voluble Jackie Robinson.

In Pelican Field we encounter Robinson angry, indignant, given to invective. Jackie Robinson in a mode "too hideous to be shown." Jackie Robinson venting, maybe even ranting, against injustice. "You stupid bastards." Words spoken quietly, although the "object"—the intended audience—of his address is not immediately identifiable, with one, or two, notable exceptions. Other than that, we are free to speculate. Was Robinson speaking to Pee Wee? To the crowd? In truth, it matters not, because, one way or the other, no one can possibly be excluded from Robinson's address. Robinson was speaking, first, to himself, and, then, most importantly, he was addressing the entire world. Whether or not what he said was, or was not, audible for everyone to hear, what it is he said belonged in and to the world. Robinson's address was for all to hear, for it encompassed everyone. No one was outside it, there was no place for anyone—any American, black or white—to hide.

In this way what is of consequence is that for once, at least this once, we now have on public record (or a public, ethnographically transcribed, record) Robinson displaying an Othello-like propensity for direct, politically unambiguous speech. Moreover, here Robinson marshals direct speech but without the Moor's (later) prevarication and, like all Shakespeare's tragic heroes (think only Othello and Hamlet and the point is instantly well made), self-doubt: "Haply, for I am black / And have not those soft parts of conversation" (*Othello*).[78] In place of "softness," of muted anger, here there is the authoring of black anger—"bastards," "bastards." There is nothing, we are sure, "hapless" about the utterance of that word "bastards." The "soft part" of the conversation has been dispensed with, and, in its place, the affirmation, which is to say, the rejection of qualification: "I am black." What we are confronted with is not "for I am[,] . . ." where the preposition "for" "softens," if the pun might be permitted, the impact of Othello's "blackness."

It is, of course, impossible to miss, the imprecision of speech, the multidirectionality of the accusation. We do not know exactly who these "stupid bastards" are. These "stupid bastards," the object of Robinson's opprobrium, who are they? Is one constituency of "stupid bastards" distinct from those "bastards," those ones being "cheered?" Are the black spectators at Pelican Field immunized against Robinson's invective? Hardly, as we later see. Racial affinity with the other is no protection against critique. At first glance we can determine that those "bastards," the ones who should not be applauded, are, of course, the police and the white authorities. Those "bastards" (let us name them "B") should not be "cheered" because it is within their power, and their power only (as Robinson is so bitterly aware), to make the accommodation for the historically large black crowd. However, the discrepancy in power, the injustice that is so palpably being demonstrated, is but one cause of Robinson's anger.

It is from the place of history, as it were, that Robinson admonishes the black spectators (let us name this group of "bastards" "A"), "Don't cheer," a constituency that is putatively and existentially his. Consequently, we would expect a certain degree of sympathy for his fellow blacks. Anything but. But Robinson does not restrict himself to (self-)admonition. He extends his (self-)critique to the issue of rights so that what he is most angered by in the behavior of A is the perversity of their gratitude. The force of (southern) law may be such that an enlarged seating arrangement for blacks is the exception, but that exception is itself, in the fierceness of Robinson's logic, the problem. There should be, as Robinson insisted on that military bus ride at Camp Hood, no proscription. Its existence, its perpetuation, is against the law, which lends Robinson's injunction, "you got it coming," its vehemence. There should be no gratitude for what is a right. In that (unspoken but politically and historically audible) rebuke is where we encounter the true force of Robinson's denunciation of A and B, "bastards" of one stripe or another, "bastards" who are coconspirators (mutually implicated) in the perpetuation of this perversity. As such, the "Negroes" must know that they are not, that they should not consider themselves, "hapless." They must not be party, on this score Robinson is clear, to their own degradation. To act with gratitude is, in this instance, to render the (black) self, a constituency in which Robinson, of course, situates himself, as a self-subjugating being. It is precisely because Robinson understands himself as part of the black whole that he so intensely refuses the perversity of his fellow blacks' gratitude. The self is never so vulnerable, so politically destitute, as when it underwrites its own subjection. This is not what Robinson signed on for when he became a Dodger, when he broke the color barrier. He did not seek to implicate himself or his community in their continued degradation through the perversity of gratitude.

The Expletive

> Its exterior form would be that of a *rupture* and a redoubling.
> —JACQUES DERRIDA, "Structure, Sign, and Play in the Discourse of the Human Sciences" (original emphasis)

There is in every expletive a threat, a warning, the promise, almost, of violence. Every expletive speaks of the danger that is coming, of the rhetorical desire to make the threat a language in itself, a politically reliable language where the signifier, the word, will culminate in the signified, the act promised by the word. Every expletive, in its speaking, encodes an act of public violence and must, as such, be understood as an event in the sense that Derrida offers in his "Structure, Sign, and Play" essay. The expletive is the event that secures a "rupture" in the discursive regime that surrounds, which emanates from, which is imposed on, Robinson. After the expletive, Robinson can no longer be cast as, say, "long suffering." In the expletive his capacity for endurance meets its limit, a limit that is reiterated in its repetition. (The repetition might be understood, in this way, as analogous to Mandela's negation, as Chapter 2 shows, because the expletive being uttered again and again speaks as the refutation of that which proscribes Robinson, both politically and racially—racially, that is, in the sense that he speaks against his own; at least one of the "stupid bastards" is a bitter critique of the Negro spectators' gratitude, a response with which Robinson, as just remarked, takes serious political and historical issue.)

In its repetition the expletive acquires a singular force. In its being repeated, its effect is redoubled, and then redoubled again, giving it a rare political life. So much so, that it becomes possible to cast the expletive—"bastards," "stupid bastards," its every iteration—as something akin to the radical kernel, the hard verbal core of the event of, the event that is, Jackie Robinson in MLB. Through this "rupture and redoubling" the event of the expletive disperses, displaces, and "distances" itself so that the event achieves a new directness and temporality. The "rupturous" effect of the expletive (which makes it "rapturous" too, of course, since the "rude break" offers a possibility that is not discontinuous with the erotic; at the very least, it promises the rush of adrenaline) is to disperse the event from player (Robinson) to player (Reese) to journalist (Kahn) to crowd (black-white-black and white, thus establishing a racialized "private-private-public-geo-historical," North-South/subjugated-power continuum) and, as such, it makes itself heard across time itself. Furthermore, in Robinson's "private" mutterings we detect the many valences of a threat issued by the overburdened Negro player, a threat that cannot find its proper target, U.S. racism and the political structure founded on that racism. As such, that threat is handed down, in its being made "properly," repeatedly, rupturously/rapturously public, into a succession of temporalities. The threat is there for every succeeding generation to inherit, issued as a political challenge to be addressed and taken up. As such, we can say that the threat contained in the expletive "distances" the event from itself even as it establishes the event, even as it allows the event to become fully itself. The event, then, expropriates, "outsources" the threat, all of which makes it possible for the event to erupt again in any moment, ours included, of course. The event of the expletive, because of the historical resonance and audibility that issues from it, makes it possible to apprehend the event as the expletive that has been—and will be again in the future—removed from itself.

However, and because of its repetition and its "public privacy," the expletive also stands as the inscription of a certain political futility. The expletive is, in its own way, politically "bilingual" because it represents, simultaneously, a form of proscription (the impermissible) and love, thwarted—the most violent, incendiary, in-felicitous kind of love imaginable because it too is impermissible. In this way, to borrow from the philosophical poetry of Abdelkebir Khatibi, the expletive constitutes the violent "limits" of language: "language was mad"[79] so that the expletive—"bastards," "bastards"—is language made "mad" by love, language made maddeningly unlovable, un-lovely. (In the reciprocal logic of Martin Luther King Jr.'s "Letter from a Birmingham Jail," "There can be no deep disappointment where there is not deep love.")[80] All love is founded on a violent in-expressibility, on the maddening, frustrating inability to say what the self imagines it has to say, wants to say, wants to say more than anything, wants to say in a language that bears/bares fully the self's love for the other. More than any other form of human interaction, love tests the limits of language and, as such, forces language to think itself again, forces language to bear more than it ever imagined it could or would be asked to. Love extends language because of its inexpressible demands; love reveals what it is language cannot say. The imperative to say what cannot be said reveals to language itself, simultaneously, its own elasticity and its limits, its lack of as well as its capacity for improvisation, for making itself anew, yet one more time. Its own detestation of the limits of the limit—the limit language imposes on itself. Love is the struggle of language against death, and, as such, the determination to find a language even in death.

In this way, Derrida's notion of resistance is helpful in that it seems to bear directly on that U.S. political history (we could as easily suggest that

Derrida draws from this history) in which Robinson is such a key actor. A history that must always be approached with ambivalence and a certain flexibility. "In the political order," Derrida writes:

> This principle of resistance would inspire, as one of its figures, the right to what the United States names with that very fine phrase for the most respectable of traditions, in the case of *force majeure*, where the *raison d'état* does not dispense the last word in ethics: "civil disobedience." (*Without Alibi*)[81]

Through his expletive Robinson crystallizes the anger of the disenfranchised (or the incompletely enfranchised MLB player; Robinson possesses what we might name a "limited franchise"—the right to play but not to resist, the right to hit but not to retaliate, the right to field spectacularly but not to speak back in the face of white violence and injustice) that cannot be contained. And yet that anger must be contained. After all, these are the principles of the civil rights movement: to resist, to resist in the face of anger, vitriol and the possibility of incurring physical and psychological harm (racism), but to resist without responding to that anger on its terms. (Martin Luther King Jr. makes this clear in the question that the civil rights movement posed to its members: "'Are you able to accept blows without retaliating?'")[82] In response to the unethical "force" of the unethical state (what Derrida names, as discussed earlier, the *état voyou*, the "rogue state"), only the ethical act—the ability to endure, to endure without violence, to endure through "passivity," in the many iterations that *The Burden of Over-representation* assigns that politics—will suffice. In order to resist the unethical it is necessary, for the sake of resistance, to articulate a resistance that is not overdetermined ("contaminated," to render the notion crudely) by that "*force majeure*" that is being resisted.[83] As such, resistance can be conducted only under the provision that it is first grasped as its own ethical difficulty. (That is, to "accept blows without retaliating.") Nevertheless, the open secret of the expletive is that it brings into full "public" view the anger that is at the core of the expletive—its uncompromising kernel—and as such it ruptures the public discourse about the event of the expletive. For a second, it blows the discourse of respectability and the limit wide open.

The expletive, because it is functions here as a kind of *jouissance* (interrupted pleasure), inscribes that which cannot, yet, be wished for and yet is precisely what is, more than anything, being wished for. The Robinsonian expletive, the repeated invocation of "bastard" (the rapid-fire interplay between A and B) becomes, in this rendering, the language of frustrated—or interrupted—political desire. Jackie Robinson's "bastards"

articulates the deep-seated need for a radical-ized black political consciousness, at once rooted in the ethics of King's nonviolence and impatient with it—no longer, if only for a moment, willing to "accept blows"
without "retaliating." The expletive expresses the un-fulfillable desire to
replace "stupidity"—the "stupidity of those bastards," A, those among
whom Robinson takes his place—with finely honed political knowledge.
(It is, at once, a one-size-fits-all application of "bastards," and an exercise
in finely honed discrimination. The line that separates one from the other,
however, is so precarious as to be non-existent most of the time.) Robinson's explosion of expletive(s) is the call for a mode of political being that
at once understands and wants to exceed, for A more than B, of course
(that is, to set A against B, to "bury" any proclivity for perverse gratitude),
the limits of the extant political. The expletive stands as Robinson's Socratic refusal of the delimitation of black anger. He will not, whether he
intends it or not, keep his anger to himself. His anger belongs outside him;
it can be properly named only as the desire to render A indistinct from B.
Robinson's expletive is a rhetorically violent demand for racial equality, a
demand that knows—historically—that it cannot guarantee democracy.[84]
As such, the expletive "bastards" constitutes the act of the self being true,
in its moment, to itself, to its own anger. In his moment of anger, Jackie
Robinson is ir-reconcilable to himself, in no small measure because he can
be said to be beside himself, literally, almost, with anger, an anger that
begins as much inside him (A) as it derives from the disproportionate
power that B, the "rogue democracy" that is white-dominated America,
has over A, the de facto disenfranchised black minority. In this explosion
that is the Robinsonian expletive, we can detect the impugning of all "bastards." Or, in this moment, for Robinson all "bastards" are equal or have
made themselves, in the acts toward each other, equally unequal to Robinson's demands.

From this location of remove (constitutive alienation), of being meta-
physically outside of himself, Robinson recognizes that it will always be
the time of "stupid bastards" for Negroes if they do not resist the propensity for perverse gratitude. In this regard, as always, there is the Fanonian
caution about the time of the proleptic conflict that must be heeded: "the
great showdown cannot be postponed indefinitely."[85] It is a precondition
of knowledge and intelligence that politics can commence only once "stupidity" has been overcome, dispensed with; Robinson knows, as Fanon
did, that his anger—and, we presume, the turbulent undercurrents of res-
sentiment surging, known, unknown? through the crowd in Pelican
Field—cannot avoid the "great showdown" that would become both the
civil rights campaign and the Black Power movement (as well as, of course,
the struggle between these black political tendencies). It is the event, like

Robinson's entry into the "Majors," that will be, that must be. It will be made, of course, through struggle, violence, and never without significant costs to America's black population, but it is the moment that will know and be in its own time. That is the value of Nietzsche's (as contemplated by Derrida) "prediction: 'Alas! if only you knew how soon, how very soon, things will be—different!' (*Ach! Wenn ihr wußtet, wie es bald, so bald schon—anders kommt!*)" (*The Politics of Friendship*).[86]

It is for this reason that "Don't be stupid" represents, as the articulation of a taut, historic pain, as the perverse scripting of the predictive, Robinson's imperative, his appeal for reasoned if not yet radical political thought. (Or, his always incipiently radical, impatient proclivity toward action, his inclining toward "retaliation.") Robinson's invective is directed at the black spectators at Pelican Field (in actuality), Hartwell Field (metonymically, by necessary political extension), and all those other ballparks where the Dodgers played their exhibition games because, in his (just) estimation, every black spectator has the right to make a claim on every American public space. The injustice is that A, or the black population in the United States, has for too long been denied this right, for too long been discriminated against, lied to. This history extends from the nondelivery on the terms to Reconstruction to the Jim Crow laws to this event in Pelican Field to the denial of the franchise right in the Bull Connor era. To, in a more contemporary moment, what is known as Ferguson, Missouri, and Charlottesville, Virginia. That is why the event of Pelican Field inaugurates, in Robinson's stipulated opposition to the enactment of perverse gratitude, in his anger (so evocative of disgust at the self, A, if not self-loathing) at the "cheering," the beginning of the political question— the question of a civil rights movement already under way, the question of black nationalism that would redefine the "race" debates of the 1960s and 1970s, the question that would become, after 2008 saw the election of Barack Obama, most especially, of "postracial America." In the terms of Derrida's timely reminder, "In principle, then, we should also think . . . even if we are not thinking *it*—about *the* political crime" (*Politics of Friendship*).[87] There is no political question that does not, in some way or other, relate directly to the law, to the "force of law," in Derrida's memorable critique. The law, then, rendered "profanely," always raises "criminality," transgression, or the inefficacy of the law as a question for the political, a condition raised by and out of the political. However, as importantly, what must be kept in mind, what must not be lost sight of (even as it might not yet have occurred—"even if we are not thinking it") is "the political crime." It is that possibility that must be acted against even as it is anticipated as an inevitability. Politics, as always for Derrida, demands absolute vigilance, diligent preparation, comprehension of the highest order, and the willingness to—as he repeats on countless occasions—conduct politics as if we were undertaking it, as if we were committing ourselves to it, for the "first time." The magnificence, the thrill (always tinged with the erotic promise of the variety, we might suggest, captured so soulfully by Betty Wright in her "melody" "Tonight Is the Night") that marks the "very first time."[88]

Two Simple Sentences

"Don't be stupid." "Take what you got coming."

These two tightly constructed, compact (simple) sentences constitute a remarkable moment. They affirm, more than anything else, Robinson's ability to understand and identify the moment of exception in the moment itself. That is, to know the event as the event in the moment of its eventality. Robinson comprehends, forcefully, trenchantly, that the significance of the event is that it reveals the injustice of history in a single, publicly visible, instance. Therein lies the import of the transcribed phrase "had it coming": It functions according to the principle of "just desserts" and, in so doing, lends an urgent, even violent, drama to the issue of conciliation. That is to say, in the articulation "had it coming" is already inscribed the emphatic refusal of reconciliation and the demand for historic justice. The phrase "had it coming" makes the debt—nominally, the right to seating—visceral and, as such, unjust or linguistically "visible" in the segregated South; justice for the Negro is unattainable because of the racial politics that obtain in the South. Through the expletive Robinson is speaking out against, back to, B, the white authorities in New Orleans, in Alabama, across the nation, and, finally, to Dixie Walker and his ilk. That is the force of Robinson's irruption into MLB.

The event, then, is not to make small or symbolic claims in the moment (of the exceptional other subject) but to reveal, in—and through and because of—that moment, how the inexhaustible right to rights, and their unjust denial, postponement (in the terms of the legal maxim, "justice delayed is justice denied"), and deferment, should inspire not perverse gratitude but anger. "Had it coming" stands as nothing so much as a critique of the postponement, in the temporal inscription and the force of discrimination (distinguishing one thing from another) that constitute Derrida's notion of *différance,* of the right (to all seating, to an integrated MLB, to—extending the argument into our contemporary—the U.S. presidency, of Barack Obama, that is) that is always only ever grudgingly ceded. This right, among many others, is what should have "been had"— should have been known, unspectacularly, as a right—generations ago. (These are the terms that the conclusion of the Civil War should have

settled, decisively, once and for all. That it did not, that Jim Crow was allowed to come into being and, worse, to flourish so that it became both the
de jure and the de facto law of the land is the "political crime" that, in
Derrida's thinking, should have been struggled against and prevented.)
That the claim has to, in its many iterations, always be made in the now
not only speaks of the struggles waged in order to secure contemporary
gains but also constructs politics as nothing but a matter of time and the
prevention of historical crimes (of repetition, to begin again, and then
again, "as if for the first time"). Or, more grammatically phrased, it presents politics as, first, a matter of tense in that it pits the present continu-
ous "have," a time that can be traced to the past, against the bitterness of,
awkwardly rendered, the immediate future present, "got it coming," and
its medium- and long-term successor—the "political crime" of the future
that finds its first fertile soil in the (always) insufficiently conscious now.
Robinson understands politics as nothing but a temporal problem: What
the now requires is invariably rooted in what the historic "then" refused
to yield—what, in Robinson's keen terms, white America refused, not
failed (because it disregarded, brutalized, through Jim Crow legislation and
legally sanctioned practice, and manipulated the law against equality), to
"give" its black subjects.

Hence, the Robinsonian stipulation that militates, through violent
negation, against reconciliation: "Don't cheer those bastards." White
America, embodied in the police and the authorities in place in New Orleans, should be critiqued—made subject to the "pregnant" force of the
expletive—because of its refusal to honor black America's (just) claim on
the polis, on the fundamental terms of American democracy, because of
its determination to offer its black subjects, to subject its black constituency to, an enfranchisement that is, effectively, disenfranchisement, Jim
Crow. It is this force of law, these "criminal" political practices, that should
be attacked, that must be, time and again, held up to scrutiny for their
institutional failure, for their institutional disregard for the rights of
black subjects. For, as much as anything, their lack of historical vigilance.
We are always warned, both implicitly and explicitly, about the "political
crime *l'avenir.*"

The Verb Is Active

"Take what you got coming."

The Negroes who swarm, in their Sunday best, as Kahn reports about
the black fans who stream to Hartwell Field in their "reds" and "yellows,"
and with such pride in Robinson's ascension to the "Majors," must be aggressive. They must, as Robinson says, "Take what [they] got coming."

They must be like their hero Jackie Robinson on the base paths, always a threat to steal, always unnerving pitchers, catchers, and infielders alike. According to Kahn, there were few sights in baseball, in all of sport, perhaps, as that of Jackie Robinson on the base pads. (He was always threatening to steal home from third base.) "The rundown was his greatest play," Kahn writes. "Robinson could start so fast and stop so short he could elude anyone in baseball, and he could feint a start and feint a stop as well" (*The Boys of Summer*).[89] On the base paths, Robinson was master; he used his speed, his strength (it is no easy thing to stop on a dime and then start back up again), and, most importantly, his intelligence to "elude" opponents, to steal a base, sometimes two, and to "manufacture" a run out of nothing for the Dodgers. (The phrase to "manufacture a run" in baseball is a tribute to ingenuity, a recognition of the ability of a team, or a player, to make the most of every resource at its, or his, disposal. Let us say, for example, that the batter "works a walk"—the language of baseball here is replete with the Protestant ethic; that is, the batter fights off strikes, fouls off good pitches, in order to secure a "pass" to first base. Once at first base, the runner steals second base, moves to third on a ground ball, and then scores on a fly ball to the outfield. And, if you're Jackie Robinson, you might not even need that fly ball out, because you can steal home. Stealing home is the most difficult play in baseball because all the odds favor the fielding team. Robinson was a master at "manufacturing" a run for his team, especially when, as Kahn relates, the Dodgers needed it most.)

For their part, black subjects must make the time of American history accountable for its violence toward them. Black America, here in Pelican and Hartwell Fields, must not, either metaphorically or literally, doff its cap at or put its hands together in either perverse gratitude or undeserved praise. There could be no surer way to "desecrate" the achievements, fledgling as they were in those early days (Hartwell, Pelican, and so on), of Jackie Robinson than not to match his aggression, pride, fierce competitiveness, and (appetite for confrontation which lent substance to) his deep hunger for justice. What Robinson incarnated, what he enacted in every game, was the black subject staking its unarguable (but denied) claim to his rights. Therefore, what Robinson was advocating was that every black subject must "take" that which rightfully belonged to him or her, they must always "take" what they "got coming." Black politics *l'avenir*, Robinson-style.

The verb that girds the Robinson expletive is active, the intention that verb iterates is, within the oeuvre of Robinsonian moments, approaching incendiary. The act is political. Robinson seeks to both, through his presence on the field and his having broken the "color barrier," integrate the game and then divide the polis. Robinson is committed to making the present unrecognizable from the past and to divest the future of its Pelican Field propensities. He insists on equality and freedom from racial discrimination as the first condition of politics in America. In Heidegger's terms, we might say that the act of "taking" must become, simultaneously without and because of thought, Being (*Sein*). (Or, vernacularized, it must become unexceptional, ordinary, nothing but the stuff of everyday life. It must simply be how things are.) Metonymically, Pelican Field must become, as it were, "hapless" in the face of the future incarnated, imagined, and articulated in Robinson's anger. ("Taking" assumes the metaphysical urgency of Heidegger's "*Da-sein*" in that it functions as the inexplicable, unbending force of the Negro self. It *is*, constitutive, undeniable.) Within any act of conciliation, there is always the propensity for a new ir-ruption, the demand for another condition on which to conduct politics. No act of conciliation is ever complete in itself. Only conciliation can make the force of the debt wholly public.

The name of the ir-ruption is the Fanonian conjuncture: "that place of bubbling trepidation from which knowledge will emerge" (*Wretched of the Earth*).[90] In the event of Pelican Field, Robinson is close enough to recognize that he is in the midst of an intense political activity ("bubbling," even if he is anything but "trepidatious") and, critically, that he is giving voice to ("surging up," "emerging," if you will, with) a new kind of "knowledge" about the effects of race and racism on his psyche. For Robinson, Pelican Field is the site of a profoundly unsettling self-confrontation that leads to a new distribution, the re-distribution, of Jackie Robinson. That is to say, Robinson, constructed after the event in such a way as to make visible (and audible; we can "hear" Jackie Robinson as never before, "hear" Jackie Robinson in his "own" voice, "hear" him speaking to us as he speaks, putatively, nominally, to himself; we can "h/ear" him anew) (a) Jackie Robinson such as we have never seen (or heard) him before. Because of this, and this is crucial, Jackie Robinson is making Jackie Robinson in such a way (philosophy, Nietzsche, Derrida, Butler, Foucault) that it makes of Jackie Robinson a (black) subject that could not have been anticipated. Through thinking the event of Jackie Robinson, Jackie Robinson is shown to the world, as much as to himself, as neither the world nor Robinson might, at first glance, recognize him.

The event, it turns out, might be only provisionally cast as "Pelican Field." The event, the eventness of the event, is nothing other than Jackie Robinson himself. In this way, the "gift" of philosophy, the truth of philosophy, is the political intensity of Jackie Robinson, a political intensity that can be fully grasped only by thinking Jackie Robinson in terms that are entirely unfamiliar, but remarkably well suited, to him.[91] Because of what Jackie Robinson says, in what might, on the face of it, be considered an offhand comment, the thought of Jackie Robinson can be traced through, as we have just seen, the thought of Nietzsche. Through Nietzsche, Jackie Robinson is made the gift of Jackie Robinson; through Jackie Robinson, Nietzsche finds a language—a veritable discourse—that he could never, in the moment of his writing, have anticipated. Friedrich Nietzsche is as much of a surprise to Jackie Robinson as Robinson is to the philosopher from Röcken, which is very close to the center of Germany's Protestant Reformation.

Socratic Thought

> For one thing, nothing could be done without friends and loyal companions, and such men were not easy to find ready at hand, since our city was no longer administered according to the standards and practices of our fathers.
> —PLATO, Letter VII

"Don't cheer," do not applaud the very bastards who have done, who do, Negroes wrong. "Don't cheer" because it is the wrong political gesture, perverse gratitude. That perverse gratitude constitutes an inappropriate response to the "beneficence" of the white authorities (in the South and elsewhere) that should be, following Robinson's ethics, the ground zero of political "common sense" for every Negro. Naming his fellow blacks "bastards," condemning them through the expletive (as he vents his anger at the white authorities as well), is Robinson's rebuke to all the black fans here to see him at Pelican Field, to see him play alongside his white teammates Pee Wee Reese, Carl Erskine, and Clem Labine, as well as Roy Campanella and Joe Black. To "cheer" is not fitting, it is a response that does not meet the ethical standard/demands of a Jackie Robinson. That is because it is not gratitude, black gratitude, that needs to be expressed here. Any cheering on the part of A fails the historicity of the moment. And, as such, A renders itself incapable of recognizing the failure of American history up to that point and, as we well know, it is a history that extends far beyond the event of Hartwell Field. This is a moment that runs, in its shortest articulation, from the racist intransigence of Mobile, Alabama, to the intractable and systemic racism that led, of course, to Martin Luther King's "March on Selma," an event, of course, made by Rosa Parks at least as much as by any other figure, a moment that remains integral to our time.

It is on these grounds that Robinson issues his injunction, "Don't cheer." Do not applaud the white authorities because it does not address what should be spoken: the grounded, morphological sense of racist injustice and historical debt. The opening of a part of the whites' section amounts to little more than the (infinitesimal—even as we ask ourselves whether a right can be infinitesimal) righting of a historical wrong. The act of police "benevolence" constitutes no more than that, no more than recognizing the right of black spectators to occupy those seating facilities unjustly denied to them. Moreover, this "right" that has no institutional support, sustenance, or longevity. (And certainly did not have any until legislation such as the Voting Rights Act of 1965 took effect.) It is understood, on the part of the white authorities, to constitute a moment of exception—a momentary exception to the law of segregation, suspended for the unprecedented situation: a black player in the "Majors." This "right" that has no institutional or structural life, is issued belatedly and under the pressure of historic black expectation: the unprecedented experience of being able to witness, for themselves, here, in one corner of the "hookworm belt" or other, a black man taking his place on the field with white baseball players. A Negro who is, on the field if not off of it, the equal of all MLB players. The black player, Jackie Robinson, within the confines of the "white lines" that demarcate the playing field, equal: like all others, the exceptional incarnation of the un-exceptional, for a historic moment in Alabama or Louisiana, equal. Here, on the baseball diamond, this was, for a moment, where equality was possible because this was, to borrow a phrase from C.L.R. James writing on the history of black cricketers in the Caribbean, a "sphere where the competition was open."[92] It was on the cricket field, and nowhere else (broadly speaking), that black cricketers in James's *Beyond a Boundary* were able to stake their claim to equality. But, unlike in James's native Trinidad, where scores of black cricketers abounded, for a moment, for the moment that is Hartwell, Jackie Robinson remained singular, exceptional.

White beneficence constitutes nothing more than an act of momentary statutory suspension (we must not mistake it for "justice" because the laws governing segregation are suspended for only the duration of the game) that has, finally, and with great reluctance, been acceded to black Americans. Robinson stands firmly against white beneficence. For him, the acts of the white authorities are long overdue, a direct consequence of the failure of Reconstruction America to deliver on its promises to its black subjects. Robinson is aggressive in asserting his right, even in—and especially because of—the absence of that right: "You got it coming." The right to (equal) seating, to the franchise, to freedom from white violence, of the official and the vigilante variety, is what has been owed the black subject. The logic of the right to rights is that there must be, when those rights have been abrogated, no expression of any form of gratitude when the transgressive authorities relent, relax their subjugation for the time it takes to play nine innings.

Hence Robinson's preference for the imperative. "Take," as an act in history, as the act of appropriation that history demands, as an act that recognizes itself as an event. "Take" "it"—these new seats, this rupture in the spatial politics of Pelican Field—as yours because it is owed to you, has long been owed to you. Claim it, without apology, without ever raising the possibility of self-denigration. Any gratitude, any show of public appreciation, demeans the act, undermines, minimizes, renders vulnerable, black rights; what rightfully belongs to black America must be "taken" as its (overdue) due. The right to rights can never be "lost to" history, notwithstanding its non-implementation; the right to rights is infinitely renewable. The enacting of gratitude, we might extract from the fierceness of Robinson's language, serves to, from Robinson's privileged location within the confines of the field, undermine and demean him—as a ball player, as a Negro—and the daily struggles attendant to bearing the burden of over-representation as the icon of MLB's integration. In Plato's terms, Robinson seeks to make common cause with his "loyal friends and companions." Or he seeks to make out of the Negro spectators—and not only for the duration of the game—"loyal friends and companions." If not that, perhaps he imagines that he might at least be able to count on them as fellow travelers.

The Contradiction Inherent in "Bastards"

There is, clearly, in the repetition of the invective, "stupid bastards," "those bastards," "bastards," a sharp contradiction. On the one hand, the expletive iterates the force of rhetorical violence that is intended for his fellow blacks because Robinson is impatient with and intolerant of their perverse gratitude. On the other hand, there is the facticity of Robinson as unable to address his fellow blacks. All he does, which is to raise the question of what it is, is precisely all that he can do. What he can do is mutter angrily "to" or "at" the nearby journalist (Kahn) and maybe not even to Kahn but to himself and to his friend Pee Wee Reese who is in earshot. Here, in the event, we encounter Robinson, the very model for an un-eventful integration of the "Majors," railing against the effects of the very integration he is spearheading. Jackie Robinson, a black man, a historic athlete, anything but devoid of anger. Devoid, we now suspect, as we must long have suspected, only in public, and even this—the "privatization" of his anger—we now know to no longer be true. Jackie Robinson, at Pelican Field, roiling, roiling with anger.

Moreover, because he is expressing himself audibly (it matters not whether it is intentional or not) within hearing distance of a journalist and teammate, this is a Robinson who definitely wants to be heard. Robinson wants, we might say, to hear himself; he wants to speak to himself about his own role in producing this moment of "cheering," this act of racially self-demeaning gratitude, this catalyzing of the perversity that is black self-abnegation. All this provokes Robinson refusing, in the manner of Desdemona's father Brabantio, to commit "treason of the blood!" (*Othello*).[93] Robinson, that is, recognizing (trying to account for, calculating) his implication in the production of so perverse an effect as gratitude, and in so doing joining himself to that painful struggle between understanding what spurs the cheering and his irrepressible (so that we can only mark it, as a qualification, "silent") condemnation of it.

In the event Jackie Robinson seeks to concile himself to his self because, as Derrida explains, "*At the center of the principle, always, the One does violence to itself, and guards itself against the other.*"[94] In the course of his attack on both A and B (the Negro spectators as much as the white authorities), Robinson finds himself "guarding" against both, locating both as "other"—incommensurate with his project for racial justice, equality, and meaningful, post-Reconstruction citizenship. This is no small undertaking, so much so that it is possible to figure the event of Pelican Field as the site of Robinsonian displacement. At the very least, we must ask if the event constitutes the occasion when Robinson is reminding himself, perhaps bitterly, of his own complicity in the system. Moreover, how could Robinson vent his anger at the black natives of New Orleans or Mobile when he, under much greater public scrutiny, performs his own kind of gratitude to the white authority of the South? Robinson could not be accused of subservience or perverse gratitude as such, but his career was marked by inhabiting a mode of what we might term political non-engagement (or provocation) on the field. (He was as tough a competitor, athletically, as any—more so, writers such as Kahn would argue, given the violence he had to endure.) Much of this, and here the burden of overrepresentation must once more figure in our political accounting, was necessary to the success of the "great experiment." Robinsonian restraint demanded, among other repressions, the refusal to take the racist bait that he routinely encountered when stealing second base, or, as we remember so well, stealing home.

Conciliation

> The black man's alienation is not an individual question.
> —**FRANTZ FANON**, *Black Skin, White Masks*

If this is indeed the case, and we have reason enough to believe that it is, then Pelican Field should be named the event of the black self confronting itself and attempting the impossible act of disavowing that same self. Robinson simultaneously trying to castigate his fellow blacks while not, at least in any way visible to us, subjecting himself to the same political scrutiny. Where, we might ask, is Robinson's demand for self-reflexivity? In the moment of ir-ruption, provoked by conciliation, conciliation becomes instructive in, as, and for itself. For Jackie Robinson, conciliation begins with a struggle within and, simultaneously, against the self—as much, that is, as it is a struggle for himself as other and for those like him, needless to say. The act of conciliation, in this intense mode, challenges the self to face its own name: the "great experiment," "integration," "Nigger," "Jackie Robinson." These are names, especially in pejoration, that are never only "individual questions." They are, against the will of the (individual) other, "shared" names, names that can be applied indiscriminately because the other is always presumed to be without singularity. That is, the other marks a morphological, unquestioned sameness, an indistinct one-ness.

Because these names are, in the case of Robinson, shared, they also concatenate, illuminate, and trouble each other. Most importantly, however, they are, finally, impossible to disarticulate from each other. The event of Pelican Field reveals the violent intensity of the act of (self-)conciliation. (The threat of "reconciliation," as Derrida reminds us, is violence of a nature that is all too "identifiable." Conciliation produces no less familiar a violence.) In its own way, of course, the pejorative or the epithet— the racist term, the misogynist remark, the language of offense—articulates the particular violence of the expletive because such a name can, even if only for a moment (as in Fanon's *Black Skin, White Masks*, "'Dirty nigger!' Or simply, 'Look, a Negro!'")[95] overwhelm the subject of its virulence. The epithet can, as *The Wretched of the Earth* so amply demonstrates (in its critique of the nonradical native intellectual), "return" the subject to a pejorative inhabitation of its im-proper "name": "Rediscovering one's people sometimes means in this phase wanting to be a 'nigger,' not an exceptional 'nigger' but a real 'nigger,' the sort defined by the white man" (*Wretched of the Earth*).[96] In his anger, Jackie Robinson refuses himself as the model MLB integrationist and becomes, instead, a "real (Fanonian) 'nigger,'" un-grateful, above all else. In forswearing gratitude and, Socratically, struggling against the (Rickey-imposed, acquiescence before, and after, all else) politics of the diamond, Robinson is politically "conciled" to his Negro self. Through the event, Jackie Robinson demonstrates a fidelity to himself, a fidelity at once publicly impossible and yet publicly palpable. "Out of joint" with himself as integration icon, Robinson's "out of jointness" with his Pelican Field time makes him conjunctive with the political that is, literally, *l'avenir* (to come) but is, more importantly, ar-

ticulable as the already radicalized within—within the self, within earshot of teammates (a teammate, and, at that, Reese, the teammate of record), and the public. Robinson's expletive marks a break with the present,
an opening to the future as well as a recognition of the moment of first
articulation, all of which might be thought of as a break on the order of
Derrida's reflection on the mother and "birth." For Derrida, "'birth' is perhaps a question of the future and of arrival, a newly arrived (*une question
d'avenir, une question toute neuve*)."[97] The "question," as such, is not only
"newly arrived" but also "arrives" from a time that is not now, a time "out
of joint," necessarily so, with what is extant. The question, then, is always
unprecedented. It establishes itself as the rupture that makes *d'avenir* possible.[98] It is the function of the precedent to demonstrate, through itself
and, possibly, against itself, "how very soon, things will be—different!"
Robinson was, of course, already "different"—incommensurable with the
time and the politics that obtained in, as, and through him.

It is in this event, on this occasion when historical debts are invoked
and asserted, "take what you got coming," when the division of public
space is struggled over, that we might understand Robinson's "private"
anger as an engagement with that salient moment in James Madison's
Federalist Papers. Allow here a borrowing from Eric Cheyfitz's analysis of
Madison's role in the failure of American democracy: "At the end of *Federalist X*, fearing a general rebellion against the property-owning classes,
Madison warned against 'an abolition of debts' and 'an equal division of
property.'"[99] The concepts "abolition of debts" and "equal division of property" are Madison's—an anxious scribe of the Constitution arguing for
the "proper structure of the Union." Madison's concepts resonate with the
situation in which Robinson finds himself. At no point in American history has there been any real public support (the time of the Great Depres-
sion, potentially, excepted, and yet not even then—not even at the height
of Lyndon Johnson's "Great Society" experiment of the 1960s) for the
"equal division of property" and yet, we might say, within the confines of
Pelican Field, that is precisely the claim that Robinson is making: All spectators should have equal access to the seating in the stadium. But perhaps
it is more than that.

In equality, in acknowledging the inalienable right of all to the "field"
that is America, what should not matter is the preemptive racial division.
The right to every seat, in every stadium, at every game, should be indivis-
ible—class distinctions apart, of course, Madison would insist. It is that
right that Robinson is urging (the fundamental right of equal access), in a
mumbled monologue (in his iteration of the "two-in-one" Socratic modality—except, of course, that Robinson is not truly alone, given Kahn's and
Reese's proximity), his fellow blacks to "take" unto themselves, without

any deference. Robinson wants his fellow Negroes to leave behind, to re-
ject once and for all, that tendency given an unforgettable name, a sting-
ing pejorative, by Harriet Beecher Stowe—"Uncle Tom." (Robinson, lest
we forget, was more or less convinced that his fellow black Dodger, Campanella, had a certain predisposition to acquiescence. "'There's a little
Uncle Tom in Roy,'" Robinson once remarked [quoted in Kahn].)[100] Instead,
the only act worthy of integration is to understand the right of access as
unqualifiedly black American, denied by white America since the antebel-
lum days. Still, the right is theirs, unavailable but theirs, theirs as guaranteed by the terms of "*une question d'avenir, une question toute neuve.*" The
black self, if we might extrapolate from the "Moorish monster" in Robinson's thought, cannot thank itself for what is its own. Such an act would
be "too hideous," would it not? It would amount to a "monstrous" act: the
self annihilating its right to rights.

In Robinson's terms, the opening of an extra, unused (at this particular
game, for reasons directly connected to the racial economy and politics
prevailing in the nation) section at Pelican Field is nothing more than a
small installment on the repayment of a much larger, perhaps unpayable,
historic debt: "You got it coming." This was, as Cheyfitz notes, the deepest
fear of Madison the great author of the Constitution: The "Constitution
was instituted during a time when small farmers in Massachusetts were
rebelling against the foreclosures of their farms by large land owners, a
class represented by the founders."[101] The rising up of those victimized by
power—class warfare—was Madison's greatest fear. In this case the fear
was provoked by the late eighteenth-century Shays's Rebellion, led by Daniel Shays and Henry Gale against Massachusetts courts intent on seizing
property from debt-ridden farmers, many of them newly returned from
fighting the Revolutionary War, only to see Boston British loyalists make
claims against the—poor, relatively and in absolute terms, patriot—farmers' property. (These claims were supported by Massachusetts governor
James Bowdoin; this was an "underclass" rebellion that saw Samuel Adams
instrumental in drafting a Riot Act that suspended habeas corpus; this was
a rebellion that prompted, famously, Thomas Jefferson, then ambassador
to France, to remark in a letter to William Stephens Smith, with a cynicism
that nonetheless bears its own veracity, one ventures: "A little rebellion
now and then is a good thing. The tree of liberty must be refreshed from
time to time with the blood of patriots and tyrants.")[102]

Alexander Hamilton makes precisely this point about the fragility of
the American state in the opening book of the *Federalist Papers*: "to decide
the important question, whether societies of men are really capable or not
of establishing good government from reflection and choice, or whether
they are forever destined to depend for their political constitutions on

accident and force."[103] Hamilton also feared the "force" of the unproper-
tied classes to "decide the question" in a form unfavorable to that of the
founders and their landed compatriots. That is why Madison was so ada-
mantly against the "abolition of debts": It would free the small farmers
from their "responsibility" toward the "large land owners." Debts must be
paid; failing that, the standing of these owners would be undermined,
perhaps even jeopardized, by the "monstrous force"—if we could, just for
a single instant, conjoin Othello and Hamilton's very different fears—of
a rebellion. These fears, of course, are not so dissimilar, since they both
turn on the question of the stability of the state, either the American or
the Venetian one. Othello's "masters" were acutely concerned with the
ambitions of the Turks in relation to Cyprus—a fear, as it turns out, the
Christian Cypriots and their Greek cousins had every right to express,
and, having done so, to then anticipate the worst.

Maybe Madison's insistence, what we might term his class loyalty, is
precisely—insofar as one can be exact almost two hundred years after the
fact—Robinson's point. To "Take what you got coming" is to recognize
that gratitude is the wrong response to a historic injustice: The right of
equal access constitutes not only an instance of repayment[104] but also the
articulation of the demand. Debts cannot be abolished, they must be paid
through the politics of conciliation: that act in which the terms of the debt
are struggled over, without precondition, as if there were no precedents
for this conversation, as if this conversation were its own precedent. They
will, these "unpaid," outstanding accounts, remain spectrally present,
haunting like that most venerable of Shakespearean figures, the ghost of
King Hamlet, whose return sparks a massive upheaval in the functioning
of the Danish state. What Robinson is advocating is that there should be
no perverse gratitude, and certainly no obsequiousness, no "Othello-like"
haplessness, no act of penitence in the process of accepting the payment
that derives from history. The event of Pelican Field makes, because of the
terrain that Robinson delineates, imperative the need for the politics of
conciliation.

Within his psychobiography, Pelican Field constitutes Jackie Robinson's "apology"—the act of displacement reconstituted as contrition for
the self's implication in the event—and the old Brooklyn Dodger's gift to
the future, his *une question d'avenir, une question toute neuve* to the black
generations to come, and the entirety of America *l'avenir*. Robinson spoke,
Socratically, to himself, and, Platonically, the Greek student allowing the
slain master teacher's philosophy to be made available to us through the
ages, to those within immediate range. As a Neoplatonist, it would be fair
to say that Jackie Robinson did not speak, often enough, loudly enough,
publicly enough of himself as a Socratic being, as the teacher whom Plato

idolized. Jackie Robinson did not "take" what he had "coming": He did not demand, except in the event, what he "had coming." Here, of course, we acknowledge the difficulty of making his claim as much as we acknowledge the precariousness of his position because it is never easy to bear the burden of over-representation. But he bore his burden felicitously, making of it always the "question" of his rights, a "question" that is best understood as an uncompromising demand: that his opponents, the predominantly white fans, and some of his more recalcitrant teammates treat him as a player who was a Dodger, that they acknowledge his right to be a Dodger. To be a Dodger, to play in MLB, for no other reason (which is to say that we submit to the palimpsest that is historical reason) than he had "it coming."

Pelican Field as the provocation, the effect of, that derives from, that is located at the core of, the event, the event that bequeaths us the gift of the interrogative, an interrogative that bears as much the imprint of Derrida as it does of Fanon. Not, as such, that "accurate" historical "answers" might be acquired but that we should, in the spirit of Robinsonian anger and fierceness, as if he did, and, if he did, how did he demand "equal treatment." We ask not only because he should have, and, in light of this fierce outburst, we are sure that he knows—not after the fact, but in the moment itself—but also because of what it must have meant to live with the fact of not doing what it is he knew he should have been doing. Robinson is angry at his fellow Negroes because, like them, we might sacrilegiously suggest, he is a "stupid bastard." Moreover, he is the most "stupid" kind of "stupid bastard" because he is so intensely conscious of himself as a politically "stupid bastard."

Jackie Robinson not only knew what he did not do; he also knew, more importantly, what he should have done. There are many reasons to admire Othello, even as we recognize how deft and canny an operator Iago is, but for the purpose of conciliation the most important one is that he troubles us and because he is committed, even in his moments of most profound self-doubt, to the interrogative. He issues, to us, an injunction: "Speak to me as to thy thinkings" (Othello).[105]

Indeed, to speak these "thinkings" about the politics that obtains in the moment, in the mode, between perverse (Negro) gratitude and the radicalized within (which takes the form of the expletive) verges on public articulation so that it is, already, without, outside of its circumscribed self. If the most recent gift of The Boys of Summer (not least of which is its standing as one of the three great books on sport, the others being James's Beyond a Boundary and Eduardo Galeano's Football in Sun and Shadow) is to reveal Jackie Robinson's failure to make (more) public his "out of jointness," then, as such, it continues to figure as a challenge to the future, to how it is we think race and conciliation. How should the subject respond to conciliation? By submitting to the forces that threaten to overwhelm the self? Or how does conciliation make possible political access to the Robinsonian radicalized within?

It is a simple, but an ethically signal, choice, one that resonates, perhaps now more than ever, now long after the event was recorded out of a historic fragment. How is it possible to make the unforgettable forgotten moment returned to us by Kahn as the radicalized inscription of—that is, if it is not designated as the first question of—a conciliation? Best, perhaps, to remain felicitous to Derrida's *une question d'avenir, une question toute neuve*. Best perhaps to begin there, to begin there as the first act of the interrogation not only that conciliation makes possible but, rather, that the "thinking" that is conciliation demands.

2 Thank You, in (a) Sense

> Singularities are turning points and points of inflection; bottle-
> necks, knots, foyers, and center; sickness and health, hope and
> anxiety, "sensitive" points.
>
> —GILLES DELEUZE, *The Logic of Sense*

A singularity can be understood as a moment or a day on which things "turned." In the instance on which this chapter turns, it is a day on which the "knots" of apartheid and postapartheid became ever more entangled, a day on which the "sensitivities" that inhere in those "knots" revealed themselves as "points" of hope, as markers of intense historical "anxiety" and prospects for a nation struggling to come

PHOTOGRAPH: *From Thomas Reuters Markets LLC*

into itself. June 24, 1995, marks a singular moment in postapartheid South African history, the day on which the South African rugby team, known as the Springboks and led by the white Afrikaner François Pienaar, beat the New Zealand All Blacks by the score of 15–12 to win the rugby World Cup final. The "singular point" that is June 24, 1995, shows how this day is "opposed to the ordinary" and why we might propose the "singular" ("singular point") as explicable only within the logic of the event— that is, the logic of the "exceptional" or "extra-ordinary" day.[1]

South Africa was newly democratized in April 1994. Just over a year later, and against considerable odds, the Springbok team emerged victorious over a superior foe, the supremely talented New Zealand All Blacks. Not for nothing has this All Black team been ranked as arguably the greatest in the history of rugby union. (The New Zealand team is known as the "All Blacks" because of their all-black uniform, adorned with the crest of a silver fern.)[2] Composed of fifteen players, rugby teams are divided into two units, designed to act in concert with each other. There are seven players in the backline: a fullback, two wings, two centers, a scrumhalf, and a flyhalf. There are eight players in the pack of forwards (often referred to simply as the "pack"): two props (loosehead and tighthead) and one hooker, who make up the front row; two locks, who constitute the middle row; and, finally, two flankers (open and closed side) and a number eight constitute the back row. The 1995 All Black backline boasted the sublime and captivating talents of Glen Osborne at fullback, the supremely talented Jeff Wilson on the right wing, and inside him the centers Walter Little and Frank Bunce, who rank with the best combinations in the game, alongside, I would suggest, the likes of the 1974 Lions pairing of Richard Milliken (Ireland) and Ian McGeechan (Scotland). (Wilson was a remarkable athlete. Not only did he represent New Zealand at rugby, scoring forty-four tries— think the equivalent of touchdowns—in sixty international matches, but he also represented his country's cricket team, the Black Caps, as an all-rounder, a player who bats and bowls with equal distinction. During his high school years Wilson was also a standout basketball player.)

The 1995 All Black pack was led by their hooker, the redoubtable and canny captain Sean Fitzpatrick, who was joined in the front row by outstanding props Craig Dowd (loosehead) and Olo Brown (tighthead). The lock forwards were among the greatest duos, featuring the imposing Robin Brooke and the massively skillful Ian Jones; in the back row was the formidable Josh Kronfeld (open-side flanker) with Robin Brooke's older brother, Zinzan, a commanding, fierce, and proud player, at number eight. The star of the All Black team, however, was the brilliant and powerful right-winger, the late Jonah Lomu, then the best player in the game. During the semi-win against England, Lomu dragged four would-be tacklers with him over the goal line to score a try that will never be forgotten.

Against Fitzpatrick's Kiwis, Pienaar's Springboks offered a solid full-back in Andre Joubert, a strong left-winger in Chester Williams, with the irascible James Small on the opposite wing, a solid prop in Os du Randt, and a quietly gifted number eight in Mark Andrews. For his part, the open-side flanker Pienaar was a committed and self-confident captain. Pienaar's outfit was not a team to be sniffed at, but, by all expert accounts (rightly so), the Springboks were decided underdogs for the final, played at Ellis Park in Johannesburg. In strictly rugby terms, emerging with that 15–12 win against this All Black team, and with the odds stacked against them, was a significant South African victory. It was not, however, what made the final memorable or historic.

The historicity of the final has three sources. It was the first time that a rugby World Cup final went to extra time. Second, it is the only final in which only two players scored all the points. For the All Blacks, flyhalf Andrew Mehrtens kicked three penalties and a drop goal, to which the Springbok flyhalf Joel Stransky replied with three penalties and two drop goals. Stransky's second drop goal, with extra time expiring, sealed the victory for the host nation. The moment Stransky's drop kick (as it is also known) sailed over the crossbar, just barely, it became a storied part of Springbok rugby lore. And, third, it was the first time that the Springboks participated in the rugby World Cup. Until 1995, South Africa was banned from the competition because of its apartheid policies.

Singularity

> Each singularity is the source of a series extending in a determined direction right up the vicinity of another singularity.
>
> —GILLES DELEUZE, *The Logic of Sense*

The singularity of that World Cup final, however, can be traced to an entirely different source. It derives from the postmatch encounter between the newly elected black president, the first president of a democratic South Africa, Nelson Mandela, and Pienaar. After the Springbok victory, Mandela handed the Webb-Ellis Trophy to the beaming captain. Mandela offered, audible to the world, his thanks to Pienaar:

"Francois, thank you for what you have done for our country." Pienaar, with extraordinary presence of mind, replied, "No, Mr. President. Thank you for what you have done."[3]

It is possible to apprehend this "exchange" (it is not the proper word, mind you, but please indulge me for the moment) as the Deleuzian "extension" of "singularities," as the event of what ensues when one singularity encounters its successor. The event of conciliation, the event made by François Pienaar ↔/and Nelson Mandela, is what happens when the singularity in motion (Mandela's language of thanks) "lines up," to use a sport's metaphor for one body coming into contact with another (in rugby, unlike in American gridiron, the contact is intense, sustained, and occasionally brutal, especially in a "scrum" or a "loose scrum," because the colliding, competing bodies are unadorned—it is simply body, in bare uniform, shirt and shorts, against body),[4] against the singularity next in line—the contact between singularities, achieved through the movement of one in the "determined direction" of the other always raises in the encounter not only the possibility of the dialectic but also the Heideggerian injunction that originates directly in Mandela's language of thanks, of giving thanks. In Heidegger's terms, *Danken ist Denken*: "thanking is thinking"↔/"All thanking belongs first and last in the essential realm of thinking" (*Was Heißt Denken?*).[5] To give thanks is to think, is to think about giving thanks, to think about what it means to give thanks, about how it is that thanks will be received, about how it will register, how it will affect the other. Thanking cannot be thought without thinking; to *thanc* is to already be in the "essential realm" of thinking. (In Afrikaans, "Thank you" is *Dankie* and "thinking" is *dink*, so that Heidegger's terms are eminently evocative. It is possible, as it were, to "hear" Heidegger "more easily" in Afrikaans than in English. Rendered in rudimentary, barely grammatical Afrikaans: "*dink is dankie; dankie is dink.*"[6] "To think is to thank; to thank is to think.") The very act of giving thanks is inscribed in and as a commitment to thinking, a presentation of thanking (thinking) fundamental to thinking conciliation. This also means, of course, that every act of thinking—and this is where Heidegger's formulation truly comes into its own—is simultaneously an act of giving thanks. Of, that is, giving thanks to thinking. That is, in thinking we are paying our respects, showing our regard for, that which matters: paying tribute—thanking—to thinking. "Real thanks," as Heidegger phrases it, "never consists in that we ourselves come bearing gifts, and merely repay with gift. Pure thanks is rather that we simply think—think what is really and solely given, what is there to be thought" (*Was Heißt Denken?*).[7] As a circular logic of the highest order, to think is to give thanks to thinking, to be able to think about (thanking) thinking is to thank (thinking) for making thinking possible. As such, thinking is nothing less than the act of giving thanks for what Hannah Arendt—that most famous of Heidegger students—understands as the "life of the mind." Thinking is life itself; it is what gives life (to) life. The only proper way to thank, the "purest" form of thanks, is to give the self over to thinking. It is, to risk a repetition, to think what it means to thank. Pienaar's "thanks," his negation of Mandela's "Thank you," is what rises to the level of thinking. Mandela's formulaic "Thank you" does, following Heidegger's demands, not achieve this status.

At the level of Deleuzian "subsistence," then, what this chapter undertakes is to think the language of thanks that is exchanged or, in the terms offered by *The Burden of Over-representation*, "conciled" as the first articulation of politics. The "exchange" that can be cast in the "line" (or series) of gift→refusal→conciliation between Mandela and Pienaar resonates with the "force" of a Deleuzian paradox: "The force of the paradoxes is that they are not contradictory; they rather allow us to be present at the genesis of the contradiction" (*The Logic of Sense*).[8] The "genesis of the contradiction," as we later see and as can be discerned from the quote itself, turns on Pienaar's refusal, as it is provisionally named here.[9] This refusal informs much of the thinking of the "exchange," but it also marks, as such, the "genesis" of the politics of conciliation. That is, conciliation instantiates a politics in contradistinction to the discourse of reconciliation that was then (and to a far lesser extent, now) the preeminent mode of politics in South Africa. This politics is most familiar, of course, as the founding act and the subsequent actions of the Truth and Reconciliation Commission (TRC). (The TRC, broadly speaking, staged encounters—direct confrontations, face-to-face meetings—between the historically disenfranchised and those agents of the apartheid regime, the police, security forces, black South Africans working on the side of the regime, that had enacted violence against them or their family members or, as was sometimes the case, between survivors of those who had been killed in their struggle against apartheid. The TRC, televised nationally, and headed by then-archbishop Desmond Tutu, sought to achieve "reconciliation through truth," the condition being that amnesty would be granted only to those who made a full account of their transgressions. The deeply Christian paradigm of forgiveness was an obvious inspiration for the TRC.) Pienaar's *refusal*—again, "refusal" as the provisional, first term to describe the event inaugurated by the "Thank you/No, thank you," a term whose "inadequacy" as such demands that its many iterations be thought—to accept Mandela's thanks demonstrates, even if it cannot be said to inaugurate, the thinking of conciliation as the first act of politics: conciliation refuses forgiveness and reconciliation as the first and last horizon of politics; conciliation is politics as that first and potentially telling encounter between self and other, between other and self that neither forecloses "violence" as a possibility of the encounter nor presumes, in advance, to understand what the outcome of the encounter will be. Conciliation as politics, and with politics there can be no proscription, there can be no determining the outcome in advance. In a word, conciliation as the absolute political commitment to the event.

At the very least, conciliation as, following Fredric Jameson's critique of the "equation" in *Representing Capital: A Reading of Volume One,* "introduc[ing] temporality into synchronicity."[10] The time of conciliation, the temporality it insists on securing for itself (it "cuts," in Deleuze's terms, into the time of . . . reconciliation, in this case), draws the "temporality of synchronicity"—those "meaningful coincidences" (the term is Carl Jung's) that appear to have no causal relationship but evidence a meaningful relationship—into question. And, as such, it draws them into history because it insists on "understanding" how it is that "temporality" makes possible the "meaningful coincidences"; that is, Jameson's "temporality" attends to the forces, such as the discourse of reconciliation that predominated, as has just been acknowledged, in the South African political after the February 1990 release of Mandela and other political prisoners and the unbanning of the black liberation movements (the African National Congress [ANC] and the Pan African Congress [PAC] most notable among them) that sought to fetishize the "coincidences" without thinking their politics. That is, the "submission" to reconciliation at the expense of political critique; that is, conciliation politics as the first and most enduring "victim" of the TRC discourse and the ANC's underwriting of it. By inserting a Jamesonian "temporality" into "synchronicity," the constitutive elements of the "meaningful coincidences" are laid bare, and the effects of their coinciding (the politics of reconciliation, the costs of that discourse, for which Mandela stands as the preeminent, almost Christ-like figuration) are called to account—to account for both what it did make possible (e.g., transition to black majority rule, a democratic South Africa, a nonracial democracy, all of this without too much more bloodshed) and what it did not (e.g., the effective redistribution of resources and addressing the vast material inequities that distinguished disenfranchised and enfranchised life, such as continuing disparities in health, education, and social resources). Jameson's "temporality" re-introduces "synchronicity" as a political event to be thought, not reified à la celebratory turn to reconciliation that obtained in South African politics in the wake of February 1990 and, indeed, for a very long—too long by far, some would argue, with complete justification—afterward. (In fact, we could say that the "Afterword" of "apartheid" is not "postapartheid" but, rather, "reconciliation," so much did that discourse consume, so much did it absorb all other political critiques into itself.)[11] As such, Jameson's thinking of the "temporality of synchronicity," or "synchronicity through temporality," works to interrogate all discourses that do not reflect on, in the South African instance, at least, the "happy coincidences" of history. (They are, as we well know, rarely "happy," these "coincidences.") Jameson, as is his wont, insists on the thinking of history. Most memorably, of course, there is the opening injunction, "Always historicize!" from *The Political Unconscious: Narrative as a Socially Symbolic Act*.[12]

Conciliation, as the rude interruption into history, as the determination to "make history," as a fidelity to history as such, stands as the absolute rejection of the terms of the extant political. Conciliation is, instead, a thinking that proposes a direct confrontation with what is in order to make immanent what should be. (Let us say, for argument's sake, conciliation would be the commitment to the complete fulfillment of the vision of the "Freedom Charter," the ANC's guiding articulation of its governing principles—sharing the land, sharing the resources, equality before the law, and so on.) Conciliation as, in Jameson's terms, *"Luft aus anderen Planeten . . . is a momentary breeze from the future* (not yet Benjamin's storm)[;] it is a faint and garbled message from outside the system and its seemingly airtight closure" (*Representing Capital*).[13] Conciliation is that "momentary breeze from the future" that offers a brief, specific glimpse into an opening of what the future might be—that is, what possibilities it might yield. However, it might also be possible to recognize in conciliation a signal, singular proposition, precisely a call for "Benjamin's storm." Or, meteorologically phrased, for the "breeze" to fulfill itself (as a mark of its fidelity to history) as a "storm" and, as such, to grow—through mutation or organic political development—from within the "system" into a clear and unambiguous "message," it will no longer countenance the extant "system." It is, instead, dedicated to its undoing, permanently. To phrase it in the terms of Jameson's Benjaminian poetic, the "gentle breeze" of reconciliation will be swept away by the force of the "storm" that is conciliation—the "storm" that erupts despite the best efforts of the "airtight closure" that is reconciliation. As such, conciliation and reconciliation are irreconcilable because only one of these is felicitous to the terms of politics.

In this regard, Deleuze's "genesis" recognizes what the "force of the paradox" can make possible—a thinking of the paradox to which will be added a Jamesonian element. Pienaar's refusal, "No, Thank you, Mr. President," points to a language that seems of a piece with that wonderfully elusive (what is it that Deleuze is saying? what does he mean?) and evocative provocation that Deleuze offers as *"language without articulation"* (*The Logic of Sense*).[14] "Language without articulation": language that exists both "outside" (a discursive impossibility, to be sure, but all the more thought provoking in that we can never designate it "pure language," tempting as that prospect is) of language as such, and language that can truly come into its own only when it "speaks as itself." That is, the language of politics that is characterized by its sparseness and its fidelity to—its sticking strictly to, its hewing unabashedly to—addressing and inscribing that force of language that is utterly and only political. Its "genesis," in this instance, is clear: "language without articulation" begins a line of reasoning that Hegel and contemporary philosophers such as Jean-Luc Nancy (*Hegel: The Restlessness of the Negative*)[15] and Slavoj Žižek (*Tarrying with the Negative*),[16] among others, would surely endorse, with the negation that makes us responsible to thinking. To thinking negation, to thinking negation as the condition of thought.

Pienaar's refusal is, so understood, nothing less than the displacement (it is rhetorically stronger than mere replacement because it pushes, forces, out, that which resided there) of *Danken* with *Denken*. This is a thinking whose "genesis" can be clearly traced to the negation that animates—politicizes, it constitutes *the* act of conciliation—Pienaar's "No," which is by no means prefatory to (his, in his turn) *Danken*. Pienaar's "No" can be taken as the "crystallization of the contradiction and not its effacement," as Jameson phrases it in his discussion of money (*Representing Capital*).[17] What conciliation makes immanent—and, potentially, imminent—is the incompleteness of the political project, reconciliation, that works to "efface" politics as such. Through the event conciliation restores the imperative of politics, it reinstitutes the logic of politics first, last, and always. As such, the prefix "re-" (as it constitutes reconciliation) is implicitly critiqued because it figures as the grammatical marker that expresses the desire for no politics. That is, "re-" conciliation speaks of a desire to instantiate that which comes after politics, precisely that political scenario that must be scrupulously guarded against, that moment in history that must always be foreclosed as an outcome; "re-," as such, stands as the grammatical mark of the desire to, impossibly, "end" politics.

As such, there is a strange, paradoxical "unity" that holds the contradiction in a unity grounded in tension—in itself, of course, a "founding" contradiction. The tension is located in the desire, explicable in some way, for an "end" to politics after the racist violence and trauma of apartheid; this desire (and the antipolitics that emanates from it) cannot but, again, make politics matter more than, so to speak, the discursive, the rhetoric of "reconciliation" and its intention to inscribe "postapartheid life" as what follows the interregnum between the declarative moment (February 1990) and the effective moment (April 1994, the occasion of the first democratic elections). By holding in tension the desire for the "end" and the inexorable lurch toward several new political "beginnings," what emerges is the possibility of politics in its rawest, most unadulterated articulation, a politics bound to the past that desperately, determinedly wants to address and undo that past (apartheid) in order to achieve the condition of *nunca mas* ("never again"). In this way, the work of "crystal-lization" (in the South African case it amounts to properly understanding the antipolitical desire that motivates the "re-") is to function as a bul-wark against "effacement" by reinforcing/enforcing attention to history, to how the (racist) legacy of inequity continues to effect all aspects of the political, to begin to understand again what it is that makes history work—work, that is, in a temporal register, much like Jameson's render-ing of "synchronicity."

Subtending the desire for reconciliation is always something more than what can be contained or articulated in the discourse it mobilizes. There is always another set of historical forces—let us name them "dialectical," in play—subtly, if not at the level of the surface, then indisputably at work "just below," "visible" just beneath the surface (or palpable at a more subter-ranean level) and unarguably "audible" (it can be heard in the murmurings of discontent, in the barely suppressed critiques that circulates among the disaffected, and so on; here we have the example of Jackie Robinson's ex-pletive to remind us) in the very discourse that militates against it. The "dialectic," as such, represents an irrepressible if not immediately mobiliz-able force that manifests itself despite the predominance of the discourse that seeks to overwhelm or liquidate it.

The "Nonpower at the Heart" of "Mere" Reconciliation

What is this power at the heart of nonpower?

—JACQUES DERRIDA, *The Animal That Therefore I Am*

As much as Mandela's "Thank you" speaks as/of the desire for (mere) rec-onciliation, it also, as we see momentarily, opens onto a politics more re-vealing than (merely) that. As a bare/base iteration, Mandela's "Thank you" constitutes an act of political artifice—a call from and for the present that cannot obviate how subject it is to the force of past and future but is, equal-ly, as is later discussed, never a politics that is without a sacrificial ele-ment[18]—that does not rise to the level, in Deleuze's terms, of a "solution": "Even if the problem is concealed by its solution, it subsists nonetheless in the Idea which relates it to its conditions and organizes the genesis of the solutions. Without this Idea, the solutions would have no *sense*. The prob-lematic is both an objective category of knowledge and a perfectly objective kind of being" (*The Logic of Sense*).[19] The problem, the politics of conciliation that Mandela will not address, the constitutive necessity of confrontation and thinking (or the thought that makes the confrontation possible in the first place) that is (that cannot be) "concealed" in his *Danken,* is what sustains (girds its political life) and maintains (gives it public "visibility," voice, volubility even) the very "Idea" of conciliation. The problem, because of its fidelity to the "Idea," because of its imbrication in negation, "subsists" in Pienaar's negation. Or, rather, its subscription to the "Idea" is what secures the opening to Pienaar's negation. The "solution" that Mandela maintains, the politics of reconciliation, amounts to, following Deleuze, a politics sans *sense*: there be can no advocacy for a present, figured here as postapartheid South Africa, which fails to understand that "only the past and future inhere in time and divide the present infinitely. These are not three successive dimensions, but two simultaneous readings of time" (*The Logic of Sense*).[20]

Mandela's "Thank you" seeks to bring his (desired) present into alignment with the "future" while not grasping that the present is a mere "cut," a short, sharp incision, in temporality and that the logic of the event "moves in two directions at once," the past and the future, and that it is only through conciliation (treating the present as the event, the present as made by and still in the process of making the event) that it becomes possible to fully apprehend Deleuze's "two simultaneous readings of time"—the cut that is the present, "overwhelmed" by the bidirectionality that is always inaugurated, again and again, by the event. The present is, as such, inherently insufficient because it cannot countenance the very possibility of (a) "becoming" that "always eludes the present" (*The Logic of Sense*).[21] With its refusal of the present, conciliation stakes itself on the moment that the singularities come up against each other. If the motion (Mandela's language) of the singularity continues in a straight line, it is inevitable that the two singularities will be brought face-to-face with each other. And it then becomes possible, because of the event, for the *Denken* that is conciliation to come into its own and for thought (Pienaar's "language") to superannuate *Danken*. (French Huguenot by descent, Pienaar's first language is Afrikaans, so that Heidegger's formulation might indeed "translate" without too much effort for Pienaar.) No thanking without thinking so that it becomes possible to assert that all *Danken* is made by, and, as such, subject to, *Denken*. Although it cannot be guaranteed, it is always likely that all tendencies in the direction of reconciliation will, at a crucial moment, be made accountable to the political force that is conciliation. This encounter marks not only the moment of irreconcilability but also that moment when reconciliation is no longer sustainable—no longer sustainable because it has no political *Grund*.

The event is "characteristic" of the "reversals" between future and past, active and passive, cause and effect, more and less, too much and not enough, already and not yet. The infinitely articulable event is always *both at once*. "It is eternally that which has just happened and that which is about to happen" (the event can be rendered dialectical [future/past, and so on] but can never be divided), but never that which is happening (to cut too deeply and not enough). "The event, being itself impassive, allows the active and the passive to be interchanged more easily, since it is *neither one nor the other,* but rather their common result (to cut—to be cut)" (Deleuze).[22] The event of the "Thank you," conciled as it is here in the figures of Mandela and Pienaar, allows for thinking the apartheid "past" and the postapartheid "future" as a series of necessary "reversals." That is, in and through the way in which the event works on (and through, of course) these figures, the one who was a historic ("admired," more of which, momentarily) political "activist" (Mandela) is rendered "passive" because what he says is, at once, "too much and not enough" (making his "Thank you" excessive, effusive, and, as such, insufficient to the terms of the event). "Passivity" is an important element in Derrida's critique on animals, specifically the cat in Lewis Carroll's *Alice in Wonderland,* refracted as it is through the "*first* and *decisive* question" that Bentham poses in his discussion about animals in *The Principles of Morals and Legislation*: "'Can they suffer?'"[23] For Derrida, Bentham's "question is disturbed by a certain *passivity.* It bears witness, manifestly already, as question, the response that testifies to a sufferance, to a passion, a not-being-able" (*The Animal That Therefore I Am*).[24]

Saliently and no less paradoxically, what Mandela's "Thank you" "bears witness" to is, within the logic (the context, if you insist), precisely the question that so vexes Derrida in his engagement with Bentham. It is not so much that Mandela's "Thank you" is a mark of his "nonpower" as his "Thank you' makes evident the shifting terrain, the interplay between "power and nonpower," between apartheid and postapartheid, between past and the desire for an "eternal present," between, reductively rendered, black and white, that is constitutive of the Ellis Park event. Through Pienaar's refusal, his "No, thank you," his ability to tilt the balance of—rhetorical—"power," if nothing else (although the dynamic is such that there is surely something else, something in addition to the "No," so that when we operate on the terrain, always, of "No, thank you," there is always something more [+] and less [-] at work, in play, producing a political effect), the precarity of Mandela's "power" (which makes it, for an instant, indistinguishable from "nonpower"), of the new political dispensation, articulates, renews, renovates, speaks itself (as precarity itself), and the provisionality (it will last only a moment; it will outlast Mandela and Pienaar too, arguably) of Pienaar's power, reveal themselves. In the face of Pienaar's "No, thank you," Mandela is, following Derrida's Benthamite language, made "to suffer": to suffer in silence, to suffer in the silence of the "nonpower" that constitutes, to deliberately subject the self to violence against itself, that is, we might venture, the "heart of his power."

There is, of course, an intense political reality, a hard political edge, within the context of Ellis Park, to Mandela's "nonpower." A "nonpower" that stands in a dis-proportionate relationship to Pienaar's "power." The vast majority of fans at the World Cup final were white, white Afrikaners, making of Pienaar the most emblematic figure—incarnation—of this newly dis-empowered Afrikaner minority in a black majority nation, a nation headed, of course, by Mandela. Within the context of Ellis Park, then, Pienaar instantiated a cultural (and former political, insofar as this constituency had just yesterday dominated the nation) majority, a majority not exactly sympathetic to the (newly enfranchised) political majority whom Mandela represented. In addition, Mandela, more than any other figure in/ of/the black political, symbolized the black majority long opposed to white minority Afrikaner-dominated rule. Within the confines of Ellis Park, within the context of the euphoria of winning the World Cup, Mandela stood if not quite alone, then certainly as a figure made salient (disruptive, a symbol of Afrikaner defeat, if such a rendering might be permitted) by his difference, by his marked otherness: black, the very personalization of the transfer of political power (at the ballot box, if not in the larger economy of power—that is, as it relates to capital) from the white minority to the black majority in the new South African political dispensation.

The Stranger Is He Who Must Suffer

As such, we can say that Mandela was both made to "suffer" his difference and, importantly, that his presence on the podium at Ellis Park was entirely due to his being endured, tolerated out of political necessity—a rendering that I undo shortly; that is, Mandela's presence on the podium with Pienaar owed everything to Afrikaner "sufferance"—their willingness to put up with him in this cathedral of their "passion," willing to "suffer," in their turn, his presence, politically painful as it may have been for them. Politically painful as it was for them at that very historical juncture: World Cup winners with reduced political authority, an authority that until 1994 they had monopolized.

However, what such a figuring of the event does is assign Pienaar's negation, his willingness to betray the self on the very occasion of the fulfillment of the self's "passion," a scriptural significance. The burden of "passivity," the difficulty of "not-being-able," of being dependent on the non-self, is historically one that has been borne by the stranger.

It is a burden that must, per the force of history, be endured as a mode of sacrificial violence against the subjugated self; that is, the other endures, and must endure in the face of, its own propensity, or the political

necessity, for self-sacrificial violence. In this regard, Derrida's terms resonate: "Religion is responsibility or it is nothing at all"[25]—if, for an extended moment, we signal his "religion" clearly. In this instance (as in in
many others), when Derrida invokes "religion" he often means Judeo-
Christianity. One must be, as Mandela is understood to be here, "responsible" to Christianity's sacrificial history—a history that culminates, of
course, in the event of the Crucifixion, that radical act that makes possible
nothing less than universal salvation. The one, the One, who is sacrificed
so that all may be saved.

Nelson Mandela understood, then, as not only the Father of the (postapartheid) nation but also its "savior." Like Jesus-the-Christ, Mandela's
"sacrifice," his willingness to endure the violence (of the apartheid state,
twenty-seven years in prison), makes it possible for everyone else (the
postapartheid citizenry, now all rendered equal by his/"His" sacrifice) to
be "saved" from the prospect—and the threat—of such violence. This is
the force of "responsibility" at work, at work in its most extreme—and, as
such, life-demanding—articulation. "Responsibility," as such, demands
nothing less than the life of the other, the life of the other who is a stranger, who can be rendered a stranger, who can, as in the Crucifixion, have his
otherness revealed to him in order that he might be sacrificed. The figure
of sacrifice, as such, the stranger in our midst (as the New Testament
promises, or threatens, if you insist), must, for the sake of history, remain
estranged from the rest of the populace. The stranger must, per force,
stand alone, as Mandela does before the Ellis Park crowd—stand alone,
that is, until he is "welcomed," made at home, by Pienaar. The paradox, of
course, is that the stranger's estrangement is the way in which the self can
fulfill her or his (Christian) "responsibility." The stranger's "outsiderness"
is all that can secure salvation for the self.

As such, the stranger who is out of place, who is (very likely) without
a place familiar to her/him and denied the possibility of returning home,
is precisely the figure who must, following Matthew's Gospel, make the
Christian responsible. Christianity's injunction (one shared by not only
the monotheisms but other forms of faith as well—to do good, to do good
to the other, to tend to the other emerges out of the scriptural significance
of the stranger. As the Gospels remind us, in one form or another, the
stranger "incarnates" (to use the term loosely) nothing less than something epic. The stranger poses, again and again, that relentless question:
who knows whether (how can we be sure) the stranger is not Jesus-the-
Christ? It is the possibility of this not-knowing and therefore treating all
strangers as though they may be something other than other, as though
they may be Jesus-the-Christ himself, that is ominously—it is a warning,

a demand made by the Word of God—present in Matthew's writing: "For I was an hungered, and ye gave me meat: I was thirsty, and ye gave me drink: I was a stranger, and ye took me in."[26]

It is not so much that it falls to Pienaar to enact Matthew's word and to fulfill the political responsibilities as set out by the New Testament, as, paradoxically—entirely unexpectedly (which is why it belongs so emphatically to the logic of the event)—it is through his negation, through his pronounced "No," that he is true to the obligations of Matthew's Gospel. It is not, of course, that Pienaar provided Mandela with "meat" or "drink." It is, rather, that he, through his negation, takes Mandela "in": takes him to himself, eviscerates, if not for a moment, but, even so, what a moment, a moment that we now remember as the event, that which stands between self and other, and, in so doing, shows love to the other. Because of this, the other is welcomed, made safe, treated with the peculiar tenderness and love that only, on this occasion, the "No" can enable. Where just an instant before Mandela's presence was that of the stranger (Afrikanerdom's ugly history of racism—apartheid), Pienaar's negation transforms the stranger into, not to put too fine a point on it, the brother: two South African men sharing in a historic triumph, both wearing the number 6 Springbok rugby shirt. In the words of the Dire Straits lyricist and front man Mark Knopfler, they were in that historic moment "brothers in arms,"[27] standing together, facing the nation, drawn together, drawn into each other, by the sheer power of negation. ("In my fear and alarm / You did not desert me / My brothers in arms.") Or, in Marx's terms (which are captured by Knopfler), Mandela and Pienaar become, in that moment, "comrades in arms," linked together, bounded together by a political pursuit that is at once crystallized in them (and as them) and far exceeds them. Like the figural stranger of Christianity, together they bear the weight of historical expectation, of a nation's fate, a weight only they can bear. This is the Christian promise, fulfilled according to the Gospel of John: "For God so loved the world, that He gave His one and only son, that everyone who believes in Him shall not perish but have eternal life."[28] The reward, especially for those who are not worthy, is "eternal life," a promise guaranteed by the sacrifice of "His one and only son." Mandela and Pienaar do not rise to this level, but they are, together, in the moment of the event, because of the negation that makes the event, reduced to a political instantiation of John's promise. And here Pienaar's is, strangely, pointedly and ironically (history's workings, inscrutable as it sometimes is), the pivotal role. His negation enables him to "welcome" Mandela as the stranger so that, together, the iconic son of Afrikanerdom and the first black president can promise a politically new future for the nation that was, for decades, riven by racial strife and violence.

The Self Is Responsible before the Other

> You can't live on
> In that way
> In the past
> Them days
> Is gone
> Gone
>
> —JOHN LEE HOOKER, "Serves You Right to Suffer"

Self and other "belong," to render Derrida's critique of Jan Patočka's notion of "demonic" in the affirmative, to that "space in . . . which one hear[s] the call to explain oneself [*répondre de soi*], one's actions or one's thoughts, to respond to the other and to answer for oneself before the other" (*The Gift of Death*).[29] It is through his negation, "No," that Pienaar registers his determination to "answer," symptomatically (metonymically), for apartheid, for its disenfranchising violence. It is through the event that the white Afrikaner can be said to come to know what it means, what it entails, to undertake the very difficult task of "explain[ing] oneself before the other." More than anything, however, what matters is Pienaar's wherewithal, his ability to recognize that what is of consequence is the historical imperative to "respond" in, through and because of the event. The "space" of the event (the podium at Ellis Park), which also marks its time (the ceremonial that is transformed out of itself and into the event), is what makes it possible for Pienaar to "hear," to understand, what is necessary—that is, what the moment (the event) demands, a demand that is uncompromising in its call to "responsibility." As rendered by Derrida, we might suggest that the event, read in terms of Patočka (and his opposition to the Communist regime in Czechoslovakia), is the political encounter through which Pienaar must, like Mandela (but in a distinct political register), "suffer." That is, Pienaar must account for himself, he must speak, personally and metonymically, of the transgressions of his people. In the spirit of John Lee Hooker's lament for a lost love, it is Pienaar (rather than, in this moment, Mandela) who understands the utter finality of the event: "Them days / Is gone / Gone." It is Pienaar whose negation speaks the incontrovertible need for, as it were, a "new day."

Through the event, through explaining (an act that can never be distinguished from supplication, from a confession, forswearing the past—"Them days . . . [g]one") himself in the event, Pienaar pronounces himself, implicitly as responsible before(/for) the other. The event is, for Pienaar, something on the order of a "sacrifice." Pienaar's negation, in this way, belongs to the (religious) order of the event because, as Derrida argues, "society organizes sacrifices" (*Gift of Death*).[30] (And, following this logic, we might say that the blues is, certainly in U.S. culture, black and white, among the more important "organs" through which "society" arranges its sacrifices. This is a culture that runs from at least Robert Johnson through Muddy Waters, Billie Holiday, Sarah Vaughan, Ralph Ellison, Elvis Presley, Miles Davis, Bob Dylan, and Tom Waits, with many other, contemporary, iterations.)[31] That is, "sacrifices" proceed according to a structure, according to rituals, according to terms that have been set up—"organized"—in advance. The force of the event resides in its "ability"—to phrase the matter loosely—to insert itself into this preexisting "organization," to impose itself on this structure, and, importantly, to dominate the time and ritual of the "sacrifice" and, in so doing, to completely overwhelm the sacrificial order of things.

The event, understood in this way, as politically opportunistic, the event as innately capable of appropriating existing structures to itself, of turning the structure of the "sacrifice" to its own (impossible-to-know-in-advance) ends. The event as responsible to only itself—the event making of Pienaar his people's (Abrahamic/Jesus-the-Christ-like) "sacrificial lamb," that figure of the self utterly, if unknowingly, willing to lay down his (political) "life" not only for the other but also so that his people might be saved. (The self can "sacrifice" itself unknowingly only because there is no way to, in advance, grasp the scope, enormity, or even the immediate effects of the event.) The purpose of "sacrifice" is always salvation as such. Through his act of "self-sacrifice," Pienaar metonymized himself, accepting in the place of his fellow Afrikaners responsibility for the violent transgressions of their collective past. Standing in for them on the podium at Ellis Park, his negation—"No"—saved them from their anger at the new political dispensation that rendered them a minority. And, in so doing, we might proffer that Pienaar saved them from themselves, from their worst propensities: propensities such as bitterness at their displacement, militant recalcitrance in certain Afrikaner sectors, enduring racism, and so on that are well known to recent South African history. By force of history and his own intellectual disposition, Pienaar is made, the figure who, unknowingly, unknown to himself, takes it upon himself to save himself (metonymically conceived) from himself. Pienaar, then, as something of a latter-day Afrikaner Moses, come—without knowing it—to lead his people out of apartheid, their self-constructed captivity. (How they conducted themselves once he had led them through the miraculously opened Red Sea, well, for that they would have to bear, each in her or his own way, responsibility for themselves.) All this through the power of negation.

However, before the power of negation takes effect, the newly elected black president must, as it were, silently endure the negation of his "power" (a "power" that can be named putative only in that moment of negation?)

that is shown to be politically contingent in the moment of his reconciliatory gesture. The "nonpower" of Mandela's "Thank you" derives entirely from Pienaar's "power," his "powerful" "No." Not only can we then deduce that power is shifting, or that it depends on the dynamic at work between or among the various forces; we can also assert, in this instance, that what distinguishes "power" from "nonpower" can be liquidated (to use the harshest political language) or obfuscated, to phrase the matter more ambivalently, with a single word: "No." Paradoxically, however, what this liquidation or obfuscation produces is not the effacement of "power" or the sanctification of "nonpower" ("passivity," the capacity of the other to endure, no matter the difficulties arrayed before it), but how the event can render "power" utterly helpless, certainly rhetorically vulnerable, before itself. However, complicating this dynamic even further is the recognition that there is always a pacifist element at the core of "nonpower"—an element best apprehended as the burden of "passivity." That is, the decision to endure, the politics of suffering, as such, raises the difficulty of not so much "not-being-able" as the "act" of "not-doing"—"acting" through not-resisting, not standing against, the willingness to "absorb" rather than "inflict." Epigrammatically phrased, the "act" of "not-doing" functions as a metonym for the discourse of reconciliation—the decision by the ANC, Mandela in particular, not to exact retribution (revenge) from the apartheid regime and instead pursuing a politics of reconciliation, the artifice of working for a coming-together after centuries, in one form or another (colonialism, the qualified franchise, apartheid), of strife, violence, and a politics of recrimination. Here, if nowhere else, Hooker's anthem reverberates with a cutting edge, an edge possessed of an irrefutable cynicism: "Serves you right to suffer." (Or, as Jackie Robinson might have phrased it, in a similarly acerbic tone, a tone that is unmistakable in its political rancor, even without the expletive appended: "You had it coming." In this instance, however, there is a more favorable inevitability that awaits those who "suffered": postapartheid democracy, notwithstanding its severe limitations.)

More than anything, peaceful (insofar as it could be achieved) reconciliation is what Mandela worked for in post-1990 South African politics. It is precisely the politics that he advocated for that, we might say, "pacified" him so before the Ellis Park crowd. Ironically, then, it is only through Pienaar's negation that Mandela's political desire can be given voice, if not fulfilled exactly—before the Ellis Park faithful, at least.[32] Nonracial democracy, in the instance of this event if nowhere else, depends upon negation in order to come fully into itself. In order to achieve itself as a true democracy, democracy must first be capable of enduring the force of negation; negation is that political act that affirms democracy.

The event is, as such, what allows us to see how "nonpower" is at the very "heart of power," but it also enables us to understand there is no "power" that can immunize itself from the "nonpower" that makes up its very core. Power, then, in the event, is endemically, constitutively, autoimmune—possessed of, we might say, an autoimmune "heart." Power, then, is that which is inclined, both despite and because of itself, toward an inexorable capacity to sacrifice itself, to be sacrificed by itself. (Power always lives with the prospect of, just there, somewhere on its horizon, "nonpower" presenting itself.) The possibility of suffering, the right to suffer, the (political) decision to suffer, is a prospect (a choice) that cuts at least two ways, as Mandela and Pienaar demonstrate (albeit in distinctly different forms and historical moments, and, certainly, in very unequal modalities—twenty-seven years in an apartheid prison is entirely incommensurate with the Ellis Park podium negation), across the political landscape, with unequal force but always with political effect. In this way, although it must be said that this applies infinitely more to Pienaar than Mandela (Pienaar's power derives more directly, and consequentially, from the event), the event undertakes what Derrida names the "passage to accidental subjectivity" (*Gift of Death*).[33] The event is what facilitates Pienaar's access to a historic "subjectivity." Pienaar's subjectivity derives from his being one of the two principals of the event; Pienaar's historicity stems from his articulation of the negation.

It is out of this particular, peculiar, autoimmunity that, in the event of Ellis Park, Mandela's beatific countenance emerges. Mandela, his head pointed slightly downward, his face an admixture of a faint smile, and his eyes betraying a look that suggests that he is, ever so slightly, overwhelmed. Head inclined, Mandela, bears the burden of "passivity" with a saintly patience. He has, of course, no choice but to bear Pienaar's refusal, to accept the historicity of negation (in Žižek's terms we might say that the "long suffering" Mandela is "tarrying with the negative").[34] Furthermore, Mandela must understand—intuitively understands—that Pienaar's negation is also inscribed with the welcoming of the stranger who is not a stranger but who remains other to the predominantly white, Afrikaner crowd. In this regard, Mandela's strangeness is best grasped politically: in terms of his race (black in and against the body of the spectators, the large majority of whom are white) and, not to put too fine a point on it, culture (rugby is, in historical terms, *the* sport of white Afrikaners). Rugby is the Afrikaner's "passion" and, in invoking this term from Derrida we cannot but, in the event of Mandela's beatific look, acknowledge how it evokes Jesus-the-Christ's Passion so that it is entirely possible to figure Mandela, in a single gesture, because of a singular (white) refusal, as the political incarnation of the Christ. There is, in its specifically South

African articulation, a trinity of acts at work here: Mandela as the figure who was "crucified" (imprisoned for twenty-seven years), "buried" (left for dead, together with the dream of liberation of all the disenfranchised: equality and democracy in the land of their birth), and "resurrected" (not by the work, the divine intervention, of His Father but because of the political calculations of the apartheid state, specifically, the actions of President F. W. de Klerk). It is, finally, after centuries of European colonialism (Portuguese, Dutch, British), the violence of Afrikaner nationalism, and the politics of apartheid, Mandela and Mandela alone who can "save" not only his black compatriots but also, in fact, the entire nation, Afrikaners not least of all. To repeat, it is he alone who can, who did, give them back (access to) their "passion"—that deep yearning to participate as a "nation" (the racism that overdetermines the "passion" is not easily washed away; it cannot be dissolved by the waters of democracy) on the international rugby stage. It is not, then, only a matter of recognizing the stranger, as Levinas so rightly insists, but also, in this moment, for the metonymic white Afrikaner (for whom Pienaar at once stands in for and stands apart from), what the political, racialized stranger, and that stranger alone, makes possible.

All desire, as such, can be fulfilled only through the other, through the one (such is the paradox of history) who was previously most despised and vilified (named "Communist," "agitator," "revolutionary," "Marxist," and racist epithets of a worse order). It is the stranger, this particular iteration of the stranger, who makes the self's most deeply held desires and dreams possible. Without Nelson Mandela (sans his release from prison), there would have been no rugby World Cup hosted by South Africa; without Nelson Mandela, François Pienaar would never have been able to play in the rugby World Cup, never have been able to get his hands on the Webb Ellis trophy, let alone hoist it aloft before a throng of adoring (Afrikaner, in the main) fans. The self's dream come true, before the world. Without the other, there is nothing but the withering—through increasing sport's isolation—of the self's "passion," the constriction of the self's "passion" into an intense provinciality, a "passion" contained to the borders of the apartheid state. Through the other, the self (Afrikaner) gains entry to the world. Through the other, the (W)/world (Cup) becomes possible; the World (Cup) can be won through the other. To phrase the matter declaratively, the other *is* the world. The stranger alone can give the self access to the world (and the World Cup). Such is the perverse and historic promise of the stranger. It is almost not necessary, to ride roughshod over Matthew's Gospel for a second, to clothe and feed the stranger—though, of course, these acts are all constitutive of the hospitality that must be extended to the stranger[35]—but simply to take the stranger "in," and, in so doing, to shield the stranger from the vitriol (and worse) that is intended to drive the stranger out, to keep the stranger at a remove (in a historic moment, no less) from the "passionate" victory that the self is luxuriating in, lest the stranger be overwhelmed or "contaminated" by the self's passion.

The burden of "passivity," then, that Mandela must "suffer" is, to follow Derrida's thinking, not the act of laying down or submitting, but of patience. The other must know itself and understand the politics of the moment so that it can endure that moment; the other must endure so that it opens itself to the world, in a way that is at once utterly distinct from and reminiscent of the way it inadvertently opens the world for the self. The other endures in order that it remains open to the possibility of the event. The other neither abjures nor abjects itself. It merely remains faithful to its own capacity for endurance. No figure in South African history has, of course, ever demonstrated such a capacity for fortitude, endurance, and fidelity to the event (twenty-seven years in an apartheid prison testifies to that capacity, needless to say) as Nelson Mandela.

The burden of "passivity" is borne as an active faith in the event. In the face of such historic endurance, the moment between Mandela's "Thank you" and Pienaar's "No" is but a fleeting insignificance, and yet, it is all it takes, that single, simple, historic negation, to fully reveal the workings, the uncanny workings, of the burden of "passivity." To not refute the negation is to allow, knowingly or not, (for) the event. At the very least, to open up (to) the event as a possibility. To keep that possibility always, "passively," open. Such openness testifies to the "power of the nonpower," to the power of endurance, to the possibilities, as Derrida phrases it, of "radical finitude," a possibility that cannot, as we well know, be thought without raising the specter of Heidegger's "being-toward-death," a political outcome that Mandela, more than most, must surely have considered. (In the terms of John Lee Hooker's blues, the reward for "suffering" is the event— the reward that is as integral to the event as the rebuke and mockery that he offers in his title.) The prospect of death that Mandela must, surely, have endured, that he must have "suffered," must have "suffered" because of, a prospect that he must have faced, have faced as intimately as the gentle harshness that constitutes the core of Pienaar's "No."

Already/Not Yet

The event of the "Thank you" makes clear that the desire for democracy is both "already," by virtue of the black president handing over the trophy to the white rugby captain, and "not yet"—leaving aside that which must never be ignored or foreclosed, the ongoing material inequity that marks the disparity between the lives of the historically enfranchised and the disenfranchised. (But, suffice it to say that, according to the ANC's core principles, inscribed in the "Freedom Charter," the basic terms for a political democracy—such as "The land shall be shared among those who work it" and "There shall be houses, security and comfort"—have not been obtained. They have, almost three decades into the postapartheid era, still not been secured. Nor does such an achievement seem possible anytime in the near or, for that matter, even in the long-term future.) The black president is, then, not "yet" in possession of a "language" (or in command of a democracy, for that matter) that can address—for "that which is about to" and, indeed, "should" "happen"—the realization of a democratic and just society; that is, Mandela shows himself subject to "articulation," to saying what is expected rather than committing to a "language" determined to account for the divisions and the reversals at the core of the event. Because the event is "both at once," past and future, neither fully active nor moribundly passive, but subject to the logic of "infinite division" (both and neither at the same time), what emerges most vividly from the "Thank you" and its negation is nothing so much as the violence—"to cut, to be cut"— that is present in every event.

The event, more than anything, demands that we think conciliation, because the very first commitment of conciliation is the rejection of reconciliation. It is impossible, in the stringent terms of conciliation, to conceive of reconciliation as anything other than a politics sans politics because it risks nothing, so steeped is it in the extant postapartheid discourse of achieving national "unity" against the history of racial difference, subjugation, and violence. We have already heard this as the "Rainbow Nation of God" and "Ubuntu" (we are human only insofar as our humanity is affirmed by others, through others acknowledging our humanity—shared humanity), so that we know its intention is to suppress the possibility of "infinite division." That is, the violence of *Denken* that makes possible a political future that is entirely imbricated in the violence of the past but yet does not succumb to that violence on its own terms, insisting instead of "proceeding" from the event to a "language" of the past and the future that is "without articulation." That is, a "language" fully committed to thinking for the reversal as a historic responsibility that is simultaneously anticipatory and reflective. The "language" of conciliation recognizes the past as inherently politically instructive and immanently and imminently "recuperable" but will not submit, out of responsibility to the future and out of fidelity to the event, to replicating those patterns of violence. The past is, before all else, subject to *Denken*, which is also, of course, a form of *Danken* to the past and a mode of thinking what it means to give thanks to what was and to offer *Danken l'avenir.* The "language" of conciliation crafts out of the event a political imaginary that can sustain the future, again, an act of fidelity to the event, while locating itself in an interminable past/future but never limiting relation to the logic of reversal. The future is free to make, as Jean-Luc Nancy phrases it, "sense of the world." It is the responsibility of the future, subject as it is to the logic of reversal, to make "sense of the world" in such a way that is entirely untainted by the "halo of sentimental generosity" (Nancy).[36] Figured as such, there is nothing for Pienaar to do but to refuse Mandela's offer of thanks. Pienaar must refuse because his negation is "tightly woven and narrowly articulated" and it "constitutes the structure of sense qua sense of the world" (Nancy).[37] Through his negation, Pienaar offers the possibility of instilling "sense" into the postapartheid world. The postapartheid world can be comprehended, made "sense of," only through the negation. The other comes to it-self through the negation of the self; an intensely racial dynamic requires the "sense" that only negation can impart.

The Event Is Not Knowing Your Place

> There is no law without a mirror. And in this properly reversible structure, we shall never avoid the moment of admiration.
> —JACQUES DERRIDA, "The Laws of Reflection: Nelson Mandela, in Admiration"

> It fails to observe its place.
> —JACQUES LACAN, "Seminar on The Purloined Letter"

> Split apart, incomplete by nature or in relation to itself. Its excess always refers to its own lack, and conversely, its lack always refers to its excess.
> —GILLES DELEUZE, The Logic of Sense

The "genesis" of conciliation resides in the exchange that is the event of the "Thank you/No, thank you." This "exchange" is marked by the interplay (which always invites the possibility of "reversal") between the sincere (Mandela, who comes, of course, overdetermined by a political "halo" whose only name is "reconciliation"), so to speak, and the disruption (into conciliation, Pienaar) that inheres in the asymmetrical "No, thank *you*." The exchange amounts to, in and because of the inaugural sincerity, a "moment of admiration" that is constitutively inadequate to the politics of conciliation. The president expressing "admiration" seeks to forge an iterable moment— "Thank you, François"—in the incipient (intending to achieve hegemony) history of reconciliation. For his part, we may say that if Pienaar, a lawyer by training (like Mandela), understands the law as Derrida proposes, then his is the response of nonconsummation. Pienaar is the recipient who does

not so much "reverse" the "structure of the law" as invert it by subverting—
publicly sabotaging—the discourse of reconciliation.

Pienaar's is the enactment of conciliation through violence. He does not
"reverse" things. He turns them upside down and inside out; he smashes
them. What Pienaar reveals in his refusal is the philosophical "triumph" of
negation (*Denken*) over sincerity, over sincere affirmation, which is a refusal that is also an inversion that is also a disruption, a "splitting apart"
that enables the negation to come fully into its own as the cornerstone of
the event, as that "language" of the event that is bound both by its "excess"
(the "simple" negative, "No") and its "lack." Simply put, Pienaar's "language"
"fails" to meet expectations. Pienaar's "language" "lacks" what, the element
of acquiescence (quiescence, dutifulness, replying to Mandela's "Thank you"
with an innocuous "Thank you" of his own), is apposite (appropriate) to the
exchange—what is apposite in the terms of reconciliation, that is. And this
"lack," as much as the "excess" inaugurated by the "No," is what makes the
event. This "lack," Pienaar's "No," opens the possibility of something other
than a rote exchange of pleasantries. True to the inimitable logic of the
event, Pienaar's "No" is what is least expected. And, because of the hegemony of reconciliation, it is what has been overlooked, neglected, ignored.
Reconciliation constitutes, in Nancy's terms, nothing other than—through
its neglect—the "singular logic of a reply that does not answer" (*Speculative
Remark*).[38] There is no room for thinking Pienaar's negation in the "singular
logic" that is reconciliation. Pienaar's "No" must be, in its being ignored or
glossed over, at once reduced and elevated to the status of a Hegelian *Aufhebung*—a concept at the core of Hegel's notion of thesis and antithesis
being contained in the same object, means simultaneously "lift" something
"up" to a higher level and to "lower" it by preserving it, so that "sublation,"
as the term is generally translated, makes it possible for something to be at
once "suspended" and made transcendent, "elevated" (as in, say, the difference between physics and Newtonian physics) and preserved, out of sight,
maybe. In this way, the most enduring specter of reconciliation is conciliation (thesis-antithesis, both eminently visible in the same political moment
that is the Mandela-Pienaar event), because it demands a reply when none
is forthcoming from the prevailing "singular logic." Conciliation is never
satisfied until an "answer" is proffered, until, at the very least, the political
work of "answering" is undertaken.

The "Failure" of the Ceremonial

The exchange between Mandela and Pienaar begins as an overdetermined
routine. It begins with the "mirroring" of images that is an optical replica-
tion (the desire to mimic an "object") that is also a duplication (to make

two where there was, previously, only one), a mirroring that is character-istic of the performances that constitute victory celebrations. And so it began as an eminently recognizable exchange.

Nelson Mandela was smiling. He was clad in a replica Springbok num-ber 6 jersey, "Pienaar" emblazoned on the back, as if he were reflecting the blond Pienaar back to himself in an elderly, black form. Atop Mandela's head was a baseball hat in the traditional Springbok colors, green and gold, emblazoned, of course, with a springbok. Smiling, Mandela present-ed the Webb-Ellis trophy to the victorious captain with a rote, almost formulaic, but nonetheless joyful "Thank you."[39] Notwithstanding, of course, that no one aspect of this exchange could be pro forma, so envel-oped was this moment by the historicity of the black, democratically elected president, just more than a year after South Africa's first demo-cratic elections, offering thanks to the white Afrikaner rugby player. What was expected, of course, was reciprocation. And, why ever not, so legiti-mized by history was that expectation? After all, it was not a great deal to ask of the white captain, was it? And, could there have been more power-ful a political gesture of reconciliation than for white South Africa, in the person of Pienaar, to thank the Nobel Laureate black president?

Is that not what the "law of the mirror," to say nothing of the laws of decorum and political sensitivity, dictated? And yet, we must ask, what is the role of thanks, a question as much for this event as for any other. Is it ever possible for the "Thank you" to stand as an adequate response to the generous or magnanimous act of the other, to the love of the other? How should the "Thank you" be spoken? What is its proper language? And, if we thank the other, from the heart, as we like to say, is that not already an iteration full of judgment about the sincerity of the thanks? (As if we suspect the other of insincerity, a priori?) Does, or can, the "Thank you" (ever) mark the end of the exchange? Or is the "Thank you," by nature of the "debt" it creates, inherently infinite, so that any suspension of thanks is always provisional and temporary? All of which makes it imperative to address the difficulty of how we think thanks? *Wie Danken denken?*

Mandela's "Thank you" is, because of the subsequent political possibil-ity it opens up (later, that is, immediately after its speaking, because it has been spoken), the "genesis" of the event made in "thanks." It is his "Thank you," offered in the spirit of reconciliation, that sets in motion the discur-sive exchange that leads to the politics of conciliation. Mandela's histori-cally overdetermined but still ceremonial "Thank you" invites, expects (such is the conventional script on occasions such as these), in return, an equally ceremonial "Thank you" from Pienaar. Instead, the ceremonial is entirely disarticulated, undone by the force of negation, all because Pienaar, as Lacan puts it, "fails to observe his place." Pienaar, of course, is at once *in* place (in his own place), on the podium as the World Cup–winning captain accepting the trophy (it is the only place he can be, is logically/ logistically supposed to be), and without regard or deference *for* place. He speaks, as it were, in the terms of conciliation, which are decidedly *out* of place, not in concurrence with the demands of *this* place, in this moment. Pienaar's *Denken* will not allow him to observe the rules, the norms, the protocols, the decorum of this place (podium). Pienaar's place, whether or not he grasps it (and his negation suggests that he is, at the very least, in some measure aware of his "transgression"),[40] in the terms of conciliation, within the structure of the event, is to be out of place in order that the politics of conciliation can take its place as that act—that intervention, in the form of the event—that history demands. It is Pienaar's refusal to, as it were, know his place that makes of the ceremonial podium the space of and for the event.

Conceived as such, it becomes possible to understand Pienaar's act on the order of a Deleuzian "schizophrenic." "For the schizophrenic," Deleuze argues, "it is less a question of recovering meaning than of destroying the word, of conjuring up affect, and of transforming the painful passion of the body into a triumphant action, obedience into command, always in the depth below the fissured surface" (*The Logic of Sense*).[41] Deleuze's presentation of the schizophrenic makes it possible to understand Pienaar's negation as deriving from its refusal to "recover" or uncover new or lost meanings in the "word(s)" "Thank you" because he is, in essence, intent on "destroying the word" as such. Moreover, he is able to "conjure up affect," a series that proceeds along the lines, each constituting its own particular point, each interchangeable with the other, no one point absolutely set in its place, through *Denken,* conciliation, violence, the reversibility of past and present, all of which, together, give us the event. Most significantly, however, we can say that Pienaar "transforms the painful passion of his body"—the "passion" of the Afrikaner rugby player who has led his nation to victory, the "passion" of the Afrikaner made to confront the effects that inhere in his body because of its violent past and, potentially, the violence that it might enact in the future—"into a triumphant action." Pienaar's triumph must be understood as the force that made the event so that his "victory" is not merely that of beating the favored All Blacks, but it marks the incipient—politically desired—"triumph" of conciliation (the exceptional Afrikaner) over its favored political foe, reconciliation (incarnated in the black president, whose exceptionality is transcendent). In this way, Pienaar's dis-"obedience" (his nonquiescence) is the ultimate "triumph" because it enables him to "command" the podium, to "command" (by usurping it) "language" and to proffer, through the event, conciliation as the first "commandment" of (postapartheid South African) politics.[42]

All this because the reciprocal "Thank you" does not follow. Or it follows only after an immediate negation, "No, thank you," that has violently "split" the inaugural "Thank you" "apart." However, the negation derives from that order of *Denken* that belongs to the Hegelian *Aufhebung*. The negation is in itself impossible without the first "Thank you." But Pienaar's "language" is, first, and above all, a negation ("No") historic in its political effect that makes, in its turn, Mandela's "Thank you" historic and, also, excessive (it is too much) and a lack (it is devoid of the politics of conciliation). Most importantly, however, the negation lends the "Thank you" an entirely new and unforeseen political and philosophical aspect.

The negation makes the "Thank you" because without the negation the "Thank you" has no philosophical value. It would have only ceremonial standing, and, as such, it would be lost to that ceremonial present, entirely without the logic of the reversal, entirely without philosophical prospect. At best, Mandela's "Thank you" bears within it the transmission of sincerity from one subject to another, from other to self, from black to white. Not insignificant, but by no means worthy of the name "event." Without the negation, Mandela's "Thank you" would have been lost to history, lost in the history of the moment, relegated to the status of a Nancian question without an answer. The negation is what not only makes the "Thank you" singular, which instills an entirely unexpected Hegelian "logic" in it, but also brings the "Thank you" to our attention—makes it relevant; here *Aufhebung* highlights elevation. Singularities, we can affirm, are nothing less than significant philosophical "turning points," inflected with the structure of the event, critical to the *Denken* of the event. But Deleuzian singularities, as we know, belong to a "series," and the "moment that two series resonate and communicate," as is happening in the event of the "Thank you," "we pass from one distribution to another. The moment that the series are traversed by the paradoxical agent, singularities are displaced, redistributed, transformed into one another, and change sets. If the singularities are veritable events, they communicate in and the same Event which endlessly redistributes them, while their transformations form a *history*" (*The Logic of Sense*).[43] In these terms it is possible to figure Pienaar as a Deleuzian "revolutionary" of a sort, given that it is he, rather than Mandela, we can say, who sees the need to not so much create "sets" (or "teams," to suggest a metaphor more appropriate for our discussion) but to "redistribute" his "singularity."

It is Pienaar, then, and not Mandela (who may be too constricted by the "history" of reconciliation, that is, by the repressive aspects of *Aufhe-*

bung) who is free/freed up to fulfill the role of "paradoxical agent." Pienaar appropriates this role because he opens himself up to the future and the past in that he "willingly" passes, we can say, "from one distribution" (the logic of apartheid, which would have inscribed him as "in excess" of Mandela) to "another" (the logic of conciliation, which demands that he "communicate" an event that can transform into a history that can truly undo apartheid and its residual effects, many of them debilitating, at least some of them still operating to confine Mandela to the ceremonial when "redistribution," the "transformation of history," and, yes, deliberately, consciously, changing "teams" is what is demanded by both the past and the future; *Aufhebung* come fully to life). The violent "cut" that is the present offers this opportunity to both Mandela and Pienaar, and it is the Afrikaner who acts—carpe diem—by "redistributing" his "singularity" with a memorable flash of historical violence. Through his "redistribution," through his openness to the series that is not his, Pienaar shows how the paradox establishes what Deleuze names the "*other* term" (*The Logic of Sense*).[44] And that "other term" is, of course, conciliation.

Negation

The force of conciliation resides, in the event of the "Thank you," in the negation. Because of the historic stage on which the "Thank you" and its negation are exchanged, the negation has achieved its own historicity. As a historic language (and not as an "articulation"), *Danken* has the political force to impose itself as the law of the "Thank you." Mandela's "Thank you" sets the stage for an inclusive (such is the desire for the triumph of a politics of reconciliation that animates his giving thanks), national (nation-making), tailor-made-for-history "Thank you" exchange. Nelson Mandela, like everyone else present at the event, anticipates (how could he not?) the fulfillment of the script. Like everyone else, Mandela adheres to a technocratic view of discursive exchange. Technocracy is rooted in the predictable, which is to say it is everything that the event is not, in that the event is marked by the predictability of the unexpected; we watch sport in no small measure in expectation of the unexpected. In technocratic terms, every "Thank you" is, must be, met with its reciprocal ("mirroring") equivalent. The only proper response—this is the law—to a "Thank you" is an equivalent (à la Newton's law of "reactions" functioning in accordance with the "equal and opposite" principle) "Thank you." In this instance, an equally sincere and heartfelt "Thank you." For his part, Deleuze (and Pienaar, through the extension of this argument) is totally opposed to the "technocrat" (whom he proclaims the "natural friend of the dictator") and advocates for the "revolutionary" who "lives in the gap which separates technical progress from social totality, and inscribes here his dream of permanent revolution" (*The Logic of Sense*).[45] Here, again, we see how it is possible to parse Pienaar as a Deleuzian "revolutionary of the gap" (that is, of the present, of the event).

However, the intention here is not to linger (not too long, anyway) on Pienaar as a Deleuzian "revolutionary." It is, rather, to understand conciliation as the politics that stands against what is on both sides—that is, to locate Pienaar as opposed to both the empty promise of technocracy (as embodied in the presidency of Mandela's successor, Thabo Mbeki) and the perfunctory techniques, the niceties of polite political society, of the "Thank you." Instead, what is proposed here is to understand Pienaar as rupturing the precious, and precocious, optimism of the "social reality" that was the "new South Africa," the "new South Africa" that pivoted on nothing so much as the nation and the world's "admiration" for Nelson Mandela.

At the risk of being reductive, but in order to appreciate the full drama, gravity, and impactfulness of these expressions of (mutual, but, massively unequal) gratitude, we must, per force, read the first "Thank you," heartfelt as it might have been, as peremptory. It was, in dramaturgical terms, mere fodder for what followed. The negation of the "Thank you" was not, as we see in the following section, a negation at all but the act of the self's responsibility toward the other.

Pienaar's negation reveals the "solution" ("Thank you") as insufficient to the "problematic" so that the "problematic" persists in the "solution" that masquerades as an answer. (Or, in Nancy's terms, the "logic of the reply that does not answer.") Pienaar's "No" not only disrupts the ritual exchange of thanks, de rigueur in such a sports ceremony, but also transforms the interplay of "Thank you" and "No, thank *you*"—the rugby captain's emphasis is unmistakable—into conciliation. That is, conciliation as the politics of first encounter, that first encounter in which politics as the necessary (rude, if you will, in the same way that Shakespeare's Moor is "rude") disruption of "social reality" takes place. Moreover, conciliation as the refusal—the outright rejection—of its counter, reconciliation: the discourse addressing the nation's history of racial animus, antagonism, and violence, and restructuring postapartheid South Africa as either a biblical promise (as the Joshua-ite "Rainbow Nation of God," as the deeply ethical Archbishop Desmond Tutu conceived it) or a new, African, humanist philosophy by the name of "Ubuntu" (as previously noted, that political condition under which the humanity of every being is dependent on and imbricated in the humanity of every other being). In the moment that was postapartheid South Africa's infancy, it is—and here the paradox must be noted—the white Afrikaner who inserts conciliation, politics for the sake of the past and the future, politics that turns in two directions at once, politics that keeps Deleuze's two temporalities alive, simultaneously, into the national discourse. "Past and future" located in an "always reversible continuity," making the present at once the time that is "eluded" and the time necessary yet "superfluous" to thinking the event (*The Logic of Sense*).[46]

The event, moreover, that is not recognizable (at first) as the event, the event that Pienaar enacts before the nation. He does so (by) facing it, (by) facing the newly democratized nation's supreme face, its most admired representation and instantiation, Nelson Mandela. As such, Pienaar creates a critical possibility for being and becoming. "The event is coextensive with becoming," writes Deleuze, "and becoming is coextensive with language; the paradox is a series of 'sorites,' that is a series of interrogative propositions which, following becoming, proceed through successive additions and retrenchments. Everything happens at the boundary between things and propositions" (*The Logic of Sense*).[47] The logic of "sorites" (so the logic) resonates in this instance because it provides a modality for thinking Pienaar and Mandela as figures who can "cross," contradict, trouble, and interchange with each other, toward an end that, while expected to be predictable, raises itself to the level of event. The logic of "sorites" proceeds as a line of argument that derives from a major and a minor premise and concludes in a generative way (except in its final conclusion) in that the last premise of the "minor" thread marks the first iteration of the (next) major thread, and vice versa. Thinking in terms of the "sorites," it becomes possible to understand how Mandela's "major" articulation provides the premise—the starting point—for Pienaar's (ostensibly) "minor" language.[48] Mandela's "Thank you" is the condition of thought on which Pienaar's negation is premised. As such, because the logic of "sorites" tends toward a (final) conclusion, we can say that the conclusion can be found in conciliation, in which the "minor" premise comes fully into its own as a politics. Or the logic of "sorites" becomes a singular premise for thinking the event and a critical premise that enables us to understand "becoming" within the "infinite reversal" that is postapartheid/apartheid.

If "becoming" can be thought for a moment as the logic of "sorites," it is possible to argue that "becoming" is conceivable only through conciliation because "sorites" follows, as Deleuze explicates, the difficult trajectory of "interrogative propositions." "Becoming," so configured, submits—which is to say it initiates, makes necessary, wills itself to do the work of politics—to thinking what is at stake in every "successive addition and retrenchment." It thinks every major and minor premise; it makes their "substitution" mutual so that major and minor exchange places, facilitating their transmission from one figure to the other. As such, the "sorite" logic of conciliation fixes itself at the boundary between "things" (the triumph of the World Cup, the—most—admired personage, the institution of the democratic state) and the "propositions" that found these "things" (the discourses of "newness," "democracy," and "reconciliation" not least among them). Through negation, a specific and rigorous kind of opening, as defined by Nancy, is made available: "the 'open' is neither the vague quality of an indeterminate yawning nor that of a halo of sentimental generosity. Tightly woven and narrowly articulated, it constitutes the structure of sense qua sense of the world."[49] The political stakes of the "open" are high because of the political work the "open" performs.

In Derrida's (Heideggerian) terms, the "open" undertakes its task with the "imperative urgency of an 'it is necessary.' . . . It must necessarily proceed from some alterity exceeding the circle of the same or the self, the sovereignty of *autonomy,* but without, all the same, taking the form of a duty or a debt that would have to be discharged so as to reclose the economic circle of exchange. This then is what, remaining to be thought, would still resist what is called 'thinking'" (*Without Alibi,*).[50] "It is necessary" that the mode of politics that must "break open" the way things are and the ways in which they operate must do so in an "excessive" form. "It is necessary," as it were, to access an "alterity" that lies beyond the "circle of the same or the self," all the while demonstrating a break that can be pronounced "autonomous" only because it does not adhere to the terms of extant discourse. However, what "is necessary" must also break with an "economy of exchange" so that, in taking this "necessary" action, nothing on the order of a "debt" is incurred. That is, nothing is expected in return because, we might say, of the "autonomy"—the absolute singularity and unimpeachable "sovereignty"—of the act. The act is true to itself, to the particularity and peculiarity of its own terms, and its own terms only. Furthermore, the act must "exceed" that which can bind the subject through what we might name a "call to duty"—there is no obligation to undertake this act except what we understand, following Derrida, as "responsibility." The act is, as such, "responsible or it is nothing at all."

And so it is with Pienaar's negation. "It is necessary," absolutely "necessary," for Pienaar to say "No" to Mandela. In saying "No" to Mandela, Pienaar is, of course, also saying "No" to the discourse—to the history—of Afrikaner nationalism (apartheid), so that his "autonomy" is complete, so that it lies beyond (even as it operates in the space between) South Africa's two predominant nationalisms: an apartheid whose effects remain palpable and a black political majority coming, however problematically, into its own. Pienaar's negation speaks of a "No" that seeks to "exceed" the dialectic as much as it is bounded on every side by its effects—apartheid/postapartheid, black/white, minority/majority, and so on. It is only the commitment to "alterity" as such that can secure the "sovereignty of autonomy," even as the precise "delimitations" of what this "alterity" entails remain, as they properly must, unclear. The "sovereignty of autonomy" remains always to be worked out, to be determined. It never knows itself in advance; it is always in search of itself, always reaching for an effect that maximizes the possibilities of "alterity."

In short, this is what Derrida intends when he speaks, in the title of his work *"Without Alibi."*[51] In Pienaar's negation there are clear echoes of the determination to address himself to the world "without alibi." In refusing Mandela's "Thank you," Pienaar decides to stand before the world, white and black, before an audience at once "passionately" local and internationally wary (after all, the 1995 rugby World Cup signaled South Africa's return to the international sports community on its own soil, a historic first; the world, literally, was watching, at least the rugby-playing world), and to take the risk of incriminating himself and all of white South Africa for its past, apartheid being only the most immediate of enfranchised South Africa's transgressions. *Je suis accusé.* Through his negation Pienaar implicitly indicts himself: "I stand accused." Pienaar's *Je suis accusé* for this reason verges, with a deliberateness, on *Je suis coupable,* "I am guilty." It is because Pienaar presents himself as "culpable" that he must refuse propriety, that he must refuse Mandela's thanks. In this moment, wittingly or not, Pienaar shows himself to understand—more fully than might at first blush seem possible—the burden of history.

Through his negation Pienaar opens himself (and, in doing so, he stands metonymically for all other Afrikaners/all white South Africans) to the harshest possible political and ethical judgment. Through his negation Pienaar stands before history, rendering himself as the "culpability" (the beneficiary of a racist, unjust political regime—what Derrida names "'culpa-responsibility . . . juridical, ethical, political'") that is the history of apartheid (*Without Alibi*).[52] The Afrikaner Pienaar, who traces his roots to the French Huguenots, is, then, perhaps best made to stand accused in Derrida's French *Je suis coupable* as the opening into the linguistic fullness of the event of negation. Pienaar's negation achieves the dual end of self-indictment (metonymically understood) and historic "sovereignty" over/of the moment. Through his negation Pienaar is, simultaneously, declaring himself "culpable," mea culpa, and determined to address himself to the significance of the moment, carpe diem. However, in his seizing of the moment, Pienaar at once makes the moment declaratively his and, paradoxically, draws Mandela (and black South Africa, again, through the force of metonymy) inexorably into his self-indictment. "I stand accused before you" is how Pienaar declares himself. Rendered in a 1990s popular, we might say that Pienaar, in the terms of *Wayne's World,* both pronounces himself "culpable" and, as Wayne might have it, says (sans the self-mocking jocularity), "I am not worthy, I am not worthy."[53]

And yet, of course, it is Pienaar's historical acuity, his recognition of the "necessity" of self-indictment, that casts him as "worthy" precisely because, in Derrida's Heideggerian terms, Pienaar grasps what the moment demands. That is, he must have been "thinking" (*Denken*) about something along the lines of a "proper"—or, rather, an "im-proper"—response to exactly the moment when Mandela would "thank" (*Danken*) him. (Here we recall Derrida's famous lament from *Le Monolinguisme* about Vichy France's long-suppressed desire to repeal the Decree of Crémieux of 1870: "They must have had it in their heads all along.")[54] When thanks are offered, thinking must ensue. (Or, when thanks are refused, *Nein, danke,* the effect might be to make thinking even more "necessary." The main effect of the event is *Denken*.) It is, then (only, but it is never "only," as we well know), because Pienaar refuses Mandela, because Pienaar flies in the face of propriety and decorum,[55] that he makes a thinking of his ("No") thanks imperative. There can be no *Danken/Nein, danke* without *Denken*. The burden of over-representation is/as the responsibility to think responsibility; the responsibility, if you will, to seize the moment—carpe diem—in its singularity; the responsibility to be, above all, felicitous and responsible to the singularity of the event.

The Birth of Responsibility

> On what condition is responsibility possible?
> —Jacques Derrida, *The Gift of Death*

Through his negation, in accepting negation as his responsibility, the white Afrikaner rugby captain turns the tables on the black president. In negating Mandela's "Thank you" with his "No, thank *you*" (here the italicized "you" marks rhetorical emphasis), Pienaar puts Mandela's "Thank you" in its historic place. Through his negation Pienaar is recognizing that he must, out of sheer regard for history (for Mandela's history of resistance, imprisonment, release, the foreswearing of revenge—a kind of lifelong fealty to justice, in short), deny the president's thanks. Mandela's thanks must, in order to gain their proper historical place, be made improper, if not feeble (although the "Thank you" is weakened considerably by the negation it elicits), in the face of Pienaar's negation.

To hear, in a highly ceremonial setting, "Thank you" (*Danken ohne Denken*), which is then followed so spectacularly by "No, thank *you*," is to recognize the rhetorical power of negation. What negation can do is make politics possible in a way that affirmation, of the (empty) echoing (or mirroring) of one "Thank you" in another, cannot. The power of the second "(No), Thank *you*" resides in its ability to reveal not so much what is politically at stake but in its understanding of what kind of political work negation imposes on the self. The task of the "No, thank *you*" is to break down—destroy—the "Thank you" in order for any concept of the "Thank you" not only to be audible but also to amplify and as such elevate the negating "Thank *you*" to its proper political place.

In so doing, the second "Thank you" (*ein Danken, das Denken ist*) is not so much returned to itself as "white" speech, the word of apartheid history, as it constitutes the act of turning *Danken ohne Denken* into the "language" of conciliation that marks the event of self-overcoming. *Ein Denken, das Danken verweigert Denken* as such marks that act of "*Danken*" as belonging to the logic of conciliation because it is a moment in which self overcomes its own self; it is that moment in which the self "negates" its own history, speaking, as it were, a "language" that is turned, deliberately, against it-self, as well as against the discourse of reconciliation.

When Pienaar utters that "No," his *ein Denken, das Danken verweigert* is transformed into a cacophonous negation. His "No" resonates loudly in the stadium, and far beyond. In this way, *ein Denken, das Danken verweigert* absorbs, adumbrates, makes it-self one with the first "Thank you," rendering Mandela's *Danken ohne Denken* into a "sorite" premise: the major articulation has been usurped, in full view of the world, by a minor "language," to formulate a phrase out of two different but not disconnected strands of Deleuzian critique. Paradoxically (although we could easily say appropriately, given how our argument is unfolding), it is not in *Danken ohne Denken* but only in *ein Denken, das Danken verweigert* that any proper understanding of gratitude, appreciation, and pure thanks—if we can conceive of such a thing—can reside. In this way, to render the matter hyperbolically, not only does Mandela's *Danken ohne Denken* not matter, as it were; it also stands historically as nothing but the invitation to proper thanks. Its "major" role, we might say, is to open up the possibility of *ein Denken, das Danken verweigert*.

Mandela's "Thank you" stands then as the "invitation" to which Pienaar is responding, which is itself a form of responsibility. It is only through Pienaar's negation, "No, Mr. President, thank *you*," that Mandela's invitation can be taken up. Pienaar's response is grammatically precise in that it puts the (political) emphasis where it belongs: on the second-person pronoun. It is on the "*you*," and there alone, that the emphasis must fall. It is on that pronoun (Pienaar's direct address to Mandela) that the emphasis must fall—that is what our ears must catch; it must find resonance in the "ear of the other"—so that the politics of conciliation can be heard, be understood, and, for the purposes of historical drama, remain.

Mandela must know, as Lacan would insist, his place, and from his place (in his ceremonial and political place) Mandela is, in the logic of "sorites," disenfranchised. From that place, he cannot thank. Instead, in his place the role falls to him of historic recipient. Mandela must only be thanked: the president must receive. He must accept the gratitude that constitutes the core of the "sorite" logic in which Pienaar's negation is formed, has been nurtured, historically. In Pienaar's negation, we might say, out of his negation emerges (we can detect the resounding timbres of) historic white apology. Pienaar's negation emerges from the historical roiling that is (metonymically) within him, evoking in this way the "war" that Paul de Man "must have lived and endured *in himself*" for "almost half a century," rendering de Man a man "torn apart by the tragedies, ruptures, dissociations, 'disjunctions.'"[56] Derrida is writing, as a friend, as a scholar championed by de Man in the U.S. academy, about de Man in the wake of the scandal that revealed de Man to have written for Nazi publications in his native Belgium during World War II. Writing as a friend, as an intellectual collaborator (the word seems impossible to avoid), Derrida brings the full range of his critical acumen and the depth of his affection for de Man to bear in this essay. In so doing, Derrida's essay achieves a keen and complicated insight into the psychological burden—a man "torn apart" by all sorts of specters and demons, of his own making—that de Man bore for the remainder of his life, for "almost half a century," almost exactly the duration of apartheid (1948 to 1994). As such, Pienaar's negation achieves a new resonance, a resonance that is as old as political conflict, political complicity, and ethical compromise itself, when considered in light of Derrida's rendering of de Man. What inner turmoil the Afrikaner soul must have subjected itself to, what historical atrocities it bears responsibility for, what "tragedies" it visited upon the other. All of this, all these ethical and political difficulties ("ruptures, dissociations, 'disjunctions'"), finds a different historical echo in the philosophical declarative that is Pienaar's "No, thank you." How far beyond Pienaar it is distributed, how it intersects with other historical "tragedies," how such historical "affinities" shed new light on the event of Ellis Park.[57]

No wonder then that so much is audible in the negation, in that single "No." In Pienaar's negation we can hear the Afrikaner's mea culpa (and, by extension, that of the entire history of white colonization, the qualified franchise, apartheid), apologizing and accepting responsibility for the atrocities and transgressions of apartheid, for the violence done to black South Africa in the name of apartheid, for the entire history of apartheid and the role of the Afrikaners (from 1948 and long before, the nineteenth-century Great Trek, the appropriation of land and natural resources, and much else besides), and, for a moment, the specific part that rugby played in that system of oppression.

Is Negation Enough?

> The conjuncture of the same and the other, in which even their
> verbal proximity is maintained, is the *direct* and *full face* welcome
> of the other by me.
>
> —**EMMANUEL LEVINAS**, *Totality and Infinity* (original emphasis)

However, what remains critical here is the question of whether Pienaar's "No, thank *you*," for all its salience and resilience as the "language" of conciliation, is sufficient to the terms of the event. Is it absolutely necessary and, as such, non-negotiable that the white self's thanks be preceded, or prefaced, by a mea culpa? In any case, how does the white self say "Thank you" to the black self against the history of violence done by that white self against generations of black bodies? Can there be, under the conditions of conciliation, anything resembling proper thanks? Un-prefaced (which is to say, unprepared), is the speaking of the "Thank you," the very utterance of this phrase, not already, in advance of itself, im-proper, insufficient, offensive? Is the act of "Thank you" not an act against history, an act irresponsible to history? And, if this is the case, if there can be no white "Thank you" without a preceding apology, then it is possible to argue that it is only the "No, thank *you*," that can make the white self responsible to the black other.

All responsibility begins with the other, with the ways in which the self addresses itself to the other and with the ways in which the self understands itself as bound to the other. In its most "radical form," Derrida argues, responsibility "exposes me [the self] disymmetrically to the gaze of the other" (*The Gift of Death*).[58] The self must stand before the other, fully "exposed," culpable, guilty, and, for this very reason, prepared, determined, in-capable of speaking to the other: to speak in the name of the transgressions that the self has committed. To speak as the self is to speak the name, is to name the transgressions, is to make the self responsible to the violence done in its name, the violence that the self committed in its (own) name—"Afrikanerdom," "apartheid," "racism," and "*racisme*" being preeminent among them. It is in the moment of responsibility, and only in that moment, that the self enters history fully as it-self—as responsible to it-self because it declares it-self responsible to the other. In this event, structured through "verbal proximity," is the "direct and full welcome of the other," which means nothing less than holding the self accountable to the terms of the "conjuncture." Everything is proximate; everything is visible: it is the face of the other that must be properly apprehended, and it is necessary to understand the "conjuncture" as the event that is sutured by "language," and, as such, it presents the opening to the "verbal proximity" of conciliation. The "language" of conciliation, Pienaar shows us, is at hand;

it is as close as the face of the other that is "welcomed" into the politics of conciliation.

In recognizing the other as other, and self as self, Derrida proposes responsibility as the response to the "call of the other" (*The Gift of Death*).[59] What marks this "call" is its incomparable, utter singularity: "My first and last responsibility, my first and last desire, is that responsibility of responsibility that relates me to what no one else can do in my place" (*The Gift of Death*).[60] Nowhere else in *The Gift of Death,* Derrida's reading of death through the works of Jan Patočka, Martin Heidegger, and Emmanuel Levinas, does Derrida offer such a compelling and succinct definition of responsibility: it is singular. To be responsible is to recognize that "I" must do "what no one else can do in my place." "I," alone, am responsible for my relationship to the other. This is what "I," and "I" alone, must do, because no one can stand in for me; responsibility, conceived as a radical openness to self and other—which evokes the logic of the "sorite," needless to say— singularity, forecloses the possibility of substitution entirely.

There is no ambiguity about this. Responsibility is the self's to face, and to act on, and the self's alone. This is what the self, which we might name "I," must confront and, in that confrontation, speak. "I" must act responsibly because all responsibility begins in and with the self, and "I" must be responsible because my doing, how "I" act, affects, relates directly to, the other. This is what is meant by singularity: there can be no substitution for or of the self, in responsibility. As Heidegger puts it, *auf sich nehmen* ([it] must be taken upon oneself)—responsibility must be taken on by the self. Or, to render Heidegger in the vernacular, thereby lending emphasis to and intensifying the singularity of the "I," *es auf sich nehmen* (I must take it on). The self is called to "take on" responsibility by the self. In *The Gift*'s Heideggerian phrasing, responsibility is that act that recognizes that the call (*Ruf*; it is, and is not, for Heidegger, a "silent voice" that calls us to responsibility) comes from within itself (*Dasein*)—responsibility stands as that force, the force of the call, the call calling to itself, that "imposes itself *autonomously*" (*The Gift of Death*).[61]

How is this call to responsibility heard? How does it address itself to us? What event births us to our own responsibility? In this regard, the clarity of Patočka's position, that the voice—of responsibility—must come from someone, resonates with Pienaar's "No, thank *you*" as an act of conciliation. Pienaar is roused to responsibility by the call that Mandela issues to him through his formal, rote "Thank you," which Pienaar, and Pienaar alone, recognizes as historically un-acceptable and in-appropriate. In the terms of conciliation, there can be no politics in this situation without transgression. Politics is impossible without the "No."

This begs the unsatisfactory but entirely obvious question about why Pienaar will refuse ceremonial niceties and Mandela will not. It is possible that we might be better served by rephrasing this question as the need to explicate why Pienaar and Mandela understand the moment to be making different demands on them so that it is never a simple matter of one (Mandela, *Danken ohne Denken*) feeling constrained by the ceremonial and the other (Pienaar, *ein Denken, das Danken verweigert*) not—or why one is faithful to the prescribed codes of conduct and the other irresponsible to it.

The answer begins in conciliation. Pienaar recognizes that in Mandela's "Thank you" is not simply the giving of thanks, the expression of gratitude (for glorifying the nation), but something markedly distinct: the call to responsibility. Pienaar understands that this historic occasion, where Mandela is thanking him, requires him to act in a fashion true to the event, a recognition that makes him conceive of something "radically impossible," something he would never have done before, something he had no need to do before (*The Gift of Death*).[62] Under an apartheid regime, then, it would be fair to say—following the logic of conciliation—that Pienaar would have acted according to the script, without fail. He would have exchanged "Thank yous," nothing more—and, with a white president, needless to say.

However, it is the black president's "Thank you" that makes the white Afrikaner rugby captain (and, by extension, all white South Africans, Afrikaners, Anglos, and all those various other white ethnic communities: Portuguese, Greek, Lebanese, Lithuanian, and so on) responsible for what he did—benefit from the injustice of the apartheid system—and, most critically, it makes him recognize that he must, through negation, refuse the thanks offered. Instead he must undertake, in some form or other, the radically impossible. Through his negation that is only at first glance a negation because it is in truth a response to the other's call, he must seek (*Denken*) the most succinct way possible to apologize for apartheid. In his "No" Pienaar is disallowing (negation) and disavowing (repudiating, denying, disowning) Mandela's thanks and, as history demands, naming himself—he is standing, as Derrida says, as himself; he will not let anyone take his place—as complicit with the entire structure of apartheid and with it structural violence and its racist inequity, done in the name of the self, the self acting against the other. Because of Pienaar's "No," this history of violence can no longer be denied; it must be owned by Pienaar, white South Africa, and by the event of apartheid itself. "Apartheid," that is, as the proper name for what the self did to the other, how the self acted against the other, and how the self behaved with impunity, violence, and with no regard for the rights of the other. Through his "No" Pienaar is calling out (hailing/interpellating) apartheid, indicting it—recognizing the absolute need for the public issuing—in the face of the discourse of reconciliation, of an indictment against apartheid. It is only through the "No" that Pienaar can answer the call of responsibility.

Constituted as such, it is clear that in his "No, thank *you*," Pienaar is responding to a higher calling. This is a calling that comes from beyond the confines of Ellis Park, at once narrowly conceived as the venue of the final (this is the immediate call that Pienaar answers, his "reply" to the—Nancian—question posed by history) and metonymically figured as coming from an entire world that stood historically opposed to apartheid. (This is the call that resonates loudest to Pienaar, placing himself, responsibly, so that he might face the world, hear in that call his own indictment, and understand that he must respond to that charge. That is his first responsibility, incipiently achieved through his negation.) The calling that Pienaar heeds exceeds the history of the Afrikaners (and apartheid); it exceeds his (personal) history as the son of lower-middle-class Afrikaners, as one of the last sons of apartheid's racialized privilege. This is a calling that comes, as is proper, from the other. This is the "language" that is "verbally proximate." This is a calling that demands that Pienaar speak the name of "Mandela," "Mr. President," the other, as sacrosanct.

In refusing Mandela the formulaic right to thank (him), Pienaar is, even though he may not understand it as such, betraying family, friends, community, nation (Afrikaners). (It is possible to understand the event only, as Alain Badiou argues in his theory of the event, in its "supplementarity";[63] the event of dis-loyalty can, then, be properly apprehended in its aftermath only in the residues that trail in the wake of the event.) Pienaar betrays those whom he loves, has loved his entire life, because there is more, much more, at stake in his adoption of Søren Kierkegaard's Abrahamic ethics. For Abraham fidelity to God demands the betrayal of all mortals, beginning, of course, with his son Isaac (who must be sacrificed to Abraham's love and fidelity to God) and all those closest to him; for Abraham fidelity to God far outweighs love for the familiar (*familia*), love for those whom the self loves. In Kierkegaard's terms, love (that is true to God) depends on betraying the love of those with whom the self is most intimate, whom he is closest to. Pienaar is, as it were, responsible to Abrahamic betrayal (love), so that he speaks under the condition of, in the name of, self-indictment: "Absolute duty demands that one behave in an irresponsible manner (by means of treachery or betrayal), while still recognizing, confirming, and reaffirming the very thing one sacrifices, namely, the order of human ethics and responsibility" (*The Gift of Death*).[64] Pienaar's "No" is possible only if the self gives it-self over to what it is not, to the other whom it has stood historically against. Pienaar's speaking transforms the "No" into an inaugural act. It is the first conception (speaking) of conciliation and, as such, the first and certainly most public act of politics as a fully and necessarily confrontational encounter in postapartheid South Africa. An encounter staged, paradoxically, to showcase reconciliation—reductively rendered as the erasure of difference between self and other—that serves only to repudiate reconciliation. Deleuze's insight could hardly have been more timely—"the force of the paradoxes is that they allow us to be present at the genesis of the contradiction."

Derrida would name Pienaar's negation, the Springbok captain's ethical commitment that is a rejection of ethics, fidelity "*in the name* of absolute duty," a duty that demands that the self be ir-responsible to it-self, to those it has (historically) loved, to those with whom it has shared its life (*The Gift of Death*).[65] Instead, the self must be utterly responsible to the other (as Abraham was loyal to God rather than to Isaac or to his wife Sarah, who was blessed only in her later years with a child), the self must recognize that it is only in its irresponsibility to it-self that it can behave responsibly to the other. Pienaar must make himself vulnerable to the most serious indictment that the Afrikaner (nation) can subject its own: his irresponsibility must make him *volksverraier*—"betrayer of the *volk*," the self who indicts it-self and all others like it, the self who is untrue to the *volk*. In this regard it must be noted that there is no Afrikaner self whose betrayal of the *volk* would be more acutely felt than that of the Springbok captain, the very avatar of the *volk*, its most glorious incarnation of its masculinized, virile, conquering, fiercely "autonomous" self.

Pienaar's negation, while not understood as such, constitutes nothing less than the über-betrayal—the betrayal of the *volk* to end all betrayals of the *volk*. It is, of course, precisely in its singular betrayal that the self achieves (Abrahamic/Kierkegaardian/Derridean) irresponsibility, that it commits it-self to politics through conciling with the other. Together, betrayal of the *volk* and the commitment to irresponsibility form the bedrock of this (anti-)ethics of conciliation. There is, furthermore, an element of Levinasian humility to Pienaar's negation—his ir-responsibility. "It is not the insufficiency of the I that prevents totalization," Levinas says, "but the Infinity of the Other" (*Totality and Infinity*).[66] Through recognizing the "Infinity of the Other," it becomes possible for the "I" to find its place, a place, in this instance, fitted—made—by conciliation.

Conciliation

It is in his "No" that Pienaar identifies Mandela, before the world, as other. In his "No" Pienaar centralizes difference (conciliation rather than reconciliation) and offers the possibility of a radical, racialized, but not racist, politics, a politics that is truly historic because it begins from the ground of apartheid—a politics that sought to refuse the other its right to be. Pienaar recognizes but will not admit of Mandela's magnanimity ("Thank you, François, for what you have done."), the president's historic capacity for forgiveness, and in so doing Pienaar "conciles" himself to politics. Pienaar joins himself, through "verbal proximity," in political confrontation to Mandela through his refusal of Mandela's thanks and arrogates to himself, and his metonymic self only, the right to think thanks—*ein Danken, das Denken ist.*

In the history of postapartheid South Africa, Pienaar's negation is an event because it claims for the perpetrator of apartheid—in all its violence, injustice, various inequities, inhumanity—the right to refuse thanks in the cause of, we must be clear in recognizing this paradox (offensive insofar as it is constitutive of conciliation), reserving the right of refusal for the perpetrator alone.

Thanking is the work, the political responsibility, of the (apartheid) self, and of that self only. In the decision to acknowledge and/or accept the self's thanks, the other enters into the logic of conciliation. The other is bound to the self while it stands apart from, stands in a position historically different from, the self. The other cannot be reconciled to the self: that would be tantamount to a failure of politics. The self must make (provoke?) the other into a confrontation, even as, or because, the other recognizes—thinks—the self's "appropriation" (a misappropriation of sorts too, of course) of giving thanks (of *ein Danken, das Denken ist*) as the intensification of difference that is also an address to the democracy *l'avenir.* The democracy to come that is inconceivable without the rhetorical refusal ("No") that is shadowed, outlined, haunted, inscribed with, the violence of difference but will not be held hostage by that violence. Conciliation acknowledges the history of violence that marks the self-other encounter, but will not concede to it. The history of violence informs conciliation, it might even impede it, but that violence does not make conciliation impossible. In its demand for confrontation, of course, conciliation is itself a recognizably violent act.

Pienaar's "No" is, then, nothing less than the most deliberate evocation of apartheid in the moment (bringing it to life again in the most inopportune time—conciliation is always out of joint, a Shakespearean [*Hamlet,* as discussed in the chapters on Derrida] disruption of the political that restores politics to itself), a national rugby-inspired celebration (reconciliation), that seeks to overcome apartheid through a democratically elected president's routine "Thank you." Conciliation will not countenance the other's "Thank you." Conciliation assigns its political work, its political responsibilities, in the most uncompromising fashion. Conciliation knows its moment, and it acts in that moment in such a way that disrupts any possibility of reconciliation. Conciliation follows the logic of the event in that it inserts politics where and when it is least expected. Sometimes, as in this instance, it announces itself in a single negation. Conciliation invests the unexpected, out of place, "No," with the force of rare disruption, intensely Lacanian in its reverberations:

"No, thank *you*, Mr. President": "Thank *you*."

Or, perhaps: "*No*, thank *you*, Mr. President, thank *you*."

The enunciatory and political emphasis must fall on the second-person pronoun (singular, it must be noted, because English does not distinguish between the plural and the singular). The self, "I," recognizes, and then insists, that it is not you who must thank you but "I"—the singular "I" that simultaneously stands and does not stand as the royal "We"—who must thank you. It is my responsibility to thank you for what you did. You, Mr. President, made nonracial democracy possible in this country; it is only because you, Mr. President, gave South Africa democracy that it became possible for white South Africa, and the rugby-loving Afrikaners more than anyone else, to participate—for the first time as a democratic, nondiscriminating state—in international sport; it is only because of you, Mr. President, that white South Africa is no longer a pariah state (*état voyou*) in the world community. And that capacity for making the post-apartheid political possible, as Mandela would later learn, was both his gift and his greatest political deficiency. But, Pienaar, we can speculate, might have glimpsed something entirely different: *Wie Danken denken*, "who thanks thinks."

In thanking you, Mr. President, I ask for forgiveness: I thank you for the gift of forgiveness, for not exacting revenge for the violence done to disenfranchised South Africa in the name of apartheid.[67] In my name, Mr. President. That, Mr. President, is the gift that only *you* could give, could give in the name of—and this is where representation as a political absence is most palpable—who you are and who you are not: black South Africa, those in whose name you accept my thanks, and in whose name you forgive me. There is thus a profoundly Christian aspect that girds and insinuates itself into Pienaar's "No, thank *you*." His "No, thank *you*" is also a public statement, made before the world, to (the) black being (*Dasein*) itself. It is a public speaking of repentance; this repentance is not made in the manner of boisterous triumph but rather assumes the visage of a singular repentance. Humility before the other, a humility that derives from negation. Conciliation, then, as ethically productive, at least in Nietzsche's dialectical sense: "I am also your best enemy."[68] It is only the Nietzschean "enemy" who can make the self know the value of and the moment for humility, for recognizing the ethical force of the other—the "enemy."

In the insistence that is the *you* in the "Thank *you*" is the audible act of repenting: of saying, "I am sorry," in which the "I" again functions as a failed representation. "I am sorry" for what you have endured; however, *your* endurance—that begins in your first resisting apartheid as a youth, then those twenty-seven years in prison—taught me, teaches me. In my turn, let me show you, in saying, "No, thank *you*," what I have learned: how I have learned from you, what it is that you have given me, made me responsible for, as only you could. In Pienaar's refusal of Mandela's "Thank you" is his acceptance of (his singular) responsibility. Because he accepts his responsibility, Pienaar is able to present himself humbled (but not humiliated; Mandela would not allow that) before Mandela and, in that humility, newly acquired in the process of conciling—to render conciliation as an awkward verb—himself to responsibility, is the first seed of (white) repentance, the coming together beyond confrontation, but also only because of confrontation, that conciliation makes possible.

What responsibility makes possible is conciliation as the first act of politics. It is the first political act that Pienaar makes because it is, under these extraordinary circumstances (and yet, in the world of sport, a routine occurrence, because every four years there is such an occurrence), he, in the act of *ein Danken, das Denken ist,* thinks the political. Pienaar thinks, not as an Afrikaner (much as he can never slough off that mode of thought, much as he declares himself a descendent of "French Huguenots") or even as a newly democratized (the postapartheid condition liberated him from apartheid racism into democracy) South African but as a figure wrought by the event. Through his peculiar (singular) enfranchisement (enfranchised out of his racist rights that by force of law denied others theirs), in his reduction to status of white minority citizen, albeit of the most powerful and privileged variety (as such settler minority positions are wont to be), into his proclaimed position of "rainbow warrior" (the rugby captain who leads Tutu's "Rainbow Nation of God"), Pienaar emerges as a figure of, a figure for, thought.

In this act of conciliation power confronts (itself as) power in that Mandela stands as the power of the new democracy and Pienaar of the disproportionately empowered (white) minority. In refusing Mandela's thanks, Pienaar presents conciliation itself as the struggle for a politics that was, in Pienaar (and white South Africa's) case, just yesterday (until the first democratic elections in 1994), beyond him. The event of the "No, thank *you*" makes Pienaar only insomuch as Pienaar makes of, makes through, the "No, thank *you*" the event of conciliation. Politics as, before all else, the act of confrontation, the most direct, sometimes brutal (not in this case, but the potential for brutal exchange is always present), difficult confrontation between self and other, and, as importantly, self and self. Conciliation is that political encounter unmediated by the prospect of reconciliation: of seeking to bring together, to ameliorate difference, to move, before any speaking takes place, toward a place—in a shared discourse—of commonality. Conciliation insists on, is based in, that which distinguishes, that which is not shared, that which holds self and other apart (an "irreducible relation," as Levinas would have it), which insists that self (white) is *not* other (black)—that there are powerful historical forces that have produced this distinction, that those forces continue to obtain, and that it is possible for the self to confront the other only if the self speaks those forces. In his historic negation, the political force of Pienaar's "No" is that it brings those forces to light, that he gives those forces new life, and, most importantly, that he gives conciliation (its first political) life. Pienaar gives conciliation a paradoxical force of the Deleuzian variety because he establishes it as a genuine political "language" that stands determinedly against the discourse of reconciliation, which was, in that moment, arrogating to itself the force of (hegemonic) national discourse.

In speaking the (his) language of conciliation, the event produces Pienaar as a new figure for postapartheid responsibility. He is a new figure because there was, heretofore, none such as him: no white, macho, rugby-playing, rugby-loving, conciling Afrikaner had existed before him. The "No, thank *you*" is the event of conciliation in that it will not shrink, in the moment of historical record, from direct political confrontation. Not, of course, extreme or even physical confrontation, but the "No, thank *you*" constitutes a negation that cannot be disentangled from the violence of racial conflict in apartheid and postapartheid South Africa. Saliently, it is Pienaar, not Mandela, who animates that violence, gives it the vividness and vivacity of the "No." Mandela articulates to reconciliation, "Thank you, François for what you have done for our country."

In his turn, Pienaar reanimates the racial rifts; he reinvigorates the history of animosity, and his negation reveals, in plain sight, the deep cleavages of apartheid political life. Pienaar's negation demonstrates how conciliation speaks the language of Deleuze's "infinitely reversible" temporalities (past-future-future-past→ . . .). Negation understands that, above all, the moment of apartheid must be spoken to, spoken of, and, it must be spoken from the position of its slow dissolution by those who gave it life, those who sustained and nurtured it, those who were its architects, beneficiaries, and heirs. (If, in the logic of Galatians, "Whatever a man sows, he will reap in return,"[69] conciliation marks the event of renouncing, as much as possible, that which has been "reaped" and, in the same act, transforming that renunciation into the responsibility to "sow" an entirely new—political—crop. "To beat," according to Isaiah, "swords into ploughshares."[70] That may be how to conceive of conciliation, but only in the long term.) Only conciliation, in committing itself to confronting— never relinquishing, never refusing or denying—apartheid, makes such a speaking possible, in part (in the past-future-future-past→ . . .) because conciliation is an event. The event always enjoys a public stage, but it can never be staged (it is predictable only in its unpredictability), and as such it is alone can bear witness to the difficult political truth to which it, and it alone, is heir. Through his negation, Pienaar introduces, unbeknownst to him, postapartheid South Africa to the discourse of conciliation. Because of this, conciliation enables Pienaar to restore the life of apartheid, he assigns that history its proper, and necessary, place on the occasion Mandela wants to script it as a moment of national celebration. Pienaar's fidelity to conciliation disrupts that narrative, a political recognition that is impossible to understand without the requisite attention to the "No, thank *you*."

Pienaar's negation is the declamation of apartheid. It is the "infinitely reversible" public death of apartheid spoken, paradoxically (all there were present at the "genesis of the contradiction"), during the event that, by this account if no other, threw the fact of winning the rugby World Cup (white South Africa demonstrating itself as supreme among rugby-playing nations, rugby as once more joyously central to the identity of Afrikanerdom) into bitter relief. In his negation of Mandela, in and through his emphatic, still-reverberating "No," Pienaar gave voice to that "infinitely reversible" death, the most painful kind of death imaginable by the white apartheid regime and its *volk*. In the event a "new figure of responsibility" emerges, such a singular individual that her or his "existence excludes," as Derrida argues, "every possible substitution" (*The Gift of Death*).[71] Derrida's singular figure invokes Nietzsche's Zarathustra, and who would know better about that which he alone can do than Zarathustra, the *overmenschen*?

"Nel-son! Nel-son!"

> I am of today and former times. . . . But there is something in me
> that is of tomorrow and times to come.
> —FRIEDRICH NIETZSCHE, *Thus Spoke Zarathustra*

Reflecting on the moment of the Springbok victory, the normally loquacious Archbishop Tutu was able to offer only a series of fragments, and breathless fragments at that. Tutu's phrases are doubly marked. They are phrases uncharacteristic of the archbishop because of, first, their abbreviation (Tutu tends to speak in run-on sentences), and, second, the intensity of their truncated grammatical structure. In the aftermath of the unexpected South African triumph, Tutu was unable, until the very end of this interview, to form a complete sentence: "'Quite unbelievable, quite incredible, what happened . . . [a]n extraordinary thing. It said, yes, it is actually possible for us to become one nation.'"[72] Divided by apartheid, black and white South Africans managed "to become," to have become (already, just a year after the country's first democratic elections), for a moment, in the history of the moment, "One team, one country." The Springbok victory gave substance (provisional though it might have been), however premature it may have turned out to be, to the notion of South Africa as "One team, one country," the 1995 World Cup's purposefully nationalizing slogan.

In the postmatch interview Pienaar, provided (a nationalizing) numerical heft that works to substantiate Tutu's breathless incredulity. When a white reporter asked Pienaar about the support his team received at Ellis Park (Johannesburg), the Springbok captain offered an unexpected, nationalizing response. Instead of restricting himself (and his team) to the physical confines of Ellis Park or the ideological limits of the Afrikaner minority, Pienaar provided a historic reply: "'We didn't have the support of 63,000 South Africans today[;] we had the support of 42 million.'"[73] At work in this brief utterance is, at once, negation and affirmation/negation through affirmation (*Aufhebung* at work, once more). Of the 63,000 in the stands of Ellis Park, it is generally estimated that the overwhelming majority (let us say, for rhetorical purposes, 62,000) were white South Africans.[74] Pienaar's is a "reversed," so to speak (and, yes, racialized too), arithmetical logic: affirmation through substitution, negation through metonymization. Pienaar negates the smaller number, "We didn't have the support of 63,000 South Africans today," in the cause of extending it into the newly democratized nation.

That Pienaar affirms the bigger number (the—national—whole, the One) at the expense of the smaller (raced fragment) one is politically salient because it is not simply an instance of metonymy. It constitutes, rather, in keeping with Mandela's vision of the postapartheid society that could live, finally, with itself as a single political entity, a historic refutation contingent on a complex, politically critical incorporation. However, in his negation Pienaar is implicitly calling for a different politics, not one in which postapartheid South Africa is constituted into a Tutu-esque "rainbow" (the maintenance of [racial] identity while combining to compose a grand tapestry of complementary hues—much like, say, the first and, to date, only African American mayor of New York, David Dinkins, referred to the city as a "Grand Mosaic"). The "No" stands, in this regard, as the call for a politics through which black conciles with white, white with black, self with other, and other with self; after all, as Levinas reminds us, an insight that achieves an unmistakably literal political force in this case, the self, is dwarfed by the "Infinity of the Other."

Within the logic of conciliation, there is only one proper place for the "63,000." It must work toward, because the politics of conciliation dictate such a process must of necessity be a struggle, a grappling with the difficult demands of the situation, situating it-self within the "42 million," an end that cannot ever be fully achieved. It is Pienaar, not Mandela, who offers both a universal vision of the postapartheid nation to come and a critique of identitarian politics. Unlike Mandela, Pienaar will not, even for a moment, even in a moment of athletic triumph, allow the "63,000" to stand on its own. The Afrikaners cannot, despite the desire of some in their ranks, a tendency especially prevalent, one imagines, among the Springbok rugby faithful, to be ex-cluded, to situate themselves, deliberately, spectacularly in the moment of victory, outside the postapartheid, nation-in-the-making, the nation being conciled before their very eyes. However, as Tokyo Sexwale, longtime anti-apartheid activist and the former premier of Gauteng province (centered on Johannesburg), acknowledges, it is not only white South Africans who were affected by the Springbok victory. As a black South African, a politically influential one, at that, Sexwale was made to rethink himself in relation to the nation, and, in truth, to Mandela himself:

> The liberation struggle of our people was not just about liberating blacks from bondage, but more so it was about liberating white people from fear. And there it was. Fear melting away. People were shouting, "Nelson! Nelson!" And who were these people, these rugby crowds? They were our jailers, our oppressors; the people guarding the borders, the police stations. But it was, "Nelson! Nelson!" We stood there and we didn't know what to say.[75]

"Nel-son! Nel-son!" or "Nelson! Nelson!" was an act of supreme interpellation, an event made in and by the present. The postapartheid nation was made (numerically and symbolically) one/One by the triumph over the All Black through two contradictory, and not a little paradoxical, highly racialized responses. Black South Africans, newly enfranchised and empowered in the wake of the ANC's electoral victory, found themselves, surprisingly, shockingly, and literally, voiceless: "we didn't know what to say." Meanwhile, the "jailers, oppressors" were in full throat, chanting "Nelson! Nelson!" Mandela, historic opponent of apartheid, jailed by the "jailers," was wildly acclaimed—as if he were—as one of their own.[76] Sexwale offered a memorable, poetic rendering of the event in an Olympian language that speaks of a black political figure, speaking, perhaps, for generations of anti-apartheid activists—giving voice to the entirely unexpected realization of a movement's greatest ambition: witnessing, before their very eyes, coming into being. Sexwale was moved to Greek poetry, "For truly, that day," he says Homerically, "we supped with the gods."[77]

In this way, numerical, racial negation itself constitutes the act, against (it would be reasonable to argue) the wishes of some ideologically recalcitrant Afrikaners, of nationalizing affirmation. Mandela's decision to retain the Springbok name, and emblem (supplemented with the Protea, a flower native to only the Western Cape), produced what we might recognize as a moment of Afrikaner autoimmunity. In Derrida's terms, autoimmunity is delineated as a "living being, in a quasi-suicidal fashion, itself works to destroy its own protection, to immunize itself against its own immunity."[78] In response to Mandela's largesse, the black president's recognition of the ideological import of the Springbok as the name and emblem that adorns the nation's rugby jerseys to the Afrikaners, the predominantly white, Afrikaner crowd produced a memorable act of self-interpellation—an instance of the "sorite," the minor (minority) raising up the major (majority's) banner.

The white spectators broke out, upon seeing Mandela, into bone-chilling chants ("Nelson! Nelson!") so shocking, so unexpected, that, in truth, they were even a little frightening. (All Black captain Fitzpatrick remembers himself as being awed by this experience, which is the only proper response for the witness to the event—to be unnerved and, for that moment, without adequate response to it.) This is the singular force of sport, a force that no other gathering—save perhaps the political rally—can produce, a force unto itself in that moment because it caused 62,000 Afrikaners to, surely unknown to themselves, autoimmunize themselves with/in a single act, that act that is nothing short of the Derridean "quasi-suicidal."

After such a historic utterance—"Nel-son! Nel-son!"—the Ellis Park crowd was no longer capable of insulating itself, completely, if ever again, against its own interpellation into the postapartheid nation. In calling out to the other, in ritualistically, jubilantly, calling the other's name, the self was calling the other to it-self. In fact, this is the moment of Nietzschean truth: "I am also your best enemy." And, what is the "best enemy" but the misnomer, the im-proper calling out to the other who has become "friend?"[79] (Is the event the moment in which the Levinasian "I" is no longer "insufficient to itself?") The self was exposing it-self utterly to the other, the other who was now both entirely other and no longer other, yet still unmistakably different. Through the event the other becomes other on other terms, terms that are distinct from the law of apartheid. The chant was at once an invitation to the other and a profound expression of gratitude. In that calling out, that calling to, the other was being thanked: "No, thank *you*," shouted more loudly, more boisterously, more exuber-antly than Pienaar ever could in his singularity, but it was, if not exactly the same call (his borne out of refutation, the crowd's out of euphoria) then an echo incredible, deafening in its resonance, inexorable in its march toward autoimmunity. It was also the act of thinking: *ein Danken, das Denken ist.*

Indeed, such are the ways of sport's euphoria that the (apartheid) self can now no longer inoculate itself against the other. In chanting "Nel-son! Nel-son!" the Afrikaners chanted their way to their own political "suicide." And, it would seem, the Ellis Park crowd, and white South Africa by exten-sion, loved every minute of their great trek to autoimmunity. Lock, stock, and metaphoric *ossewa* (the ox-driven wagon with which Afrikaners made the Great Trek to the South African hinterland in the nineteenth century), the Afrikaners were all in, courtesy of the Springbok win, Pienaar's nega-tion, and Mandela's strategic decision to allow them the cultural and ide-ological sovereignty of their beloved Springbok name and emblem. When the other shows the self love, for Afrikaner rugby lovers the only proper response is, apparently, to reciprocate by chanting, in frenzied incanta-tion, the name of the love object who continues to be, has historically been, other, but still worthy, in some strange way, of the self's love which is, of course, also a form of self-love.

There is a profoundly Nietzschean aspect to this unexpected love af-fair, this ideological ménage-a-trois, which pivots on Pienaar's postmatch pronouncement. In the terms of the Nietzschean dialectic of love and rea-son, *Thus Spoke Zarathustra*'s author insists, "There is always a bit of mad-ness in loving. But there is always a bit of reason in madness."[80] Pienaar's negation lends an unexpected complexity of thinking this new strange love of the white, Afrikaner, rugby-loving crowd for Mandela, their erst-while sworn enemy, the incarcerated leader of an organization routinely vilified in the national media and variously characterized by the apartheid regime as "terrorists," "Communists," and a range of other racist invec-tives. In simultaneously refusing the white minority its special status (the "63,000" in attendance) and conciling it to a democratic future, Pienaar in-advertently draws attention to a critical political fact: it was a point of ideological honor for the historically disenfranchised black majority to oppose the Afrikaners' obsession with rugby—an obsession that is, as it were, Pienaar's birthright, because he is a figure shaped, in significant measure, by Afrikaner rugby culture.[81]

In his "mad love" for rugby, for his own Afrikaner *volk*, for himself, for the adumbrated nation-in-conception that he was partly responsible for articulating, Pienaar grasped the difficulty of the re-situating of the Ellis Park crowd: history had offered them a new place, one not disentangled from their apartheid past, but one that was acquiring its own distinctness nonetheless. And so Pienaar has to, under the pressure of history, "reason" it as an arithmetical formulation. Pienaar's phrasing depended on an ideological deracination that was itself a kind of Zarathustran death. It was a kind of death that was full of the promise of resurrection, that kind where "all your passions turn into virtues and all your devils into angels" (*Thus Spoke Zarathustra*).[82] The Ellis Park crowd, itself already a metonymy for Afrikaners, was displaced. It now had to learn to count itself in terms of the new political calculus—tens of thousands of Afrikaners at a rugby stadium where they constituted only a few million of the "42" (which is, of course, as history would have it, also the number Jackie Robinson wore). In the new logic of nonracial democracy that Pienaar put forward, the Afrikaner (rugby) *volk* were made to stand outside themselves, transposed from the rugby stadium (hypermasculinized bastion of Afrikaner power) into the nation; the Afrikaner *volk* were ex-posed, rendered other to themselves, made to think beyond themselves. If the apogee of Afrikaner cultural triumphalism is the winning the rugby World Cup, then it was, paradoxically, in precisely this moment that the Afrikaners were unmoored to an entirely unknown locale. The Afrikaners were projected (it might even be possible to say that they were, ideologically speaking, rudely hurled), not by the black president but by one of their own, their rugby captain, into the postapartheid nation. In the act of celebration, of requited, rugby-mad love, the *volk* were reminded, by the utter simplicity of a number (in which they confronted, baldly, the extent to which they were out-numbered), that the Afrikaners constituted a political minority, albeit one with considerable political, economic, and cultural clout. That is why, audible in the moment of triumph, in that reverberating echo, "Nel-son! Nel-son!" is the ominous, life-giving "death" knell of autoimmunity. In loving the other, the self must sacrifice something fundamental and constitutive of it-self. Is Nietzschean "madness" the true logic of love? How could there ever be "angels" without "devils"? What kind of "passion" gives itself up to "virtue"? Or, maybe we ask, does not give itself up to "virtue"?

It is in this regard that Pienaar's speaking matters so much because it reminds us of Derrida's notion that "responsibility demands irreplaceable singularity."[83] In his "singularly responsible" turn, as the "public" leader of the Afrikaners, Pienaar must, in response to the bona fides of Mandela's autoimmune democracy, demonstrate the Afrikaners' own propensity for autoimmunity as an affirmative act. It is in and through autoimmunity that the self, and/or the nation-state, can itself be opened to the other, and thus to that which is *l'avenir*. That is, the "to come" that includes, as it always does, the possibility of the event of nationalization, that is, absolute autoimmunity as well. The event of World Cup rugby triumph, then, is impossible without the *volk* risking the death of the *volk* or without Mandela risking the death of (postapartheid) democracy itself or squandering some of the political capital that he, Mandela, had acquired as icon of the anti-apartheid struggle.

For the Afrikaners, the greatest risk contained within the triumph was the subsumption of the *volk* into the black majority because of the triumph. It was in the fulfillment of the *volk*'s über-desire, winning the rugby World Cup, that the *volk*—even though neither black nor white South African fully knew this, could fully know this—was most, not least, autoimmune. Victory at Ellis Park in 1995, not defeat at the ballot box in 1994 (where Mandela's ANC won a resounding electoral victory in South Africa's first democratic elections), was what made the *volk* autoimmune. No longer was the question "How much will or can the historic 'oppressor' of Sexwale's political imaginary (now anachronistic?) risk itself in the face of its newfound, unprecedented, vulnerability?" a matter of political consequence. That issue, as the critical apartheid belief (in truth, a racial logic in itself) that the autochthonous Afrikaner was uniquely susceptible to the black majority, was no longer sustainable—it could no longer bear the weight of a political speaking. Confronted with this reality, the "responsibility" was left to the "irreplaceably singular" Pienaar to speak in the name of those who were given the right to be, to be-come, "antidemocrats," those who now had the right to resist the new state's authority, to "abuse" the freedom of expression.

Pienaar's speaking is salient in that he is direct in his symbolic rejection of local white Afrikaner predominance—if not presence at the World Cup final itself. It is for national singularity, where "42 million" can be condensed into that peculiar unity that is the nation-as-One, that Pienaar, literally, with Mandela, stands. And, of course, to which he speaks. To say nothing of how he tackled, scrummed, and mauled on the field of World Cup play against the mighty All Blacks just minutes earlier. It can be declared, with Zarathustran certainty, that "Apartheid is *dead!*" (But God still lives, one expects. Or, maybe it is only the god of rugby who survives.) The new, anti-apartheid democracy, so deeply rooted, for both blacks and whites, in Christian doctrine, must be embraced, spoken for by the *volk*'s captain.

Responsibility as such recognizes its absolutely responsibility to the other. Mandela must not thank; he cannot thank. It is not his political duty nor is it, strange as it is to say, his right to thank the self. Through conciliation the self has, pointedly, dis-enfranchised the other, again, in such a way as to behave ethically toward the other. The self conducts it-self in the language and custom of apartheid (the white self disenfranchising the black other), all the while turning that language and custom against itself. The only way to speak conciliation is through history. Conciliation is historically ethical.

It Is the Duty of the Self to Thank

In the political logic of conciliation, history determines that the duty to thank belongs to the self. The self, and only the self, must thank. That is what the self gives the other in responsibility: responsibility as a form of supplication, of subjugation, a first request for forgiveness. The self, in refusing thanks, is not offending but supplicating itself. It is not negation as such, and although it begins in negation, it would not be possible without the (prior) negation, but responsibility as inextricably bound to self-abnegation: the surrender or repudiation of the self that is achieved through conciliation. The promise of conciliation, of politics, is that the moment of self-abnegation is but that, a moment. The political struggle continues, it does not, it will not, abide condemnation or even violent retribution as that im-possible desire, as the final act.

In refusing Mandela's thanks, Pienaar is repudiating him-self for apartheid, but he is also, far more importantly, saying clearly that the work of thanks—of giving thanks, of thanking the self—is not the work of the other. The other must be thanked, even in the most routine exchange. In fact, conciliation makes it possible to conceive of every encounter between self and other as a potential event: the iteration of that routine phrase "Thank you" has been made inveterately, unfailingly, perhaps even liberatingly, political—provided, of course, that we follow the Heideggerian injunction. Or, at the very least, that we remember that *Danken ist Denken.*

The work of a responsible politics is to know whom to thank and who cannot, must not, be thanked. The event suggests that all thanks the other offers must, in the moment of politics, be put/pushed aside. Every act of thanks must begin in negation, it must trace itself to, locate itself in, the event of conciliation. Every thanks must be, without fail, thought because it demands that the self account for it-self (that is, the self is made accountable to history, history as responsibility) in every exchange of thanks with the other. In giving thanks, in refusing the right to be thanked, the self shows itself to be responding to the call of the other as other. The self must recognize where that call came from, how it first struck (what it seemed like to) the other. How the "Thank you" heard is only the secondary issue. What really matters is for whom conciliation makes the "Thank you" impermissible. "No," you may not thank me (the self). That work belongs, because of history, to the self. That is how con-ciliation figures the act of thanking: it assigns every speaker a historic role, a role made by (postapartheid) history, a role that must, again and again, be thought.

In un-doing the "Thank you," Pienaar, through conciliation, elevates it. "No, thank *you*" is the only way to begin to thank the ethical subject of his-tory. "No, thank *you*" inaugurates a singular thanks: that act of thanking that could not have known itself as a historical speaking until it began in, and because of, the negation. This is what, as Derrida suggests, it means not only to be responsible but also to do the work of responsibility as a deconstructive political act. Responsibility as such is an act that under-stands its own paradox, its own capacity for thinking toward its own undo-ing (that is precisely what it works toward), always premised on the condi-tion that the act of politics must be taken up again. The "concept of responsibility," Derrida writes, has "always implied involvement in action, doing, a *praxis, a decision* that exceeds simple conscience or simple theo-retical understanding, it is also true that the same concept requires a deci-sion or responsible action to answer for itself *consciously,* that is, with knowledge of a thematics of what is done, of what action signifies, its causes, ends, etc." (*The Gift of Death*).[84]

It is conciliation that ensures that Pienaar's "No" will simultaneously "exceed simple conscience or simple theoretical understanding" and en-able him to "answer for [the decision or responsible action] consciously." It is the event of conciliation that enables Pienaar to make the decision (insofar as the decision can be, however momentarily, extricated from the event) that enables him to answer as self to other. The event of concilia-tion also allows us to grasp that Pienaar is not simply rejecting Mandela's thanks. He is, as has been discussed, designating the proper recipient of thanks, and who, alone, is responsible for giving thanks—to the other—and, in so doing, he both produces the event out of thanks and exceeds it, by some measure. Furthermore, in being true to his conscience (a critical act, to be sure) or the ethico-philosophical framework he is constructing, he is as aware as he can be, in the midst of the event that he is speaking into being (the event that is gathered in, because of, and through his nega-tion), he has some political and historical sense of what his "No" means, and, most importantly (in terms of conciliation), he knows what ends he seeks to achieve. (Historically unachievable as they may be, of course.)

Pienaar is interrupting the postapartheid hegemony of reconciliation. In his irresponsible actions, he is striving toward its undoing. In his "No," which gains in emphasis the more we think it, Pienaar is proffering a new philosophical understanding of the postapartheid political. He is moti-vated by a "practical idea of freedom"—for all—that he speaks, without fully knowing it, presciently, from the condition of unease. Pienaar grasps, and this is what compels him to act, that the freedom he inclines toward will require, on his part and on the part of every member of the postapartheid society, re-conciliation, is unachievable, unthinkable, without conciliation. That is the critical, defining, element of his philosophical understanding.

In Pienaar's "No" can be discerned, from beginning to end, the substantial philosophical gulf that separates conciliation (Pienaar) from reconciliation (Mandela). These are iconic postapartheid figures bound by difference, a difference that demanded, from the moment of negation on, a thinking wrought in and through thanking—*Danken ist Denken*. A thinking of self and other that first speaks itself as the negation that is not a negation but the first utterance of—the first optic and audible encounter ("verbal proximity," once more) with—conciliation, an encounter entirely unremarked on philosophically. The time of conciliation came and was not acknowledged. It arrived long ago, in the speaking of the "No," addressed directly to Mandela, who was the first not to recognize conciliation for what it is: a critique of him that he could not discern because it threatened the very project, a South African society after apartheid, to which he had dedicated his life. In part Mandela could not recognize conciliation not only because he could not hear the political timbres of Pienaar's difference but also because the event of conciliation was surrounded—perhaps even overwhelmed, drowned out—by the very conditions (the World Cup victory) that made it possible.

That is, when the crowd chanted "Nelson! Nelson!" Mandela could hear only the "minor" key. What was being spoken, in the "language of the major" key, was the politics of conciliation. It proceeded, conciliation, from negation, a negation that, for all its "verbal proximity," Mandela did not, could not, grasp. He was held in thrall not only by the surprise, shock (?), of the Ellis Park crowd's adulation but also by the discourse that he, more than any other, had championed reconciliation. "Verbal proximity," as such, does not by itself constitute sufficient grounds—or the necessary conditions, to phrase the matter more appropriately—required to "hear" the "language" of conciliation, even as it is being spoken, loudly, clearly, as negation. Only when *Danken ist Denken* is properly understood, is heard as conciliation, can negation come fully into itself. It is, we might conclude, the responsibility of the other to, at the very least, open itself up to, and for, that Deleuzian "language" that supersedes "articulation."

3 I Think I Saw Jacques Derrida at the 2010 World Cup in South Africa

This interminable task, the ghost remains that which gives one the most to think about—and to do.

—JACQUES DERRIDA, *Specters of Marx*

In the winter of 2010, which was, of course, the Northern Hemisphere summer, South Africa hosted the football world. It was the first time that the football World Cup took place on African soil. In the midst of the raucous vuvuzela horn calls, since banned from football stadiums in Europe but just coming into their pomp in 2010, somewhere among the exuberance of the jostling crowds; the seats packed with spectators from Europe, Asia, the Americas (after South Africa, the greatest number of fans emanated from the United States), and a host of African countries; and the football pitches in Cape Town, Johannesburg, Port Elizabeth, and Durban, I am sure I saw a historic figure, a historic African figure. I saw an African figure in Cape Town, a figure famous in Euro-America who was born at the opposite end of the African continent. Born in the North, born in the Maghreb in July 1930, when Algeria was still a French colony.

Watching the 2010 *Coupe du monde*, I think I saw Jacques Derrida.

I swear, I promise you, Jacques Derrida was there, at the 2010 World Cup in South Africa.

Initially I was surprised to see him in South Africa, what with Derrida having died in October 2004 in Paris and all. However, what might help is a more accurate rendering of my encounter with Derrida. Let me try again.

I think I saw the ghost of Jacques Derrida at the 2010 World Cup.

As such, I allow myself the liberty of marshaling Derrida to my cause. I avail myself of this liberty because I take to heart what Derrida teaches us about the ghosts and the "phantasms" (which operate "at the crossing of the unconscious, the phenomenological *phanesthai*, the noema as an intentional but real component of consciousness, and of spectrality [*phantasma*] of phantoms")[1] who are so often, as we know from the Introduction to this work, central to his work. In Derrida's estimation, we must expect nothing other than the hegemony of ghosts (*les fantômes à venir*—the "ghosts to come") as well as anticipate the mechanisms for their proliferation, mechanisms that human beings have created. And so Derrida offers a historical prognostication, "I think that the future belongs to ghosts, the technology greatly increases the power of ghosts."[2] As much as his prediction prepared us for the "future" of ghosts, Derrida, we can rightfully assume, readied us for his own visits *l'avenir* so that it is now entirely possible to be sure that Derrida was in fact in attendance at the 2010 World Cup. Derrida as much as promised us a visit of this order.

Because of Derrida's reverence for the "revenant" (such as King Hamlet) and his ability to operationalize ghosts (the ways in which he critiques Marx's dislike for ghosts in *Specters* is a thing to behold) it can sometimes be very difficult to distinguish between the figure of the ghost and the figure of the real, between Jacques Derrida and the ghost of Jacques Derrida, so to speak. (*Specters* stages an enthralling interplay among the ghost of Shakespeare's *Hamlet*, Marx's aversion to ghosts, and Derrida's call for the ghost from the future, the "New International" for our time; all the while, of course, *Specters* inscribes—through Derrida's stirring, provocative dedication: "A man's life, as unique as his death, will always be more than a paradigm and something other than a symbol. And this is precisely what a proper noun should always name"—the ghost of assassinated South African Communist Party leader Chris Hani, so that a certain ghostly fatality hangs over the work. Politics, as it were, acknowledged as a necessarily deadly business [*Specters of Marx*].)[3]

For all this in-distinction between the ghostly and the real, not to mention Derrida's commitment to thinking the politics of hauntology, there is something entirely appropriate about such a "sighting" taking place at the first African *Coupe du monde*. After all, from his childhood in

El Biar, Derrida was a keen player—a practice he regretted giving up once he moved to France—and something of a football fan: "Playing football, one of the great passions of his youth, had not survived his move from Algeria" (Peeters).[4] What is more, in his time at Koléa (where he did his military service), he was—discernible to those who know the sport despite the awkward phrasing of a Derrida biographer, Benoît Peeters—the school's football coach. Derrida ran the "school's football," is how Peeters renders it (Derrida).[5] Like his fellow pied-noir Albert Camus, Derrida was a goalkeeper, or so the rumor goes. (Camus's reasons for keeping goal, however, were—the lore goes—strictly economic. His impoverished grandmother warned him against wearing out his shoes. As such, the only way the young Albert could continue to play while keeping the punishment to a minimum was to play in goal. Derrida's reason for serving as the last line of defense is less well known. One dare not speculate that it was due to a lack of the ability to play in the field. He might, after all, have been a talented shot stopper.)

As an amateur player who had learned and enjoyed the game in Africa, spotting a phantasmatic Derrida in the stands at Athlone Stadium in Cape Town or as a ghostly presence among the crush of spectators exiting Ellis Park in Johannesburg (primarily a rugby venue, as we know from the event of Pienaar),[6] should not have been in the least a surprise. It was, after all, no more a surprise than it would have been to see the "real" Derrida, deceased though he may have been, lining up at the concession stand at Kings Park Stadium in Durban (another mainly rugby venue). After all, there is no African country, other than his native Algeria, where one would be more likely to encounter Derrida than South Africa; after all, there is no African political figure whom Derrida admired more than Nelson Mandela, the former ANC leader and, as we well know, the inaugural president of postapartheid South Africa. Since at least 1983, when he published "Racism's Last Word," an essay written in support of a museum exhibition organized by the "Artists of the World against Apartheid,"[7] Derrida showed himself to be a staunch supporter of the ANC as a liberation movement, a committed proponent of the anti-apartheid cause, and a keen admirer of Mandela.

It is appropriate that Derrida should have been present at the 2010 Coupe du monde in South Africa because it allows for the completion of what might be termed the "African circle" in Derrida's life. It is the 2010 World Cup that links the North African Derrida to South Africa, it is the event that, through the politics that is international sport, connects the Maghreb of Derrida's youth to his commitment to justice at the opposite end of the continent. (It is also what links this author, who played a game or three at Athlone Stadium in the mid-1980s as a dedicated amateur footballer, to

Derrida; one Mediterranean author writing to, writing of, another; one amateur footballer to another.) As Peeters puts it, all of Derrida's politics runs through the experience of his native Algeria: "When he gave his opinion about apartheid and what had followed, or the Israel-Palestine conflict, he would never stop thinking about Algeria, or the Algerian within him, without which the rest would be incomprehensible" (*Derrida*).[8] In the wake of "what had followed" apartheid, in light of how he had done his bit to help make a postapartheid nation possible, it seems only proper that the young footballer from El Biar should be in attendance at the inaugural hosting of an African World Cup. Here, in South Africa, the "Algerian within him," the Algeria without which his politics would have been "incomprehensible," would have been able to enjoy an African return of the sort (the *Coupe du monde* in Africa? Surely not) that was not possible when he was a young boy keeping goal between makeshift posts in El Biar and—who knows?— dreaming of one day wearing the number 1 shirt (reserved for goalkeepers in those days) for Algeria in a World Cup.

As such, seeing the ghost of Jacques Derrida at the 2010 World Cup is, arguably, at least as interesting as spotting the real Derrida, in no small measure because the figure of the ghost is entirely true to the spirit of Derrida's work. As those familiar with his work are well aware, everywhere one turns in the Derrida oeuvre there are ghosts. They are there in the typographically inventive, philosophically challenging *Glas* (How is one to read it? In what order? This page, and then that? This column and then the one on the following page?), where the ghost of Algeria can be discerned, especially as it relates to Derrida's father, Aimé. There are more family ghosts in his exchange with Geoffrey Bennington, *Derridabase*[9]— the ghost of his Jewishness, the always present possibility (threat?) of "circumconfession," his laying claim to a "Christian body," his claims to being an extreme Marrano, the kind of Jew who keeps the secret of his Jewishness so hidden that he forgets entirely that he is Jewish. (An impossibility, but . . . .)

Then there are two more ghosts who are renowned as much for the deep influence they exert on Derrida's thinking as for their controversial roles in National Socialism: Paul de Man (as discussed in Chapter 2 and addressed again here) and Martin Heidegger. In the essay "Typewriter Ribbon," among other moments, Derrida grapples in an intensely self-reflexive way with the difficult and painful effects of his long friendship with de Man (whom Derrida will not abandon, which makes it imperative, as we have seen, for Derrida to right/write to think the complexity of de Man's war journalism). In "Typewriter Ribbon" de Man is thought together with Augustine (himself, of course, an Algerian of sorts)[10] and Jean-Jacques Rousseau, assembling a veritable retinue of ghosts. Derrida's engagement with Heidegger was a life-long undertaking, making Heidegger the most formidable ghost, philosophical adversary, and sounding board in the Derrida oeuvre. To begin with, we might locate that articulation most concentrated in *Of Spirit: Heidegger and the Question,* but it would be more accurate to assert that Heidegger is "phantasmatically" present in almost every Derrida work. (Derrida's very first words in *Of Spirit* are memorable because they invoke ghosts, bringing to mind the consistent presence of spectrality in what seems to be the entirety of the Derridean oeuvre— from *Specters of Marx* to *Cinders.* "I shall speak of ghost [*revenant*], of flame, and of ashes," Derrida promises as he sets about engaging Heidegger.)[11] The opening of the essay, "'Le Parjure,' *Perhaps:* Storytelling and Lying ('abrupt breaches of syntax')," for example, with its playful recalibration of Heidegger's *Was Heißt Denken?* as the question "What Is Called Not Thinking?," indicates Derrida's deep immersion in Heidegger's thought. As always, his subtlety of mind and intense dedication to thinking is what allows Derrida to wrestle simultaneously with Heidegger's philosophy and to stand against Heidegger's infamous 1933 "Rectoral Address" ("The Self-Assertion of the German University") and against Heidegger's refusal, after the war's end, to either acknowledge or apologize for the violence done to a figure such as Paul Celan. (Derrida, of course, explores Celan's work in *Sovereignties in Question: The Poetics of Paul Celan.*)[12]

Derrida, to use a C.L.R. James phrase, saw Heidegger "whole" (cognizant of the philosophical importance, critical of the ties to National Socialism), and as such is able to assert the value of Heidegger as a thinker, a thinker who presents the world as a difficulty to be thought.[13] It is in this warts and all spirit that Derrida engages Heidegger as a thinker, speaks of and, indeed, we might even say, stands in defense of his thinking, because, as Derrida wrote in response to the controversy that followed in the wake of Victor Farías's *Heidegger and Nazism,*[14] "no one has ever been able to reduce the whole of Heidegger's thought to that of some Nazi ideologue" (Peeters).[15] For Derrida, as always, it is the body of "[Heidegger's] thought" that must be apprehended because it amounts, in its totality (in the political complexity of that totality), to so much more than Nazi ideology, as that body of work is haunted by the ghost of National Socialism. Moreover, and here Derrida is fully immersed in the spirit of Heidegger (especially the philosophical priority that Heidegger assigns thinking in *Was Heißt Denken?*), Derrida takes it upon himself to pursue that which Heidegger does not, cannot, and, possibly most importantly, will not, think. This is what it means, in Derrida's sense, to take responsibility for Heidegger's "lack" and then, magnanimously, to cast what Heidegger does not do as something approaching an intellectual gift from Heidegger: "This absence leaves us with a heritage, the *injunction* to think what he did not think" (Peeters).[16]

In the terms of *Was Heißt Denken?*, Derrida is at once the teacher and the student: the teacher who, as Heidegger insists, "must be more capable of being more teachable than the apprentices" (Heidegger).[17] Derrida takes up the position of "teaching us" to "learn" from his "teaching" us what Heidegger did or could not. Derrida invites, or challenges, or provokes us to go where Heidegger so glaringly did not. Rendered idiomatically, we might say that, after Derrida's invitation to think Heidegger, it is only philosophers who go where angels (our better or worse angels, depending) fear to tread.

A different "injunction," then, from the one Derrida issues in relation to Heidegger is brought into play, but an injunction—borrowed from and perhaps, as such, mis-used in *Specters of Marx: The State of the Debt, the Work of Mourning and the New International*—that nevertheless obtains because of how, with deftness, Derrida assigns a privileged place to thinking and, in a moment rich with historical irony, justice. Here Derrida calls for justice, for justice for the dead, for justice in how we think the dead: "To be just: beyond the living present in general—and beyond its simple negative reversal. A spectral moment, a moment that no longer belongs to time, if one understands by this word the modalized presents (past present, actual present: 'now,' future present)" (*Specters of Marx*).[18] It will not do, Derrida knows, to indulge in the simplicity of denunciation or "negative reversal." Such an approach to Heidegger, or any other figure (but Heidegger more than any other figure), would be antithetical to thought and do little to address the "spectral" effects that such a figure casts on time—all time, *Zeit*, as such, as Heidegger does. "To be just" demands nothing less than a thinking "whole," a thinking that is replete with all of the risk attendant to what Derrida names "perilous knowledge (the knowledge of what *remains* always to be thought and thus still *resists* thinking: a trace without alibi, a difference without alibi)" (*Without Alibi*).[19] For Derrida, as for Heidegger, thinking must stand alone: "perilous" and exposed to everything, to its own uncertainty no less than—perhaps before—everything. Nothing, if thinking is allowed this register, can sustain—is able to sustain—thinking other than thinking. Only thinking, preferably of the variety that commits itself to "perilous knowledge," can sustain—that is, guarantee—thinking. As Derrida continues, such an undertaking "can always be paralyzing, to be sure, but it also offers the only chance not to give in to paralysis" (*Without Alibi*).[20] It is only thinking that not only guards against "paralysis" but also accepts this refusal to cede to "paralysis" as nothing other than an opportunity—the "only chance," no less—to think in the face of (the threat, the danger) of "paralysis." To think is to stand, directly and perilously, against the threat that is "paralysis."

Undertaking such a thinking—thinking "whole," thinking under the threat of "paralysis"—is considerable, perhaps best rendered as thinking for everything. It is thinking for everything because it demands thinking a figure's "lack" (the "unthought" is Heidegger's term; for Heidegger the riches of a thinker lie in the "depth" of her or his "unthought"), accounting for a thinker's transgressions (Heidegger's, de Man's), and, most importantly, doing so without ever losing sight of or sacrificing such a thinker's thought. Herein, we might say, lies the true value of the ghost. The real value of a thinker can be measured in terms of the force that the thinker is capable of exerting in response to the (enormous) shadow that the specter (Heidegger, in this case) casts over the thinker's (Derrida) engagement with the spectral intellectual. It is the specter that, properly, ominously, resolutely, without apology, holds all thinking, and, as such, all thinkers who engage the other's work, to account. There can be no argument, then: Derrida is made responsible to his thinking, held to account, gladly, it seems, by the specter of Heidegger, de Man, and Celan, among others.

The Ghostly Force of *Specters of Marx*

To be held responsible by the ghost, precisely because it is a ghost and "belongs to" that moment "beyond the living present," demands that the ghost be addressed, argued with, and resisted, if such a resistance is at all possible. No wonder then that one could add to the list of ghosts Derrida immerses himself in, seemingly infinitely. There is Freud, Lacan, all the ghosts who constitute *The Work of Mourning*, Roland Barthes, Louis Althusser, Louis Marin, Deleuze, Levinas.

The most direct invocation of the ghost, however, is to be found in the very title of the work that is *Specters of Marx*. In this text, ghosts abound, and they would appear to be even more numerous than usual. There is, as already noted, "revenant" King Hamlet (heir to the "revenant" that opens *Of Spirit: Heidegger and the Question*—Heidegger, of course); the king's son, Hamlet, troubled prince of Denmark; and the King as *visor effect*. Then there is Karl Marx of *The Communist Manifesto* and Max Stirner (aka Johann Caspar Schmidt, author of *Der Einzige und sein Eigentum—The Ego and His Own*),[21] a member of that group of young philosophers known as "Die Freien"—more commonly known as the Young Hegelians, a redoubtable presence in the second half of *Specters*. We are, of course, already familiar with that memorable Derrida dedication to the slain South African Communist Party leader Chris Hani: "A man's life, as unique as his death, will always be more than a paradigm and something other than a symbol. And this is precisely what a proper name should always name" (*Specters of Marx*).[22] There is, perhaps in part because of his "untimely" demise (just before the publication of *Specters*), no proper taxonomy, or categorical delimitation, for a ghost such as Chris Hani. The ghost, above all else, demands its own "proper name"—the "ghost of King Hamlet" makes this point amply. The ghost, we might speculate, can come into its proper spectrality only with time. The ghost's ability to haunt the future depends, as it were, on temporality insofar as it matters when the ghost becomes ghostly (it is a matter of time), that figure who disrupts the "modalized presents" that Derrida iterates—"past present, actual present: 'now,' future present." How does one append a "proper name" to the ghost who has just been buried? Name the ghost of the bloodied body when the fate of the nation that is not yet postapartheid South Africa and, as such, we might suggest, simply not yet a nation (hence the importance of Pienaar's "No"), remains so unsettled, so at risk, so fragile against the specter of potential racialized/racist violence? It is for this reason that Hani remains, in so rich a cast of ghosts, motley in its own way, "unique" and somewhat apart—still, as it were, so reminiscent of "life."

It is possible, therefore, that Hani's singular status as ghost—the reason for his coming first after dying last, as it were—turns on his "location" within Derrida's multiple presents. Derrida's dedication locates Hani within the "actual present," while Hani's anti-apartheid politics makes him a figure of the "past present." It is, however, the burden of the "future present" (that messianic imaginary that constitutes the "New International") that Hani is assigned; it is the hope of the "future present," that moment that "writes"—acts, speaks, thinks—for the end of apartheid, that Hani must bear. As such, Hani's ghost—the ghost coming into its spectrality, that is, its (full) political force and effect—stands, in the case of *Specters,* as Derrida's writing of the burden of over-representation.

It is for this reason, among others, that Derrida proposes politics as the experience of being haunted by the "modalities of the present." To be so haunted is to be made responsible to *l'avenir,* to the "to come" that must be struggled for, repeatedly, without the guarantee of arrival. It is, as Derrida recognizes in the notion that we must "begin again, as if for the first time" (always, we would be quite right to add, "as if for the first time one more time"), the very nature of the political to be, as it were, endless. The work of the political is to make new demands, to require new responses—and/ or resistances—of a context that a priori, constitutively, "always, remains open, thus fallible and insufficient" (*Specters of Marx).*[23] The work of the political, how it is we do politics, is necessarily *l'avenir* because it is, as Derrida notes, "fallible and insufficient." That is, it is in the very nature of the political to be constitutively un-able to anticipate every contingency; the political action taken in the "now"—the "actual present"—cannot plan for (and, as such, plan a response for) the effects of its actions, the consequences of its decisions, all or any of which can let loose a series of political possibilities that will demand a potentially new response.[24] To engage (in) the political is to acknowledge the fact of always being "fallible," of always being likely to "get it wrong" despite the best laid political plans; the looming specter of the "insufficient" is, as such, nothing other than the recognition that all politics is conducted on the premise of an encounter with the un-expected and, more tellingly, the unprecedented. (It is among the fundamental principles of politics that one will always get something, this or that, wrong. And "getting it wrong" must be followed by the determination to get it right. And so on, and so on. Once more, and then once more, yet again.) In these terms, to anticipate "fallibility" ("getting it wrong" or "being wrong" are too colloquial but do serve the purpose of conveying the sentiment)[25] and "insufficiency" is the mark of political intelligence, of historical assiduousness, and, as importantly, intellectual stamina. That is, it is the mark of political intelligence to know, to prepare oneself in the knowledge, that more will be required and to acknowledge that (all?—a truly exhausting possibility) actions taken in the "now" will be "insufficient" to the demands of *l'avenir*. In making the case for "infinite responsibility[,] . . . no rest allowed for any form of good conscience," Derrida not only captures the in-exhaustible nature of politics but also, as if to underscore the point, offers no respite from it, not even, as he insists through his wry declarative, "for good conscience" (*Specters of Marx*).[26] There is no end to political responsibility. There is no time for indulging in the demonstration of "good conscience." (By itself, we might say, "good conscience" can do very little. It is, at best, a starting point, but it must never be allowed to function as a terminal political point.) We are never done, as Leon Trotsky was quick to remind us ("permanent revolution"),[27] with politics. It is little wonder, then, that the "fallible and insufficient" constitute, in conjunction with the burden of "infinite responsibility," the very grounds—the first condition, an epistemological primal understanding, if you will—of all political commitment. The injunction to prepare for that which is not yet and, cannot, as such, be known but must nonetheless be expected, the call to act politically, is ceaseless, no matter the enormity of the victory or the catastrophic effects of defeat. In fact, in each case, what is called for is greater responsibility.[28] That is, responsibility as grounded in the willingness not only to act but also to understand what the moment demands, and what it might demand is a "lack of action." As Derrida phrases it, one must "do everything it takes to do nothing right away" (*Without Alibi*).[29] Every political action, and especially that act that demands not acting ("right away"), can achieve its maximum political efficacy only if it is thought, if the moment is subjected to thinking.

In Heidegger's curt phrasing, "it could be that prevailing man has for centuries now acted too much and thought too little" (*Was Heißt Denken?*).[30] What Derrida's call for "political restraint" recognizes is the importance of creating conditions under which it becomes possible to preserve, by holding the self in absolute reserve, the irreplaceable (singularity and) sanctity of the moment: to respond to that precise moment by exercising, so to speak, in a Spartan way, political discipline. That is, to not act—incomparable restraint—is to gesture in Heidegger's direction while holding in Derridean reserve the knowledge that action postponed, as such, is the only possible efficacious political action (in that moment). It takes a lot to do nothing—"right away." This act of doing nothing is, and here again Heidegger must be acknowledged, the greatest tribute to thinking—to thinking the political demands of the moment while "doing nothing," nothing but think.

That is, not only to think but also to do so under the most perilous conditions. That is because, even if Derrida suggests that "you lose nothing by waiting," neither he nor history can underwrite—can sign, to our satisfaction or his/theirs—this injunction, this political advice (*Without Alibi*).[31] There is no guarantee that "doing nothing" will secure the desired outcome; in fact, it is entirely possible that "waiting" can cause you to lose everything, that a struggle can run aground on the beach of inaction. However, this is the risk, this is the political calculus that must be thought, this is the way in which thinking is constitutive of politics because, insufficient as it is, it must decide in favor of "inaction" on the basis of nothing but itself. That is, political thinking at once raises the awful specter of being wrong, of doing incalculable harm, and it raises itself to the level of political trustworthiness—as a measure of political action, inaction as a political action in itself. Thinking that does not trust itself in the moment of greatest political urgency—to resist the urgency to do something and do nothing instead—cannot be said to think, even as it, as needs must, always keeps itself mindful of what it is (not) doing.

"Inventing" the Event

Because of how Derrida provokes us to understand politics, what we are made to think is nothing other than the event. (And, of course, the demands of the effects generated by the event. Politics, as we well know, permits of no imagining of the event to end all events—that is, the "culminating event," which not even a messianic politics promises.) That is, to undertake politics in the knowledge that all action, one's entire political imaginary, is un-prepared for the event as much as the event (the revolution, the overthrow of a regime) is precisely that "outcome" that the political struggle endeavors to achieve. As such, all political action—beginning with the commitment to the cause—is geared toward that moment for which it, this set of (otherwise) deliberate interventions (protests, marches, strikes, violent exchanges, and so on), has established as its ambition, and yet the ways in which that "outcome" (it is always more complex and generative in its demands than is expected) is secured refuses to subscribe to the logic of any political plan. The event (of the political movement, let us say), as such, bears the mark of invention, an invention geared toward revealing that which is extant:

> What I believe I must salute, and be the first able to do so, is an *invention*, the event that consists in *finding*, in altogether inaugural fashion, in *discovering* what no doubt *appeared already to be found there*, seeming to wait analysis, explication, unveiling (the task is not easy and it is not nothing, anything but, it is almost everything) but also in *making exist*, like a singular *oeuvre*, what undeniably, this time, *was not yet there* and what comes about as public and readable existence only at the instant an irreplaceable signature comes to interrupt the continuity of an unveiling discovery, to mark a leap into explication and displace the whole apparatus. (*Without Alibi*)[32]

In Derrida's terms, as much as the event must be "invented," the work of "invention" is the work of making visible, legible, and politically usable (this is what "discovering" does) that which is "already" ready—it lies in wait, "awaiting," respectful of no punctuality except its own—"to be found there." It is here that the work of thinking—"analysis, explication, unveiling (the task is not easy. . . . [I]t is almost everything)"—must take place, must be undertaken with all due care and assiduousness. Furthermore, this task is complicated by the contradictory nature of apprehending the event. On the one hand, the event lays bare what is "already there," and on the other, it is necessary to "make" the event "exist." On the one hand, it is already there, and on the other, Derrida determines it is "not there yet." The event is always, even in the very midst of its unfolding, what is worked toward. The event is the very definition of *l'avenir*.

The value of the contradiction, if that is its proper name, is that the politics of the event is such that it awaits—can be fulfilled, as it were, only through—interruption, through the surging up of the disturbance that underlies and runs through it. The event becomes "public," comes into a "public and readable existence," only at the "instant that an irreplaceable signature"—let us call it the "mark" that the event makes on history (say, the October revolution or the first World Cup hosted on African soil)— "comes to interrupt the continuity of an unveiling discovery." That is, the event becomes fully itself, fully "explicated," only in the moment that it "interrupts" the very process to which it is central. (It is only the event that can, as I have written elsewhere, make of the "pseudo-event"—the Wimbledon tennis championship, the Super Bowl, the Masters golf tourney—an event.)[33] The event can be said to constitute an event only at/in the moment that it disrupts its own coming-into-itself. That moment we might conceive of as the moment of "naming," that moment when the event interrupts itself in order to announce itself. What is more, the effect of this interruption not only serves to draw attention to the event as such; it also constitutes a promise to the future. (Again, here, we have echoes of Trotsky and the struggle to avoid strictures, be they of "National Socialism" or some other constriction imposed on the event.) This promise is to the "continuity" that is the ongoing, ever-revealing discovery of what it is the event "means" or how its effects manifest themselves, how the event might in the short term "take effect": here again, the work of "explication" (thinking) is called for in order to think the "displacement" that will reorganize the "whole apparatus."

The "signature" that is appended to the event is, for this reason, twofold, operating in different—but not necessarily discordant—registers. The first register, let us call it the specific one, is the signature that writes its name as a proper noun (say, the "2010 World Cup," "1917," the "Industrial Revolution," and so on), and the second, which is more important, can be understood as generic—it is the signature that can be discerned in every event, the "mark" imposed on the event that is common to every event. Derrida designates this adequately enough for our purpose: as the act of dislodging the entire "apparatus." The event, as much as it derives its singularity from its particular context, is unthinkable—is disqualified from the status of event, we might say—as event until it has been made to bear the imprimatur of the generic. Until it is like all other events in its "irreplaceable singularity." Every event, then, much as it will find and determine its own signature, its unmistakable articulation, its absolute truth to itself, its capacity to alone establish the schedule of its punctuality, also operates under the force of the generic. The event's singularity (its name, its capacity to make its mark in/on time, and so on) is singular precisely because it is "finite" (not "completed" or "finished" as such, but delimited by its own signature) and as such is open to l'avenir—as much to what is to come as to its own further unveiling of which it knows nothing. The event, as such, is constitutively (conceptually—we are never done thinking the event) insufficient to itself and, as such, fully political in its proper sense. The event is continually open to our intervention, our "invention" of it, yet one more time, if you will; the event, we might say, depends for its political life on our renewing it through invention. That is the demand of politics— to test our capacity for invention.

It is out of this tableaux, politics-sans-end, that Derrida posits the possibility of the "messianic," "messianism without the messiah." Derrida seeks not to return us to the logic of the "Great Man Theory of History" (we have every reason, in this regard, to be suspicious of and impatient with the epic, charismatic, and heroic figure, so central to the political of "phallologocentricism"—giving us grounds sufficient to steer well clear of any advocacy for the "messianic") nor to relieve human beings of their political responsibility. Instead, what Derrida raises is the need to always keep open the possibility of an intervention, an insight or inspiration (a moment of political "genius," so to speak; invention, we can now be sure, is that political requirement that is never far from pressing its cause), an entirely unexpected act—of bravery, otherworldly courage, or stupidity (by the opposition, making it a political "gift" of sorts)—that tilts political fortunes to the side of justice, the ethical, or makes possible the realization of the radical. That is, to conduct politics, to commit to a cause, on the ground that the event is the irrepressible horizon and sustaining "dream" of the political. The ghost, as it were, beckoning to us from the future.

The ghost is the promise that *l'avenir* makes to us. It is, as such, utterly impossible to prepare for either the ghost or the event, and yet this is exactly what must always be kept in mind. The ghost, as it were, is that political force—the specter, such as "Communism"—that keeps us mindful of the event like nothing else ever can. The ghost, this time as the provocation to invention and explication, is what gives us to thinking, and not only for the event. The ghost is, in the most productive sense possible, what haunts our political imaginaries into possibility. It is only by keeping the ghost in mind that we can live with politics as unending hauntology, as the promise of what might be, the promise that promises us the potential of political fulfillment.

The Ghost: A Figure of/for Thought

For Derrida, the "ghost is not just one figure among figures. It is perhaps the hidden figure of all figures" (*Specters of Marx*).[34] The ghost, the "hidden figure," is the figure of thought. The ghost is what gives us to thinking, what, we might say, brings us—sometimes willingly, more often not—to thought. It is because of the ghost that we are able to produce, at the very least, a thinking in excess of the "paradigm" and the "symbol" that "substitutes" for Hani. That is, the "paradigm" requires ("only") a broad, conceptual approach, while the "symbol" raises the prospect of not so much the "abstraction" of the figure as the "emptying out" ("empty symbolism," which is, of course, never—entirely—"empty"); that is, the invocation of the "paradigm" and the "symbol" serves to circumvent, interrupt, or short-circuit the need for thinking. Both the "paradigm" and the "symbol" run counter to Derrida's inscription—his writing—to the ghost Chris Hani and are why, to reiterate, he insists that "one should never speak of the assassination of a man as a figure, not even an exemplary figure in the logic of an emblem, a rhetoric of the flag or of martyrdom" (*Specters of Marx*).[35] The categorical, inscribed everywhere from (within) the logic of "assassination" to the "exemplarity" that attends to, that attaches itself to that violent political fate, to the "emblematic" and the "fictive representation," at once both "audible" and "visible" from the first in the language—"rhetoric"—of patriotism (or in the cause of the sovereignty that is not-yet but is being struggled for) discernible in the waving of the "flag" or in the elegiac phrases intended to honor the deeds of the "martyr."

Through the ghost of Chris Hani, and the proscriptive (and prescriptive) terms that Derrida sets out for how to think the "historic violence of Apartheid," Derrida offers a set of philosophical and political guidelines for how to properly apprehend (that act that makes a confrontation with what is to hand imperative and unavoidable), and comprehend (to come to terms with fully, or as fully as possible), what is at stake in Hani's death—that is, what it is exactly that must be subjected to thinking (*Specters of Marx*).[36] The "rhetoric of the flag or of martyrdom" does nothing to advance our understanding of what the "man" struggled for, nor does it shed light on the political motivations that might have warred within him. To speak of the "man"—Chris Hani—is to think the several registers of his politics: Marxist, proponent of violent struggle, exiled revolutionary, ANC member and yet primarily located within the South African Communist Party, and so on. It is with this caution in mind, his refusal of the paradigmatic and the symbolic, that Derrida calls for a thinking of the name.

Naming the ghost, appending it as a proper name "Chris," "Chris Hani," as the figure of thought, makes imperative the need to always think, think with, think against, think of, think despite, think, even, most especially, for the ghost. Thinking the ghost takes place under the most provisional, uncertain, unforeseeable conditions because the ghost who will address us in our "modalized present" is as likely to come from the past as from the future:

> If he loves justice at least, the "scholar" of the future, the "intellectual" of tomorrow should learn it and from the ghost. He should learn to live by learning not how to make conversation with the ghost but how to talk with him, with her, how to let them speak of how to give them back speech, even if it is in oneself, in the other, in the other in oneself: they are always *there*, specters, even if they do not exist, even if they are no longer, even if they are not yet. (*Specters of Marx*)[37]

For all his declarative uncertainty—"they are always there . . . even if they do not exist"—what Derrida establishes here is more than simply how to think spectrally. He delineates the ghost in its political relation, a matter of no small concern for either Derrida or Marx (or the Communist Hani, for that matter), to the question of the other. (For Derrida, as we know from how he distinguishes his position—in relation to language, in this instance—from Heidegger, it is what "comes from the other" that makes everything [politics, language, thinking itself] possible,[38] and, as we have seen and will see again momentarily, Derrida's position intensifies on the occasion of the political death of the other and when the ghost [the reputation, the intellectual standing] of the disgraced friend is under attack.) It is only through our willingness, our ability, to recognize what "comes from the other" that we are, finally, able to be in the world as subjects capable of imagining and as such struggling for justice and a more equitable world.

We encounter an iteration of a "debt to" and "recognition of" the other most poignantly and under extremely trying conditions in Derrida's defense of de Man after the news of de Man's writing for collaborationist papers broke. (The notion of the debt to death finds its most poetic articulation in *Athens, Still Remains,*[39] where, in the text's first two lines, Derrida confronts us with the phrase: "*Nous nous devons à la mort*" [We owe ourselves to death].)[40] Peeters writes that Derrida "did so out of loyalty to his dead friend and out of concern for justice, giving full scope to his 1984 lectures on the promise which 'has meaning and gravity only with the death of the other'" (*Derrida*).[41] Through this designation, "in the other, in the other in oneself," Derrida offers an iteration of the other whose repetition draws us away from ourselves, even from Marx, and compels us toward the other by making us wary—politically suspicious, cautious about our political motives—of ourselves; through the death of the other, the self is able to derive "meaning and gravity" in/for its own life. (It is also through thinking death, as Derrida argues in *The Gift of Death,* that it becomes possible for the self to understand itself as "responsible" to its "irreplaceable singularity." Writing about death within the context of the "gift of the law," Derrida argues that it is "from the site of death as the place of my irreplaceability, that is, of my singularity, that I feel called to responsibility.")[42] It is only through death that we are, colloquially phrased, able to come into our own; it is only (in the knowledge of death) that we are, equally importantly, able to respond to the "call of responsibility."[43] It is death, and death alone, that makes us fully human, and, seeking to be, to become fully human is precisely what makes us responsible as human beings. In this way, death emerges—announces itself—as the most provocative, life sustaining of ghosts.

Political Advantage, Ghost

How are we to know the ghost? How are we to know the ghost when we
are engaged in the difficult enough project of recognizing the "other in
ourselves?" How do we write and/or speak to the other, both "as other," as
the "other in ourselves," and, as in Shakespeare's *Hamlet,* as "this apparition come" to disturb the peace of these "liegemen to the Dane?"[44] This
"apparition," which, as Bernardo, the soldier guarding Elsinore Castle,
ventures, "looks it not like the king?" when the answer is at once as obvious as the recalcitrant ghost that "stalks away" (it "will not answer"), is so
phantasmatically disruptive of the Danish political (*Hamlet*).[45] It is out of
this sense of political unease, foreboding, and social perturbation that a
nervous Marcellus implores the "scholar" Horatio, the figure of Shakespearean thought entrusted with the work of translating between worlds,
as it were, to undertake the task of inquiry—or the most lopsided act of
interrogation in dramatic history: "Thou art a scholar, speak to it," Marcellus urges (*Hamlet*).[46] "Question it, Horatio," Marcellus goes on to ask his
colleague, all the while knowing that the appearance of the king's ghost
"bodes some strange eruption of our state" (*Hamlet*).[47] What Marcellus,
Bernardo, and Horatio's pursuit of political answers—all of which is given
voice through the urging to "Question it"—reveals more than anything,
however, is not their desire to be enlightened but their more profound
(their very real political) fear. All of these characters know that, in one
way or another, the ghost bodes ill for the present, for the political of contemporary Denmark. (The ghost, in this way, figures as the Derridean secret or, as he might have, as his postcard: it conceals nothing. It merely
iterates or inscribes what is already known. As such, the secret is the most
public of public documents. Anyone, as it were, can "read" it.)[48] Rendered
as such, the more urgent question is certainly not how we speak of ourselves but how are we to speak *to* ourselves about that which it is we know,
that which disturbs our darkest hours despite our "strict and most obser-
vant watch" (*Hamlet*).[49]

The ghost is not only ubiquitous (here, there, everywhere, in every
modality of the present), but also, as Derrida knows, it is possessed of an
unfair advantage. In order to reckon with this political inequity (it cannot
be redressed; things cannot be made equal; the ghost cannot be coun-
tered), Derrida coins his own "Shakespearean term," the "visor effect." The
ghost can be said to hide behind, and as such is protected by (which also
makes the ghost in-visible to us), the visor. In this way, the ghost ensures
that "we do not see who looks at us." This is the power of the visor, Derrida remarks, and what it shares with the mask (from which Derrida distinguishes it in other respects): the "incomparable power, perhaps the

supreme insignia of power: the power to see without being seen" (*Specters of Marx*).[50] The visor, it could be argued, exceeds even Bentham's panopticon.[51] Whereas the panopticon operates at a distance (usually vertically situated, above the observed, not quite visible even though those being surveilled are aware of the panopticon's powers of reconnaissance), the visor is more of a technical apparatus in which Bentham's operational modality is intensified by, so to speak, a Levinasian proximity. (The face-to-face nature of the encounter that must be rendered as a face-to-visor encounter, thereby allowing the ghost to be present without its face being seen. In Foucault's rendering, the king's face is always visible, always looking at us, looking at what it is we are doing or not doing, as the case might be.)[52] What is singular about the visor is how it can be operationalized as a "technical prosthesis, a body foreign to the spectral body that it dresses, dissimulates, and protects, masking even its identity" (*Specters of Marx*),[53] especially the ghostly effect achieved when the deceased but not dead king is able to not so much "mask" his "identity" as to mobilize it to political ends. By casting his identity into doubt (Is it the king? Is it not the king? What does the "apparition" want? In whose name, and with what authority, does it speak?), the ghost of the murdered king can reveal, as we know from that well-rehearsed line (shrouded in doubt and limned with unease though it be), that "something is indeed rotten in the state of Denmark." What is more, the "apparition" can be set in motion, as only a deceased sovereign can, as a force of immense disruption (the ghost can determine the political fate of Hamlet's Denmark) to his erstwhile state through nothing but his spectral return. Politically speaking, the power of the ghost is fatal to not only his enemies but also all the state's citizenry—from the royal house (Claudius the usurper; Gertrude, first widow to/of King Hamlet then Queen again, this time to Claudius, the newly crowned king; Prince Hamlet, uncomfortable with all of his inheritance, because for the prince the throne promises to be nothing other than a chalice poisoned several times over; Ophelia, driven to madness and suicide by the political intrigue that envelops the Danish court and overwhelms her lover; Polonius and Laertes, father and son, each caught in his own web of ambition; and so on) to the military (Bernardo, Horatio, Marcellus) to the lowly grave diggers (tasked with laying Ophelia to rest), all touched by the appearance of the ghost. The afterlife (and artifice) of sovereignty, when it assumes the visage (or the aspect, in Foucault's sense, of the everywhere present king in *Las Meninas*)—or, more dramaturgically phrased, the visor, when it can see without being identified, named—leads, in Shakespeare's rendering, to the dissolution of the state. The fate/fatality of the sovereign, it turns out in *Hamlet,* is nothing less than fatal to the state. If the sovereign "dies" (is murdered) and returns as an "apparition," then the

state too is doomed to die—to come to a bloody end that spans generations and transcends class boundaries.

The Ghost Looks at Us

It is in our direct encounter with the specter, such as Bernardo, Marcellus,
and Horatio experience, that we know we are being looked at but we are at
a loss as to know how we are being observed, what the fate of our being so
"looked at" might be. We cannot know how we are being judged or whether
the ghost deems us trustworthy, considering how the king was betrayed
(murdered and then usurped, both politically and personally) by his brother. The ghost has been made, by force of history, politically discriminating,
and as such it will speak to only those on whom it can rely. The effect of
betrayal (death/assassination) is an extreme, otherworldly judiciousness—
an address to only the trust-worthy, an address that finds its voice only
after several relays, first silent and then increasingly more voluble and politically consequential in its fallout. It follows a fatal sequence: the ghost of
King Hamlet→Bernardo→Marcellus→Horatio →Prince Hamlet, who cannot learn or know how "to be" (*Sein*) in the midst of the chaos that envelops
the state, and so takes his own life.

What the ghost of the king instills, then, is both the importance—irreplaceability—of the name and a deep caution about how the name is
used to address us. At worst, the ghost instills political uncertainty into
the invocation of the name because we cannot (can no longer, after *Hamlet*) be sure of who claims us, who speaks our name, who speaks in our
name, whether or not it is historically or politically proper to invoke the
proper noun—Hani, Marx ("A specter is haunting Europe—the specter of
communism" ["*Ein Gespenst geht um Europa—das Gespenst des Kommunismus*"]),[54] Marx-ism, Friedrich Engels.

The thought of the ghost is, in critical moments, what makes it specifically political, and therefore difficult, for us to inhabit our own body.
That is, the ghost complicates our ability to call ourselves by our own
name, to properly own our own names—that is, to know our names as
properly our own. Our discomfiture with our "own" name derives from the
recognition that the name, our name, much as it is "ours," is among the
very first things given to us, so that we are always the bearers as much as
the creators of our name; it derives from the recognition that we live with
it, live it (etymologically, as much as anything: What is the "meaning" of
my name?), even as we know that we must bear it, if not as a burden (although that too is possible; just reflect for a moment on that parental—
paternal/patriarchal—desire for self-reflection that is audible in the direct transmission of the name: John Smith Jr. or Peter Jones III; which

one is worse or better?), then certainly as the first act of political imposition. We have, as it were, been given no choice in the name that we bear—it has been given to us, a gift that is potentially as much a gift as a poisoned chalice. (As such, there is an unavoidable measure of an a priori, unknowable passivity involved in the name, since we are, for the most part, named, "baptized," in the Christian tradition; we are anointed with the name that we must now take as our "own.") It takes a radical act of self-disruption and self-reinscription (let us say, conversion to another faith and fate, surely) to name the self, and even such an act is circumscribed by the politics of the permissible—axiomatically, the name that designates and inscribes an-other faith is proscribed. (Even in what would seem a "small" change, Derrida's "transition" from "Jacky" to "Jacques Derrida," there is, as he acknowledges, something considerable at stake. It is not only a change from the "familial" "Jacky," what could also be understood as a pet name, a nickname, a naming that designates affection or a preference for the "formal"—"Jacques"—rather than the diminutive. It is, rather, motivated out of the desire to mark his writing. As such, for Derrida writing is always the "event: the coming of the other, in sum, of writing and desire" (*Without Alibi*).[55] Produced under the expectations that attend to writing, that writing portends, the name cannot but be the bearer—"Jacques, not "Jacky," or, as I have argued elsewhere, the process by which "Cassius Marcellus Clay" becomes "Muhammad Ali"[56]—of the event; the name, in its naming, in its appending "meaning" or the desire for meaning to a life, is a priori overdetermined by a politics, a politics over which the party named has no control. This is a struggle with which Derrida is familiar, remarking on the matter in a 2002 interview that testifies to this difficulty: "The name, in a way had to be coined and invented for myself, at the same time unique and iterable. That's what I can do to honour the name.")[57]

It is little wonder, then, that for Derrida so much turns on the body of thought, on the body as em-bodying thought and making thought articulable; the name is what demands and as such makes thought thinkable. "One engenders some ghost by *giving them a body*," he writes, "Not by returning to the living body from which ideas and thoughts have been torn loose, but by incarnating the latter in *another artifactual body, a prosthetic body*, a ghost of spirit, one might say a ghost of the ghost" (*Specters of Marx*).[58] Not only is the "artifactual body," the "prosthetic body, a ghost of spirit," of course, what preoccupies Derrida in thinking "(Derrida's) body"; the "prosthesis" as such is also the focus, as we see momentarily, of his *Le Monolinguisme*. However, what is salient here is the body that Derrida "engenders" as a ghostly provocation and as politico-philosophical/philosophico-political presence but does not address in *Specters*.

It is because of this failure to address the ghost, the ghost of Jacques Derrida, that there can be no question, then, that it is specifically the "ghost" that "gives us the most to think about." As Horatio knows only too well, the specter can be spoken to—"Speake to it Horatio[; t]hou art a scholar. . . . Question it"—only if the ghost can be presumed to have had, and will again have, for that reason, a form, an identifiable, articulable body. (As Derrida asks, "Can one, in order to question it, address oneself to a ghost? To whom? To him?" [*Specters of Marx*].)[59]

Derrida's affection for the ghost is what, he might insist, distinguishes him, in relation to the specter, from Marx. As well as for, as has been noted, Marx's implacable foe (a figure who, as we know, "disgusts" Carl Schmitt), the prototypical nihilist, anarchist, and existentialist extraordinaire Max Stirner. There is something spectrally dangerous for Derrida, dangerous but eminently explicable, about Marx's aversion to ghosts, Marx's desire to, as Derrida phrases it in his reading of *Capital,* make the *Spuk* "vanish . . . dissipate," all in the cause of securing the "end of market production" (*Specters of Marx*).[60] Derrida believes that the co-author of *The Communist Manifesto* is in great danger of being upended—and, of course, apprehended— by ghosts because, in Derrida's lyrical phrasing, "Marx always runs the risk of going after in this way his own ghost." (Uncannily, the Afrikaans word for ghost is *spook,* so that Derrida's *Spuk* would resonate in more than one language, in more than one political timbre, in South Africa.) And yet, as Derrida acknowledges, Marx is by no means exceptional in this regard. In full poetic flow, Derrida pointedly asks a question that ends in declaring (naming, situating) Marx as an "immigrant":

> Is this not our own great problematic constellation of haunting? It has no certain border, but blinks and sparkles behind the proper names of Marx, Freud, and Heidegger: Heidegger who misjudged Freud who misjudged Marx. This is no doubt aleatory. Marx has not yet been received. The subtitle of this address could have been: "Marx—*das Unheimliche.*" Marx remains an immigrant *chez nous,* a glorious, sacred, accursed but still clandestine immigrant as he was all his life. He belongs to a time of disjunction, to that "time out of joint" in which is inaugurated, laboriously, painfully, tragically, a new thinking of borders, a new experience of the house, the home and the economy. (*Specters of Marx*)[61]

Restlessness, deracination, and the difficulty of *wohnen* (dwelling), raised here as the "subtitle" *das Unheimliche* ("the unhomely" or more stringently rendered as "the homeless"), are the political conditions that Derrida raises here in relation to Marx. What is more, Derrida intensifies Marx's alienation by naming him not only an "immigrant" but also a "clandestine" one. That political category of "immigrant" who hides from the authorities, a category that has become, here in the first decades of the twenty-first century, perhaps the most volatile political subject. No other subject raises the question of "belonging" in all areas: the law (What is the legal status of the immigrant?), rights (What rights does the immigrant have, if any? Not even human rights, in its Arendtian formulation?), religion (the immigrant in the West labors under the weight of Islam, Islamic radicalism, Muslim terrorist, all afoot and the cause of violence in London, Paris, Orlando, Brussels, Berlin, and who knows where else), and race/racism (the immigrant is always from an impoverished, undemocratic "there"—Africa, the Middle East, Central America, and so on). That Marx should have foreshadowed this thinking of the "immigrant" is doubtful. What cannot be disputed, however, are the ways Marx and Marxism anticipated exactly just a figure to disrupt the smooth flow and functioning of capital. And yet, of course, also a figure whose precarious political status made it especially vulnerable to the predations of capitalism.

However, while Marx might be an "immigrant" and might be in his "host" country illegally, Derrida insists on retaining Marx's strangeness by arguing against his "domestication"—we must resist the urge to "neutralize him through naturalization" (*Specters of Marx*).[62] Under no circumstances must Marx be rendered as a nineteenth-century *sans papier*, or illegal immigrant, in order to assign him a political label familiar to us, a designation explicable in and to our time.

Above all, Derrida wants to retain Marx's strangeness and, through this, Marx's capacity to continue to haunt us. In this regard, Derrida mobilizes Shakespeare through a phrase beloved by Derrida: the "time is out of joint" (*Hamlet*).[63] In this way, we might say, the failure of two of the major thinkers in nineteenth- and twentieth-century Western philosophy (as I show momentarily), Freud and Heidegger, to properly take Marx's measure augurs well for our thinking of Marx. Because "Marx has not yet been received," because Marx has been misjudged, not once, but at least twice, because Marx is "disjoined" from us and, possibly, from every other time (every other moment in history), Marx becomes (yet again, his staunchest supporters would insist—never for the first time)[64] the mobilizing, disruptive intellectual force that makes possible a thinking of our conjuncture. "Marx has not yet been received" for the simple, and therefore telling, reason that we have not been ready to do the work of receiving him.

In this regard Derrida is not only insistent but—dare one say it?—prescriptive. He is prescriptive because he is impatient with extant engagements with Marx, critiques that Derrida deems basic, "aleatory," and, as such, constitutively insufficient. Nevertheless, if he urges us not to "send

Marx back to the border," a fate to which we might consign both the "immigrant" (who is surely "illegal") and the stranger (presuming, that is, that such a subject cannot be said to conjoin these two political classifications). The Marx that Derrida offers up for our thinking, presents for our consideration, is that "spectrological" Marx who "disjoins"—disarticulates—our entire political imaginary because of their (Marx's and Derrida's, Derrida in the name of Marx) joint call for the "new thinking" and a "new experience" that can be "inaugurated" only by embracing (living fully in) the "time that is out of joint," the time of the "New International." That is, Marx makes everything—from sovereignty (the "border") to the domestic (how it is that we "dwell," Heidegger would say,[65] in "the house, the home") to the ways we experience our late, late capitalist age, to invoke Jameson,[66] (the "economy" subject to thought)—subject in an entirely unprecedented way.

Because we have not yet, in Derrida's estimation, taken the proper measure of Marx, his *Specters* presents us with precisely such an opportunity. *Specters* offer the opportunity (as the various responses to Derrida's text in the collection *Ghostly Demarcations* suggest) that Derrida makes, in his own distinct way, immanently possible and, he would argue, necessary. However, the effect of the ghost is always, no matter who writes the ghost (or who is written by the ghost or is, to risk salaciousness, ridden by the ghost—that is, finds her- or himself [Horatio, Marcellus, just for starters] overwhelmed into helpless action by the ghost), to lead us to other ghosts. Sometimes the ghosts we encounter are those ghosts that we are, in any case, haunted by; (the "original") ghosts, surprisingly, sometimes make us wonder why we did not see—how could we have overlooked it?—the "problematic constellation of haunting" that "blinks and sparkles behind the proper names of Marx, Freud and Heidegger."

"Mirror, Mirror, on the Wall, Who Is the Ghostliest of Us All?"

> What if, to conclude, we floated the idea that . . . Marx himself,
> Marx the liberated ontologist, was a Marrano?[67] A sort of
> clandestine immigrant, a Hispano-Portuguese disguised as a
> German Jew who, we will assume, pretended to have converted
> to Protestantism, and even to be a shade anti-Semitic?
> —JACQUES DERRIDA, "Marx and Sons"

The self is the most terrifying specter of all. The self fears nothing so much as a confrontation with its own spectral "incarnation," the possibility of coming face-to-face with itself. For this reason, it is the specter that is most assiduously (and, deliberately, insofar as it is possible to rigorously avoid the specter of the self) avoided, and therefore the specter that haunts us, all of us, the most relentlessly. The specter of the self will not, as it were, be ignored. King Hamlet, arguably, knows this, which is why he wears his "visor" so defiantly while speaking in his own historic voice. The king seeks to maximize his own (political) capacity not only for haunting the "rotten state" but also because he is guarding against that impossible to (indefinitely) postpone confrontation with the specter that is the most fearsome to all. That moment will present itself to the murdered king when he has to face the specter of the deceased but not-yet-politically "dead" King Hamlet, that King Hamlet whose death has sown such havoc in his old state.

In this regard, the king wants to, as it were, have his ghost and eat it. That is, the king wants to be both heard and seen, as it were, without ever running the risk of apostrophizing himself: turning, pausing (parsing, even), addressing himself, being addressed himself, as and by the imaginary other. Clearly, what the ghost fears most is the capacity of the ghost to haunt itself. The ghost fears itself as the ghost. The king wants to be public without, in the discourse of the spectral, exposing himself to the vulnerabilities that might, to phrase it awkwardly, attach to him as a—no, the—"private" subject of the political. How does the ghost look at or address itself as itself? Would the ghost, as such, require a mirror that, after *Snow White and the Seven Dwarfs,* could help the ghost self-assess? "Mirror, mirror, on the wall, who is the ghostliest of us all?" The logic of power that informs this self-confrontation is rooted in the desire for self-affirmation. The more "ghostly" (or, in Cinderella's case, the more "fair") the subject, the more powerful that subject is.

There is, in this regard, an "implacable *concatenation*" between Derrida's critique of Marx and Stirner, both of whom exhibit their own particular fear of the revolution, and King Hamlet. It is, Derrida writes, "as if they had been frightened by *something* inside themselves" (*Specters of Marx*).[68] By its very invocation, "concatenation" compels a "physical," bodily thinking— not only of the link between (or among) two or more figures but also of a potentially disruptive conceptualization of motion, of what happens when the act of thinking figures (historical bodies) together is undertaken as Derrida does in his concatenating Marx, Freud, and Heidegger. This is because "concatenation," in itself, if not necessarily by itself, stands as an invitation to think against, to produce tension and conflict, and, above all, to provoke in the manner that Derrida advocates in *Without Alibi*: "A provocation is always somewhat 'vocal,' as one might say in English, resolved to make itself heard, sonorous and noisy. The most inventive provocations should not be vocal, but this is difficult to avoid" (*Without Alibi*).[69] Here it seems necessary to adjust Derrida's phrasing in order to fully embrace the kind of political intervention—"invention"—the provocation can achieve: The most inventive provocations should not only be vocal; they must be vocal precisely because such a "noisy sonorousness" is what makes them difficult, if not impossible, to avoid. That is, we must live with and in the discomfiting presence of the provocation; we must live with the relentless "noise" generated by the provocation. In this regard, as Derrida says, the provocation that is the ghost "echoes . . . like a spectral injunction: the order comes down from a place that can be identified neither as a *living present* nor as the pure and simple *absence of someone dead*" ("Marx and Sons").[70] The "ghost" is neither one, "living present," nor the other, the "absence of someone dead," and, for this reason above all others, the ghost, and what it provokes, whom its haunting brings to light, to life, is what must, first and last, last and first, be thought. Not only is the ghost particular (it will not speak to just anybody) and disruptively articulate (when it speaks, it demonstrates the power to disrupt the status quo from top to bottom); it is also noisy. Its presence creates a political cacophony, one that cannot be drowned out; the ghost's noisiness reverberates far and near, loudly so that everyone must hear. And, as such, encounter it. The ghost has taken to the air(waves), sonorously.

Specters is, so conceived, a provocation of the highest political order because it intervenes in a dramatic political upheaval, a political upheaval generated by the ghost who roams across, between, and alternately within both *Hamlet* and *The Communist Manifesto* ("*Ein Gespenst geht um in Europa—das Gespenst des Kommunismus*," as we by now know well the opening line of Marx's *Manifesto*: "A specter is haunting Europe—the specter of communism"): the revolution of the ghost, the revolution by and because of the ghost. Hamlet's Denmark suffers a political collapse because of the ghost; Marx and Engels's Europe, "old Europe," as well as the Europe of the second decade of the twenty-first century, stands on the precipice of massive social disruption because of *das Gespenst,* the ghost that is coming, coming from the someplace other than the "absence of someone dead," someplace what we can only speculatively name "the future." But, of this we can be sure, the ghost will arrive, and, like the event (the event of the ghost, the event made by the ghost), the ghost will follow its own timetable, it will be punctual (only) on its own terms. It will surprise us all. We will be surprised that it has been among us all along. We will be surprised by our own surprise.

The ghost is the author (the technical, writing, motor) of revolutionary history because it "appears to put itself spontaneously into motion, but it also puts others into motion, yes, it puts everything around it into motion, as though 'encourager les autres' (to encourage the others)" (*Specters of Marx*).[71] The ghost, the political force of the ghost, cannot be accounted for;

however, such is the power of the ghost that it sets others, the other, in motion. The ghost is that "something," ineluctable, implacable, im-measurable, and possessed of a radical power. It is within the political that the ghost unleashes history on, we might say, history as such. How could we not live in fear of the ghost? Live always on the lookout for it; live that is, in such a way as to distinguish ourselves from Marx, Freud, and Heidegger, key thinkers in history who, "like everybody, did not begin where [they] ought to have 'been able to begin' (*beginnen können*)—namely, with haunting?" (*Specters of Marx*).[72] Vigilance on our part is called for because the "fault . . . is repeated, we inherit it, we must watch over it" (*Specters of Marx*).[73] All thinking, to risk repetition, to admit to the necessity of repetition, must begin—*muss beginnen*—with the *Spuk*. Here Derrida, following in reluctant Hamlet's footsteps ("O cursed spite, / That ever I was born to set it right"), imposes on us, on himself, responsibility to our inheritance (*Hamlet*).[74] That which history has bequeathed to us "we must watch over." Failing that, we will have failed to begin where we "ought to have begun." It is within our rights to "curse" our fate (to rage against its "cruelty"), but displeasure at the "spitefulness" of history by no means absolves us of the responsibility to "set it right." At the very least, we must begin with that as the first task that history has set before us. It is on these grounds that Derrida develops his respect for Hamlet, the unwilling Prince, who, regardless of his deep desire to be spared this fate (Christological, in its own way: "O my Father, if it be possible, let this cup pass from me" [Matthew]),[75] steels himself sufficiently so that he can summon his own courage enough to command those who are with him to "go together" to confront a nation, a politics, "out of joint."

"Revolution" is the name we have, the conceptual framing, for what Marx and Stirner are "frightened by." But what of Derrida, especially when he proclaims, "Marx had his ghosts, we have ours," in a tone that is at once confident of itself as a pronouncement—since ghosts are everywhere, we are, per force, surrounded and alternately, and by turns, terrified and enlivened by our own—and an invitation to the question: Who, what, is our ghost? Specifically, what is the name of our ghost? ("Capitalism"? "Late-capitalism"? Surely we are done with "neoliberalism"? Or, maybe not. Injustice? The figure of the migrant? The refugee? The immigrant denied rights? Human rights? And so on. O, how many names we have for the ghost. How un-prepared we are for its presentation. How familiar and eminently known to us it will be. How well we know it. "O cursed spite.")

More to the point, however, we have arrived at that juncture where we can no longer delay the question. That is, what is that ghost, that "something" inside of Derrida? What risk does he run of, like Marx, not "going after his own ghost"? (Is such an avoidance even possible? How does one track one's own ghost? Where do you begin to look? A hard look cast inside? Behind us? Or is it right in front of our noses?) And, what is the name of that ghost, a specter capable of asking, as Derrida does, "Who has ever called for the *transformation* of his own theses?" (*Specters of Marx*).[76] We might reply, fully provocative, true to the "pro-vocation" that Derrida issued, that everyone who has "inherited," who has partaken of the gift that is Marx, Freud, and Heidegger (and many others beside), must commit to this act of "transformation." We must then undertake the work of "transforming our own theses" because there can be no tradition of thought without the "call" of transformation. After all, Derrida is as much issuing a call to himself as he is challenging the ways we live in the present-future. Under the sign of this "pro-vocation" (this call, for that which is a "vocation" is a call—to serve, to duty—that must not be ignored), we are made responsible by the ghost, the several ghosts, Derrida not least among them—to think for transformation, to work to "set it right." Interminable iterations of the work of politics, these injunctions to responsibility, give us, as any good *Spuk* would, much to think about.

Algeria

To begin, I will confide in you a feeling. . . . It is the somewhat weary feeling of an old European. More precisely, of someone who, not quite European by birth, since I come from the southern coast of the Mediterranean, considers himself, and more and more so with age, to be a sort of over-acculturated, overcolonized European hybrid.
—JACQUES DERRIDA, *The Other Heading*

He cannot refuse this community at once proposed and imposed.
—JACQUES DERRIDA, *Archive Fever: A Freudian Impression*

We are dealing here not with any "old European." We are dealing here with an "old European," and a "weary" one to boot, who is equivocal about himself as a European. Jacques Derrida, a thinker who posits himself, in an "open secret," as a "Marrano,"[77] who is, moreover, "not quite European by birth." Derrida is therefore not and can never be fully European because he is—as he reminds us both here and, with such poignancy, in *Le Monolinguisme de l'autre*—from somewhere else. He is from somewhere outside of Europe, from El Biar, "from the southern coast of the Mediterranean." But as Derrida remarks of Freud in *Archive Fever,* there is no possibility of a constitutive outside, a way out, an escape route, if you will, from this situatedness within. Both Derrida and Freud (and Marx too, we might add) are Jewish sons from "elsewhere" who are, inextricably, of this "community," Europe, the Christian West, the "community" they cannot "refuse," the "community" that is "imposed" on them and yet also, with a rare intellectual and socio-cultural force, "proposes" itself to them. (In this way, when Derrida titles his response in *Ghostly Demarcations* "Marx and Sons," as if Marx had started a venerable corporation of thinkers, which, of course, he had, it becomes obvious that Derrida is claiming his inheritance as one of Marx's grand-sons, hyper-visible heir at once to the radical tradition Marx inaugurates, an inheritance amplified and intensified by their shared—difficult, since Derrida proposes Marx as a minor "anti-Semite"—relationship to Judaism.)[78] It makes itself "available" to them; "shows" itself (without ever fully revealing itself) to them; and, in the process, draws Freud, Derrida, and Marx toward this "community" as if they belong there, as if they belong there and nowhere else.

No wonder then that Derrida is by turns affirming and interrogative of his Europeanness. Little wonder that Derrida declares himself "of" this "community," but it is a declaration that always bears within it (and, as such, betrays) the trace of something other than belonging:

> I am European, I am no doubt a European intellectual, and I like to recall this, I like to recall this to myself, and why would I deny it? In the name of what? But I am not, nor do I feel, European *in every part*, that is, European through and through. By which I mean, by which I wish to say, or *must* say: I do not want to be and must not be European through and through, European *in every part*. Being a part, belonging as "fully a part," should be incompatible with belonging "in every part." My cultural identity, that in the name of which I speak, is not only European, it is not identical to itself, and I am not "cultural" through and through, "cultural" in every part.[79]

Of one thing, then, we can pronounce ourselves certain: Jacques Derrida is not only a European. (As such, it will not do to designate Derrida an "overcolonized hybrid." What it means to be "overcolonized" begs thinking, raising at it does the Fanonian[80] specter of immersion beyond immersion, expressing as it does the other's desire for an impossible absorption into the colonizer's mode of being that, finally, must leave the colonized, perhaps like the Marrano, entirely "forgetful" of himself. In this regard, the invocation of "overcolonized" serves to return us, against our will, to thinking colonization as if we had not yet begun to understand it as a cultural and psychological imposition; the work of Fanon, Ngugi wa Thiong'o, and Paulo Freire, inter alia, notwithstanding. "Overcolonized" hints, more than anything, at a violence previously unthinkable; something on the order of death, or suicide.) Derrida is not, then, except in "part," and by no means an insignificant "part," a French intellectual.

Instead he is, in his own terms, definitively, *"more than one/no more one"*—"more than" a French or European intellectual, and, he could not, beyond a certain point, beyond a certain "crisis," so to speak, could "no more" be a French intellectual (*Specters of Marx*).[81] Excess and negation, "more than/no longer able to be," this is the to and fro, back and forth, belonging/un-belonging[82] condition of Derrida's being an intellectual who inclines toward Europe. Also, this condition of excess and negation is marked by a joining that is also a splitting, a dividing—against his will— into France and Algeria, into Algiers and Paris, into Judaism and Catholicism, into colonialism and its aftermath. In all of this, Derrida is deeply entangled, deeply immersed, because of, despite, himself, despite whatever he may or may not desire.

As such, because he is "more than one" and "no more one," rendering impossible at once "hybridity" and any opening to a radical singularity, Derrida draws us toward something other—toward the other, and, what then cannot be avoided, toward himself. Appropriately, then, this thinking Derrida as "more than one/no more one" can begin only "inside" the one, as it were. It must begin with that "something" inside of him that is, that is not, "more than one," that place that will no longer permit "oneness"—"no more one." To be "more than one" admits to the ghostly specter of what is "more than" (>), "more than" being a European intellectual or being French, an idea that so clearly haunts some of his later work.

Above all else, as becomes increasingly clear over the course of his life, Derrida is haunted by his relation to the "southern coast of the Mediterranean." In a word, as he has already told us (both explicitly and discretely), Derrida is haunted by Algeria. As in *Le Monolinguisme*, arguably the apogeic text in this regard, where, it is possible to say, it is the Arab philosopher Abdelkebir Khatibi, to whom Derrida can be said to be writing *Le Monolinguisme*, who haunts the Sephardic Jew at odds with, struggling with, his Jewishness—"Marrano?"—yet who cannot claim, without hesitation, hurt, prevarication (how are we to trust Derrida's self-representation? we are called upon to call Derrida into question), and equivocation, that which has been "imposed" on and which has been "proposed" to him.

To be "more than one/no more one" requires that the intellectual who does not "feel, European, in every part, European through and through," who does not "want to be European through and through," undertake the politics of double duty. The intellectual has to be the Algerian and the French together, by turns, occasionally claiming one without foreswearing the other—"I am. . . . [W]hy would I want to deny it?" There is no room, there is no time (or there is only the briefest moment, itself a troubling circumscription) for denial because the lack of time and space (critical as they may be) is overwhelmed by the other question that is before us, the one that presents itself more obviously and urgently before us. Namely, how does one do double duty? What is the cost of this task, these tasks? To do double duty is to understand the act of thought, of politics, as doing things not twice, which is to say in their repetition, but in their difference, as the politics of *différance*.

Double duty demands that the intellectual undertake first one task, one articulation, and then the other; the time in between tasks that is the aporia where the impossible work of thinking both at the same time, in the same philosophical gesture, must be undertaken, again and again. It is because of the responsibility that "double duty" imposes that the question of translation becomes the matter of the measure. That is, the measure of thought, the measure of what Derrida names the "cultural," the "part" that is not in "every part." "I feel European *among other things*," Derrida says. "Would this be, in this very declaration, to be more or less European? Both, no doubt. Let the consequences be drawn from this. It is up to the others, in any case, and up to me *among them*, to decide" (*Specters of Marx*).[83] In order to decide about himself, Derrida insists that he can do this work only if he is, as he is and continues to be (the ghost), "among" us—a spectral figure of thought, so reminiscent of the Christ who walks among the disciples after his Resurrection, a stranger fully conversant with the terms of the discourse, the stranger who has not only experienced violence but also endured it in the name of the largest possible political cause (human salvation), now tasked with the responsibility of explicating how he has fulfilled the Father's promise.

To do double duty is to feel now "more" and then "less European," which implies, of course, although this is never articulated in any measure, that Derrida must feel, in moments, "more Algerian" than he does French. This does not mean, of course, that he feels in that same moment "less" French because he does not exclude such an unthinkable possibility—"Both, no doubt." That is the demand of double duty: now more but not necessarily less; now one, then the other; now here and then there—doing two things, imagining the prospect of doing them once rather than twice (at once), and yet knowing that it must done again after it has been done; not repeating them but doing them again, one after the other, doing them together, in their inexhaustible, richly uncertain singularity inscribed in the answer "Both, no doubt." This is, of course, a philosophical formulation itself already overdetermined by "doubt." Little wonder, then, that, in the spirit of "more than one/no more one," Derrida expresses a preference for the collective decision in response to the "quantitative question"—"more or less," always a matter of the measure—the thinking of the place of duty, the thinking of where we think from, what we think toward, what we turn from, what is apostrophized and conjured up in this act of thinking. To think, in this way, is to know thinking as, in the spirit of Heidegger, "*Nur Denken kann Denken denken*," "only thinking can think thinking."

Thinking, in this instance, takes place under a very particular conjuncture, a historic time. This moment is marked because for a moment, just a tantalizing moment, Derrida cedes his right to the decision; at least, for a moment, he appears to. "It is up to the others," he says. They (that is, "we"), and they ("we") alone, for that moment, we presume, can decide his status, can determine who he is—that is, where he is from, what constitutes his primary alliances. And yet, as we well know and have already noted, he cedes nothing to us. He retains, deliberately, the power—the considerable political power—of the phantasmatic. He is, rendering himself in the third person, "among them," so evocative of Jesus-the-Christ, in-visible among those who should but do not recognize him.

In this way, Derrida (deliberately? as the haunting from the present-future?) disorients and dislocates us so that we are not sure as to the attribution of that inescapable "something." Should we attribute it to here or there? Nonetheless, for a moment, there is the possibility of suspending the onerous responsibility of doing double duty. Even as we think the particularity of double duty, think its particular demands, what remains—the part that remains unmovable, the part that presents itself to us, inexhaustible, for thinking—is Derrida's haunting caution. It is caution that is not only audible in the dedication to Hani, but also equally, if not more so, evocative of Marx: "A man's life, as unique as his death, will always be more than a paradigm and something other than a symbol." Double duty is always less onerous than we imagine it to be, and, in the same measure, more demanding than we can even begin to know. How, as Derrida asks, can or should we prepare to "receive Marx?" (Again, the befuddled, unknowing disciples, ignorant, in truth, present themselves to us, to us for thinking.)

Lingering, present in the form of the urgent concatenation, the ghosts (Marx, Derrida, Hani, et al.) haunt double duty as an inheritance (itself, of course, demanding nothing less than consummate responsibility). Disconcerting is the issue of how we understand the relationship of location to elocution: "the singularity of a place of speech, of a place of experience, and of a link of filiation, places and links from which alone one may address oneself to the ghost" (*Specters of Marx*).[84] What double duty compels us to "address" is not only the "ghost," or the "ghost" in the self, but, again, the imperative for self-addressing—to face the self, unflinchingly. At stake is not only how the self speaks itself, or speaks to itself, but also how the self speaks, historically, ethically, we might say, from a, or the, place—that conjuncture—where the self situates itself. Again, as we need no reminding, there is Marcellus, haunting us as he haunts Derrida, and Shakespeare haunts Marx: "Question it, Horatio, thou art a scholar."

Our question, our inheritance, from Marcellus and, much more pertinently, from *Specters of Marx,* is the question of Algeria. We must begin there; that is the only way we can understand how Derrida undertakes the "transformation of his theses." That is the ghost Derrida bequeathed us in his declaration: "Marx had his ghosts, we have ours."

It is the question of Algeria, that is, if we allow ourselves the right to situate ourselves within the "ours" that is the ghost of Algeria. Not ours alone, clearly, it is Derrida's first, we might say, but ours nonetheless: the Derridean gift to all Algerians, inherited from Khatibi the Moroccan and Augustine, the Bishop of Hippo—the Derridean gift to all of Africa, to all of African thinking, to the anticolonial project, and those *états voyous* who took the place of France, Britain, Spain, Germany, Belgium, and so on. It is our act of apostrophizing and conjuration, of making, for the sake of the ghost, "Algeria" a sacred name, the name for the *Spuk* that is "Jacques Derrida," was "Jacky Derrida." We are following the trace, following it because we are, as it were, in this regard taking Derrida at his word when he says—because he says—that the "name of the one who disappeared must have gotten inscribed someplace else" (*Specters of Marx*).[85] The primary inscription of the "name" could be "inscribed" anywhere; it is very possibly everywhere—that is, were we able to locate its trace, its "cinders," as Derrida argues elsewhere.[86] However, we are, in no small measure because of Derrida's "Dedication" to Chris Hani and his deep imbrication in Shakespeare's *Hamlet* (*Hamlet* as an act of conjuration), able to trace our tracing for the name to, as our response to Derrida's pro-vocation, before all else, our thinking of *Specters of Marx.*

With no fear of contradiction, we can assert that because of *Specters of Marx* Algeria has not "disappeared," or, to phrase the matter in the more violent discourse of the *Guerra sucia*, it has not "been disappeared." (In the iconography of *Cinders,* we might say that it has returned to us as the "erection of the pyramid," that Algeria, figured as a "pyramid," has been called on to "guard" the life of the ghost of Derrida.) Furthermore, we are confident that, conjuration or no, "Algeria" has not assumed an unrecognizable, asymptomatic form, and, even if it has, we would have no trouble recognizing its new form, the new guise it has assumed through Derrida's "construction." And no, Algeria has not been made ghostly, but, again, even if it has, it has become a *Spuk* in order to haunt us, to haunt Derrida in death, into the search for "someplace else." Algeria has, quite simply, been apostrophized—it is being addressed as though it were not present. However, Algeria's not being present does not, because of the political force of the ghost, because of Algeria as a ghostly force, as a force made out of that indestructible force named hauntology, mean that it is absent. It is addressed as the spectral presence of that which is purportedly, but always only nominally, absent.

To this end, it becomes necessary that we, like the "old European," turn to face the "southern coast of the Mediterranean" and then declare both that moniker and that geopolitical locale insufficient. Recalling, calling upon, that spirit we might name "Hani-Marx," "Marx-Hani-Derrida," we must be alert to the insufficiencies of that memorable dedication: "more than a paradigm and something other than a symbol. And this is precisely what a proper name should always name."

In the name of the ghost, this is, as Derrida says, what we "must do." We must name Algeria so that we might "put others in motion, as though 'encourager les autres,'" so that we might release the ghost of Algeria into, or for, our thinking of *Specters of Marx*. Specifically, we must know our thinking of this haunting text (the hauntology of Karl Marx and Chris Hani) as the act of Derridean double duty. As such, the responsibility that attends double duty raises a plethora of questions, ghosts of the most interrogative genus, in truth. Among these it would be necessary to ask if, since Derrida has determined that it is "up to the others" (a claim that we have challenged), would it be proper then to suggest that it is only the Algerians who can decide if Derrida is a fellow Algerian? If so, what kind of "Algerian" would he be? (Would he best be understood, as I have argued elsewhere, not as an "Algerian" per se, not as an "Algerian" of the postcolonial variety but, instead, as a "Nostalgerian?" Such a designation, as I make clear in a previous work, means that it is impossible to think Derrida's relationship to "Algeria"—it matters not whether it is under the conditions of colonialism or postcolonialism or locked in internecine wars driven by dictatorial tendencies or a certain brand of Islamic radicalism—without centralizing its, and Derrida's, relationship to France, beginning, of course, with both a structural critique and a more directly personal one; that is, one must acknowledge the long-lasting effects of the 1940 revocation of the 1870 Decree of Crémieux, which disenfranchised Algerian Jews, and how that led to Derrida's untimely expulsion in 1942 from the Lycée Ben Aknoun.)[87] Is Derrida the "Algerian," the "Nostalgerian" sui generis, and if so, would it still be possible for him to stand with other Algerians, or must he, a priori, now and into perpetuity, be indomitably other to his native land that is/not his *terre natale*? If he commits (which he cannot) to "Algeria," what kind of "Algeria" would that be? What kind of *l'Algérie de l'esprit* would that conjure up? What kind of use might Derrida have for such an Algeria? What kind of use would we have for such a Derrida?

Nevertheless, should he offer such a commitment before the act of double duty occurs; can he be counted among them, those he left (but never left, never abandoned) so many decades ago? In any case, we know that the moment of abdication, maybe even a disingenuous abjection, submitting to the judgment of the other, however allusive and full of political prospect and portent it may be, constitutes but a moment—it too shall pass; it passes away; it is always passing away. It has already passed; it will never pass away.

It is not, except for that moment (and, again, we have good reason to quibble with Derrida here), only "up to the others" to decide. Derrida wrests the power of the decision back, not by disenfranchising the other but by locating himself, in the act of double duty, now with the other (the other could, can no longer, decide by him- or herself alone; the other is always in the process of negotiating her or his status—enfranchised; disenfranchised; in the midst of losing or gaining or regaining this status; Algerian or French; Algerian or not; immigrant or not; *pied-noir* or not) and then simply as part of the broader social decision-making process: "me, among them." Is "me" the reinscription of the name of the *desaparecidos*? Is "me," surely it cannot be, a metonym for "Algeria"? The symptomatic longing for a state beyond the suffocating and oppressive nation-state? (The state—of being—that Marx and Engels promise?) For France? Again, surely not? Again, why not? Must "every part" have a "proper name"? Or is "me, among them," following as it does "it is up to the others," the most demonstrable act of double duty? The act of double duty that rises out of the possibility of infinite division and relentless, invigorating concatenation? The unjoined link? The un-breakable bond, so strong, so utterly vulnerable to the weak force that is "Nostalgeria"?

Or, perhaps, just maybe, Derrida opens up the opportunity for a signal rendering of double duty. That is, we are invited to join him (duty halved, duty shared, duty intensified through and through because of its—now—shared nature), to join him in the spirit of the constitutive insufficiency (of self) that he delineates in *Without Alibi: "I like feeling interpreted beyond what I wrote. Interpreted, that is, at once exposed and given to be read . . . a gift come from a place where, despite certain appearances, I will never have been capable of going [me rendre] myself."*[88] Derrida openings himself to what it is that is "beyond" him, that which lies on the "other side" of his grasp— that which has taken up residence (dare one say it?) "beyond" his thinking. Because of Derrida or because of what Derrida cannot do, does not want to do (?), knows not how to do, "I will never have been capable of going myself"; he not only makes it possible for us to "join" him in the execution of his "duties" but, in fact, also raises the possibility—one that is surely too tempting to resist, however foolish and overwhelming such a project might be, to say nothing of the kind of work it would entail—of us exceeding, doing what he cannot, going beyond him. In order, of course, that we "expose" what he suspects might be there but cannot—yet—wrap his arms around and, in so doing, we might become "joint" thinkers in the project(s) that he values and, in so doing, possibly enable projects beyond Derrida's ken. (Is this how we restore the time to itself so that it is now no longer "out of joint"? Derrida senses this, especially in regard to his understanding of how we write and what that writing might yield. Remarking on the ways in which "resistance" might be figured, Derrida argues that it is "resistance" as such "*that . . . perhaps . . . gives tension to writing: dispersing, dividing, decentering, delegating* [legare] *and simultaneously gathering, collecting, but also choosing, electing, selecting, thus again dividing, privileging* [legere]" (*Without Alibi*).[89] Because of writing, Derrida at once throws things open, a little wildly, a little breathlessly, "dispersing, dividing," but also calls for a recalibration, a reconstitution of this "writing." It is as if we were being asked to reassemble an archive ("gathering, collecting"), all the while careful of Derrida's critique of the "fever" that the "archive" inspires, the archive just now thrown wide open for us to rustle through without constraint but always knowing that restraint (a kind of Foucaultian "discipline") is, a priori, required. And then, most importantly, Derrida assigns the work of discrimination. Out of what has been "gathered and collected" the work of deciding begins: "electing, selecting," "privileging," all of which means that not all materials contained in the archive have equal value or are of equal value for the archive being assembled. We are called on, in conjunction with Derrida, to judge what is in the archive, and, having judged, we must account for discrimination. The archive is what makes us responsible to and for our "privilege," for, we might say, the "privilege" of doing double duty. Who could have, at first blush, have imagined double duty as just such a "privilege"?

Writing, hesitation, translation, discipline, discrimination, this is how one does double duty. Always in the knowledge, now more than ever (having accepted, insofar as we able to decide on our joining this venture-in-process), that there is the condition of writing determined by the logic of "more than one"/"no more one": Europe/Africa, Algeria/France/"Nostalgeria," old Europe/new Europe, colonizer/colonized, "not quite European/from the southern coast of the Mediterranean," and, finally, Marx's ghost, Derrida's ghost, and our ghost, all, simultaneously, in motion. Disruptive, pleasurable, provocative, elemental, in motion, in search of rest, of a place to think—all the while knowing that every other condition is as amenable to thinking as being at rest. All this, moreover, demands the work of nothing less than "writing." We have, as it were, no "alibi"—having been made aware of the demands of double duty—for not "writing."

"I Think I Saw Jacques Derrida at the World Cup"

> Regarding new forms of a withering or rather a reinscription, a re-delimitation of the State in a space that it no longer dominates and that moreover is never dominated by itself.
> —JACQUES DERRIDA, *Specters of Marx*

> They are labelled, a number is sewn on their backs as if they were playing on a soccer team the night of the big final beneath the lights, from Ghost No. 1 to Ghost No. 10. Only one of them would be missing, one may well wonder which one it is.
> — JACQUES DERRIDA, *Specters of Marx*

> Will I dare to say that my desire had a place, its place, between this call and this risk?
> — JACQUES DERRIDA, *Cinders*

I think I saw Jacques Derrida at the World Cup in South Africa. The World Cup, historic, the first on African soil. More specifically, a World Cup on South African soil. Chris Hani's soil. Hani, lest we forget, was assassinated on April 10, 1993, by Polish immigrant Janusz Waluś, just before he could make this his way to watch a football match that Easter Saturday (the most unarguable day of death, the day between the Crucifixion and the Resurrection in the Christian calendar—a day that falls in the holiest week in Christianity) afternoon. I think, I am sure, I saw Jacques Derrida at the World Cup. He was wearing the green jersey of Algeria. I am sure, I think, that I saw Jacques Derrida, at the World Cup. He was draped in the French tricolor of Les Bleus. "Labeled," "sewn on his back," I can almost guarantee you, was emblazoned the number "10." Above it, the letters spelled a Berber name, not Sephardic, like Derrida's, but still it seemed recognizable. It played easily on the ear and on the eye. It read "Zidane." The ghost, from the 2006 World Cup, a Frenchman whose family had come from the Kabyle, now playing for France. Zidane, known as "Zizou," the French captain, the very best that France had to offer. Zinedine Zidane, the best African footballer, ever? Who would quibble with that? Zidane, the best African footballer ever, born in Marseille?

And then there were the seventeen players that France, we might say, "offered" Algeria. Seventeen of the twenty-three players on the Algerian team were born in France—French youth internationals such as Habib Belaid, Ryad Boudebouz, Mohammed Chakhouri, now representing the Renards du Désert. Like Zidane, these players had been born in France, had been, for the most part, groomed in the French youth system. Unlike Derrida, born and raised in Algeria, these players "inherited" Algeria from

their parents. It required a special dispensation from the world's governing body in football, Fédération Internationale de Football Association
(FIFA), to allow these seventeen players to "represent" Algeria. To do double duty: born in Europe, wearing the colors of the Renards du Désert,
"French," "Algerian," "among other things." Like Derrida, most of them
spoke no Arabic, to say nothing of those who might trace their roots to the
Berbers, to the Berber language. Like Zidane.

They returned to France, to live and play "here," in Europe, again, and
not "there," the Maghreb, after the World Cup. "There," where many of
them had never been, thrust into a language not their own. Translation
through repetition: Is football ever, truly, a shared language? How could it
not be? How does one address the teammate from "there," the place of the
other? In what language? It mattered, it mattered not enough because
"there" had reached out, wrested these seventeen "Frenchmen" (dare one
call them that?) from "here." Seventeen Frenchmen, Frenchmen in "part
only," presented with the chance to play at the World Cup, to do double
duty. Who knew how powerful the call, the address to the self from that
ghostly place, the "southern coast of the Mediterranean," could be? How
could they have known what articulation, what precise language, their "desire" would assume? What "risk(s)," if any, did they envisage? Was the "call"
more powerful, the call to play at the *Coupe du monde*, more alluring than
the "risk"? The "risk" of not knowing "who" it is exactly they were playing
for? (Let us not speak of "representation" as such. That we will take up on
another day. But, shortly, we return to it. The matter cannot be avoided
entirely.) Long before these seventeen players did duty for the green of
Algeria, Derrida knew the force, the temptation, the inherent presence—
for the past-present, for the future-present—of that call. As *Cinders* attests,
Derrida knew the indestructibility of that call. He knew its persistence, and
warmed to that persistence. In the persistence of that call he heard the
faint, but never extinguished, embers (to mix metaphors) of that call.

What will "dominate" that which is incapable of dominating itself?
The first answer would, of course, be neo-colonialism, buttressed by quasi-
indictments about (sporting) *Gastarbeiters* (or, worse, the seventeen are
simply footballing "mercenaries," eager to play at the World Cup but unwilling to declare allegiance to the "State" of Algeria), but such an account
does not take into consideration the force of double duty.

Instead, it might be proposed that things should proceed, as Derrida
suggests in *Specters,* by a question. We might ask what happens to the
"State" that is inscribed, again, by that outside itself that is, has never
been, fully apart from it? If de-limitation is the "natural" condition of the
nation (here we recall Derrida's insistence on borders and "sovereignty"),

is it possible to ever imagine unimpugnable membership? Is im-proper membership the only politically ethical way in which to belong to, or represent, for that matter, the nation? Does all representation, in its very impossibility, emerge from that other shore, as both Derrida and Jacques Rancière (*On the Shores of Politics*)[90] have argued? Is representation, like the "spirit of the revolution," *"fantastic and anachronistic through and through?"* (*Specters of Marx*).[91] The seventeen Algerian-Frenchmen (both, neither—all at once?—always caught "between the call and the risk") make the nation non-contemporaneous with itself, in terms, it should be stressed, other than the temporal. What these seventeen figures, "spectral" to both France and Algeria (made "invisible" and superfluous to the French nation through their exclusion from the French *Coupe du monde* team, temporary sojourners in Algerian colors, "ghosting" into town, as it were, for the purposes of football—What did it feel like to be such a ghost, so real a ghost, to live for a moment as the ghost of your parents, or grand-parents', making?), make legible through this process is that of the nation doubled out, out-wards, upon itself, even as it, in the same act, dutifully re-turns to, turns back into, itself. But, never, needless to say, as itself, as what it was. The nation transformed by the act of double duty. "Algerian" names, French in part, Renards du Désert for a moment. When the time for the national anthem is called, do they have to suppress a rote turn to the words (the world) of "La Marseillaise"? Do they even know the words to either national anthem?

What the "representation" of these seventeen players marks is, as Derrida says, "new forms of a withering or rather a reinscription . . . of the State." At the World Cup, where the very idea of representation turns on the "State," the act of double duty reveals how the "State," before the world, at the World Cup, operates under the ghostly conditions of "de-limitation": the State functions from within a "space that it no longer dominates and that moreover is never dominated by itself." The State, the States, as we should properly say, lives under the terms of haunting:

> A regenerating reviviscence of the past, of the spirit, of the spirit of the past from which one inherits . . . so assimilating of the inheritance and of the "spirits of the past" that is none other than the life of forgetting, life as forgetting itself. And the forgetting of the maternal in order to make the spirit live in oneself. (*Specters of Marx*)[92]

No one, as Belaid, Boudebouz, and Chakhouri found out, forgets the "maternal," forgets the "spirit of the past from which one inherits." To wit, *l'Algérie de l'esprit*. In one form or another, in some lesser or greater measure, the "spirit" of Algeria lives in Derrida and his seventeen "compatriots"; to live, to love "life as forgetting itself" is, of course, to understand how one lives a life of not forgetting, to understand how to live in the impossible desire of achieving a full appreciation of and for the inheritance. If we cannot ever know how to live in the full complexity of our inheritance, then doing double duty demands, in the act of its doing, of its being done, that we, at the very least, struggle toward such a comprehension. After all, who among us, as Derrida reminds us repeatedly, can forget the spirit of the mother? Of our mother as she reaches out from that southern coast, especially as she offers us the prospect, so seductively inscribed on/in that green jersey, of seeing "Boudebouz" on that jersey, the opportunity to play in the "big final beneath the lights" of an African World Cup? (Only an amateur footballer, in all likelihood an enthusiastic but not very talented one, could grasp the joy of such a prospect: to "play," for a few spectators, in the "big final beneath the lights." Derrida, clearly, keen footballer that is he reputed to have been in his youth, understands this "dream come true" in its entirety.) What else did Derrida inherit from Algeria, in addition to the gift of *le monolinguisme*? What did he not inherit from Algeria? Is "forgetting the maternal" the first, most enduring trace of the non-anthropological self? Is that the very trace of deconstruction? What Algeria, in standing as the "forgetting of the maternal," gives us back, as we do our double duty, is the possibility of reclaiming a name that we had not thought with the precision and the requisite difficulty it deserved. Such is the dedication of the mother that she, in the spirit of Chris Hani and Jacques Derrida, knows "precisely what a proper name should always name."

As a footballer, Derrida knows that it matters that the jersey (which, in the era of Derrida and many others, including me, used to be numbered 1 through 11, from the goalkeeper, who wears "1," to the striker—or left wing, in the very old days—who wears "11," the doubling of the "1," as it were, but now the game has changed and players are free to choose their own numbers) bear the proper name. I know now that I was wrong about Derrida and his jersey. It was Zidane who was wearing that number 10 jersey. Derrida was at the World Cup doing, as he is in *Specters of Marx*, double duty. It is Jacques Derrida, from the "southern coast," who is the missing player; it is he who is wearing number 11—"11," "eleven"; it is the very sign (in football) of double duty: "1" and "1." Again, and again, the "1" is called to duty—not once, but once and then again, and again: "1," and "I," the "I" constituted twice in the "erection" of the "1." Double duty: another name for the burden of over-representation.

We can now be sure that when Derrida, in the tone of a New Testament scribe, warns us, "Only one of them would be missing[;] one may well wonder which one it is," he has identified for us—allowed us to iden- tify—the missing player (Song of Solomon).[93] It was him. (It was Toni Morrison, expert in hauntology, author of *Song of Solomon* and *Beloved*: "Dearly Beloved, we are gathered here today"; Beloved, the daughter who is sacrificed, who haunts, who returns; Beloved, sacrificed to the Ohio River; Beloved returned, in a flood of water, to Sethe on Bluestone Road. If Sethe were a footballer, she would, without doubt, have shared number 11 with Derrida.) It was Derrida who was "completing," in the act of dou- ble duty, Algeria, "completing" Algeria from France, completing, we won- der, his own re-turn to Algeria (?). ("Competing" for both Algeria and France, "competing," by turns, for one against the other: the internecine strife that is at the very core of double duty.) It was Derrida's ghost, all seventeen of them, multiplied by seventeen (or, perhaps, after *Specters*, should we say eighteen, now that we can officially announce Derrida as a member of the squad?), "there is *more than one* of them and they are het- erogeneous," that made Algeria a team, if not a (sovereign political) whole (*Specters of Marx*).[94]

Seventeen players born in France representing Algeria is nothing other than the act of "prosthetic synthesis" (*Specters of Marx*).[95] The Alge- rian team for the 2010 World Cup was constructed out of the "de-limited State." This team was constituted through ideological force, a clear indica- tion of the "withered State." Algeria's World Cup squad was a "prostheti- cally synthetic" unit made into a squad and then selected into a team of eleven. In so doing, the Renards du Désert ("craftily"?—dare one say?— these Renards du Désert) achieved a signal political feat, a "*unique* linking, a historical concatenation without example" (*Without Alibi*).[96] By appropri- ating the French for Algeria, by appropriating them for Algeria without demanding that they be—be-come—"citizens," nationals of the first order, the 2010 Algerian World Cup team can be said to have, and the vio- lence of the phrasing here is deliberate, forced the (French, Algerian; Al- gerian, French; French-Algerian; Franco-Algerian) other out of a (again, the litany of names can be said to "concatenate without example") self that can be properly reckoned with only as a double-duty self. A self that, like Derrida and Chakhouri, knows, lives the burden of over-representa- tion—as a double duty without political end.

Seventeen out of twenty-three, a significant, overwhelming majority, constitutes nothing if not an act of philosophical violence against the "de- limited State." This squad of footballers was made by putting the body of the others onto the self (to the point where one is in-distinguishable from the other, which means, of course, that the distinction must, again and again, without resolution, be argued for), the body of the revenant nation.

That is, the nation that has, just for a moment that is the interregnum between qualifying for and playing in the World Cup, turned its attention
away from those whom it was, just now, appropriating, incorporating (and,
yes, possibly excluding—were the "Algerian" players available for selection,
native born and bred, citizens, fully, not good enough, not adequate to
meet, to represent, the desires of the [Algerian] nation?), and addressing
and speaks, instead, to the dead through its appropriation of the seventeen. Through them it turns to face the ghost of imperialism (not, assuredly) "past," the ghostly seventeen, the "present-future" seventeen, who
moreover now function as a critical resource for—dare one say it?—the
(Algerian) nation's exhausted (or insufficient, at least in terms of football
talent) cultural resources. (As such, in the terms of Marx's critique of capital, the seventeen [eighteen?, an argument extended in the "Afterword,"
where Derrida is posited as an "Algerian philosopher"] can be said to be
"productive" for Algeria because, in the future, should their French-born
children display any football—or sport in general—talent, they would, in
their turn, be eligible to represent Algeria. The ghost of Algeria, of French
Algeria, doubling its "value," potentially, to Algeria. Not once, as we are free
to speculate, but, potentially, several times over.) Much, we might say, to
return us to the specter of Zidane (hero in the French *Coupe du monde* victory in 1998; villain, to phrase it kindly, after his *coup de boule* in 2006),[97]
like the Algerians—and those from other far-flung colonies—who have
constituted the French team for almost two decades now. Might Derrida
one day be "returned" to Algeria? Or is that missing the point because the
work of "making" Derrida, in full recognition of the difficulty of such a
thinking, has been done, already been done, by *Specters of Marx* and *Le
Monolinguisme?* Is that the answer delivered by "our ghost"? Is this the
apostrophization, this irrepressibly absent presence, of *Specters*? Is this the
ghost, so richly endowed in, and with, thought that Derrida bequeaths to
us, again and again?

But, while such a claim can assuredly be made, and is being made here,
the bodies of the seventeen double-duty players, the apostrophization of
Algeria, and the ghostly political critique of *Specters of Marx* make it clear
that the present-future has been usurped by the present-past. Yesterday,
it would seem, has taken the place of today. Because forgetting is remem-
bering, "one must forget will have been indispensable. One must pass
through the pre-inheritance, even if it is to parody it, in order to appropriate the life of a new language or make the revolution" (*Specters of Marx*).[98]
Seventeen out of twenty-three French in Algeria, Frenchmen, of a certain
sort, representing Algeria, does that not, even beyond the Algerian World
Cup squad, point to an unarguable "indispensablity"? The "southern coast

of the Mediterranean" has, as it were, come to Europe to claim itself after which it will re-enter Europe and then, perhaps, re-situate itself, for a moment, or longer, who knows?, again in Algeria—in Algeria from France, from Europe. Will the act of double duty make the "Desert Fox" players, and Derrida, more or less Algerian? We already know that Derrida, and these seventeen, are both more and less European. Is this a "parody," a culturally arresting one (it required new football laws to enable it), of colonialism? What is our name for it? Reverse neo-colonialism? Or is it simply another instance of Europe and Algeria engaging the difficulty of making a "new language" for inheritance? (Does reverse neo-colonialism not strike one as an abject term? Is this not a political indictment shorn of efficacy because it is already too exhausted, too familiar? Hackneyed in the extreme?) The demands on the "new language" in which, with which, out of which, a "revolution" will be made are, in advance (this is its "pre-inheritance"), onerous. But, that is the responsibility that attends to the "revolution," is it not?

Because of the act of double duty, it is now possible to think, in the same gesture, only beyond (Algerian) ontology (after all, who can now be said to count as an Algerian?) and beyond the history of French imperialism—old Europe, new Europe; it hardly matters. It is no longer tenable, after the event of *Specters of Marx* and the seventeen, to declare, with any political confidence, about the continuing consequences of Europe in Algeria or about how Algeria has reshaped Europe. Those declarations contain, of course, a measure of truth, but it is by no means the end of the matter. What is "Algeria," Derrida's and the seventeen others' Algeria anyway, but the haunted act of doing, time after time, addressing the self again and again to the "revivified past" and *l'avenir*, double duty? We can have no doubts now about the ghost, the ghost of *Specters of Marx* we must now claim as ours, the ghost that we have questioned in our non-/apostrophized speaking to it. Above all else, the ghost is the figure of the politically indispensable.

I could not, for the sake of thinking, be happier that I encountered, or imagined that I encountered, the ghost of Jacques Derrida at the 2010 World Cup in South Africa. I am moved because the simple act of imagining an encounter with the ghost has demanded, very much in the spirit of Derrida, that we, as he says, undertake the work of a hauntological politics. It is necessary, according to Derrida, to "transform the paralysis [we know well how the ghost, seeing it or imagining seeing the specter, can lay us low; can leave us speechless; can cause us to be, like Marcellus, without a language] into aporia, to break a path for myself, I tried, gropingly, to find my voice" (*Without Alibi*).[99] What seeing Jacques Derrida at the 2010

Coupe du monde made imperative was the need to find a "voice," "my voice," one in which I too could learn to address the ghost.

And, as is proper when one acknowledges the desire to speak to, to be heard by, to engage with, to exchange thoughts with, thinkings with, the ghost, one knows that it is absolutely necessary to prepare for the prospect—the inevitable demand that comes from the future—of not only "double duty," as such, but also triple and quadruple and . . . duty, to be performed many times over. And then again. When one commits to addressing the ghost, one must do so under the condition that one knows that it is very likely that one will unleash into public view, into thinking, not one or even many iterations of a single ghost (as *Hamlet* teaches us), but, as is far more likely, we are opening ourselves up to numberless ghosts. Some of which we will be familiar with, others, well, not so much.

The ghost, before all else, as our "interpretation" of Derrida as ghost makes evident, will compel—or encourage, or urge—us to, with prompting, through hauntology, again, go "beyond." To go "beyond" and, in so doing, "expose" ourselves to thinkings well beyond our imaginings or expectations. That is the gift of the ghost, a gift that demands that we follow lines at once both vertiginous and direct, both circuitous and straight, that is the gift of thinking. Of thinking through the ghost, of never being released from the responsibility of thinking because of the ghost.

That is our debt to the ghost that Derrida, in *Specters* perhaps more than anywhere else, urges us to, through our "writing," to never resist. It would be futile, as Marcellus, Horatio, Claudius, and, of course, Hamlet, know, to resist the ghost. We have no reason to. We are better off, much better off, making as full an acquaintance with the ghost as possible. Make our acquaintance with the ghost as Marx and Derrida so willingly, and so thrillingly, do.

Let us welcome the specter. It will do us good. It would, in any case, do us no good to ignore or resist it. One must, in this spirit, write for nothing so much as the ghost. We can never be sure as to whether or not the ghost will reply, nor can we know what the ghost will conjure up. And, like Marcellus, Horatio, and Hamlet, we can never know when the ghost will present itself to us. Just like that, entirely unexpected.

One minute you're going about your business watching a World Cup game in Cape Town and the next you're running into Jacques Derrida—or a ghostly form of Jacques Derrida that is in-distinguishable from Jacques Derrida. In fact, it is entirely possible that the politico-philosophical force of the ghost of Jacques Derrida exceeds the politico-philosophical thought of Jacques Derrida himself. The force of ghostly thought, no doubt, can be attributed to the other ghosts that the ghost of Jacques Derrida gathers to himself (and so bequeaths to us) and then sets loose. Ghosts with familiar names, but names that all are overburdened with the history of hauntology. So, to this end, let us begin again, as if for the first time, as if we have done nothing yet, to address the ghosts that haunt Jacques Derrida. Let us begin with a short itinerary for our *voyage l'hauntologie*. For now "Algeria," "Vichy France," "Khatibi," and, by no means least, the force that is *le monolinguisme* will suffice.

And yet we know full well that this itinerary will not suffice. After all, our *voyage l'hauntologie* might have begun and ended with Derrida, but in between—"between the call" issued by Derrida and the "risk" it required to address the proliferating ghosts (How could there be so many of them? One after the other, and then still more)—we wound our way through Jackie Robinson (the other "Jackie" to "our" "Jacky"), François Pienaar, and Nelson Mandela. And there too we found plenty of ghosts afoot: U.S. racism, apartheid, the event of the expletive, and the event made by negation.

French, Afrikaans, English. These ghosts, each of them, rigorously, determinedly monolingual.

And yet, each of them could be addressed properly only through philosophy, race, and sport. Maybe all ghosts secretly desire to be athletes. Maybe every ghost is, in fact, an athlete of sorts, an athlete who plays for "Team Hauntology"—What colors, whose colors, would they wear? And so, regardless of whether Derrida loves football, Robinson excels at baseball, and Pienaar is a World Cup winner, all the ghosts that they loose speak some iteration, eminently resistant to translation but full of echoes, resonances, and evocations, that makes each of their struggles with *le monolinguisme* audible, if not explicable, to each other.

Not surprising, then, that it is precisely their individual monolingualisms—their struggles against it, within it—that compel them to share *voyage l'hauntologie*.

It is a strength, not an impediment, to speak only one language, to speak that language that is not your own. Derrida, Robinson, and Pienaar each refuse the constraints—imposed by history, racism, colonialism, anti-Semitism, apartheid, and so on—of *le monolinguisme* and speak, through Derrida, to and among their ghostly selves.

If we listen carefully, we can hear Derrida, Pienaar, Robinson, and Mandela in conversation with . . . Heidegger, Deleuze, Butler, Jameson, Nancy. . . . If we stop for a minute and pay attention, we can hear them, one after the other, in chorus and harmony with all the others, rising to a philosophical cacophony of the most tempered variety. But still, unquestionably, audible. Each individually, and in concert, they declare:

"I have only one language; how glad I am that it is not mine."

"Look what this *le monolinguisme* has made me think."

"I have only one language; how glad I am that it is not mine."

"What a debt I owe, gladly, to *le monolinguisme*."

And then they quietly retire, to talk among themselves, as ghosts are prone to do. Or so we are told, since we can only guess at their conversational habits and philosophical predilections.

Notes

INTRODUCTION

1. Benoît Peeters, *Derrida: A Biography,* trans. Andrew Brown (Malden, MA: Polity Press, 2013), 117.

2. Jacques Derrida, *Monolingualism of the Other; Or, the Prosthetics of Origin,* translated by Patrick Mensah (Stanford, CA: Stanford University Press, 1998), 1.

3. In this regard Julia Kristeva's work has a great deal to say, and, what is more, the question of how the foreigner lives in the diaspora is one that Kristeva takes up in a range of registers. In *Revolt, She Said,* Kristeva strikes, predictably, a more conversational tone in her critiques of 1968, psychoanalysis, French nationalism—among others—and how this affects the "foreigner" (*Revolt, She Said: An Interview with Philippe Petit,* translated by Brian O'Keefe [Los Angeles: Semiotext(e), 2002]). In *Strangers to Ourselves,* Kristeva achieves what can almost be described as a lyricism as she addresses, through Albert Camus, the relation between the foreigner and happiness: "Can one be a foreigner and be happy? The foreigner calls forth a new idea of happiness" (*Strangers to Ourselves,* translated by Leon S. Roudiez [New York: Columbia University Press, 1991], 4).

4. Acts 20:35, in *The New Oxford Annotated Bible,* edited by Michael D. Coogan (New York: Oxford University Press, 2010).

5. Stanley Cavell, *A Pitch of Philosophy: Autobiographical Exercises* (Cambridge, MA: Harvard University Press, 1994), viii.

6. Ibid.

7. Ibid.

8. Ibid.

9. To any scholar of cultural studies the very notion of the "ordinary" evokes Raymond Williams's famous essay "Culture Is Ordinary," in which Williams not only asserts the everydayness of culture but also makes a strong argument—on

which much cultural studies work would build—for the importance, the life-sustaining quality, of working-class culture. (In Raymond Williams, *Resources of Hope: Culture, Democracy, Socialism* [London: Verso, 1989], 3–14.)

10. See Grant Farred, *In Motion, At Rest: The Event of the Athletic Body* (Minneapolis: University of Minnesota Press, 2013). The "Introduction" to *In Motion, At Rest*, specifically but by no means exclusively, undertakes the work of theorizing "the event" in sport.

11. Cavell, *A Pitch of Philosophy*.

12. Eduardo Galeano, *Football in Sun and Shadow*, translated by Mark Fried (London: Fourth Estate, 1977). To my mind, this is one of the three great books on sport. The others are C.L.R. James's *Beyond a Boundary* (New York: Pantheon Books, 1983) and Roger Kahn's *The Boys of Summer* (New York: First Perennial Classics, 2000).

13. Claude Lévesque, "That Incredible Terrible Thing Which Was Not," in *The Ear of the Other: Otobiography, Transference, Translation*, by Jacques Derrida, edited by Christie McDonald, translated by Peggy Kamuf (Lincoln: University of Nebraska Press, 1988), 75.

14. See Jacques Derrida, "Otobiographies: The Teaching of Nietzsche and the Politics of the Proper Name," in *The Ear of the Other*.

15. William Shakespeare, *Othello*, edited by Kim F. Hall (Boston: Bedford/St. Martin's, 2007), act 1, sc. 3.

16. William Shakespeare, *Hamlet*, edited by Harold Jenkins (New York: Methuen, 1982), act 1, sc. 1.

17. William Shakespeare, *Twelfth Night*, edited by Collin Symes (London: Collins, 1974), act 1, sc. 1.

18. Ibid.

19. Edmund Husserl, *The Crisis of European Sciences and Transcendental Phenomenology*, translated by David Carr (Evanston, IL: Northwestern University Press, 1970), 379.

20. After reading the New Testament in his twenties, in 1886, the Czech-born Husserl had himself baptized into the Lutheran Church.

21. Derrida, *Monolingualism of the Other*, 16.

22. Kristeva, *Revolt, She Said*, 19.

23. In her critique of 1968, Kristeva develops a theory of political action that is deeply committed to "revolt." Borrowing from Arendt and Sartre, Kristeva argues that "revolt is indispensable, both to psychic life, and to the bonds that make society hang together, as long it remains a live force and resists accommodations" (ibid., 38). The revolt, cast in Kristeva's uncompromising terms (it "resists accommodation"), is the most vital and necessary element of political life. Without revolt, the polis is doomed to inertia and *unspeakable compromise*.

24. *Love in Two Languages* (*Amour bilingue—Bilingual Love*) uses a love story between a French woman and an Arab man (from the Maghreb) to meditate on the inscrutability and untranslatability of language (Abdelkebir Khatibi, *Love in Two Languages*, translated by Richard Howard [Minneapolis: University of Minnesota Press, 1990]). It is through Khatibi, because of his novel, we might say, that Derrida is able to think his own relation to Algeria, the French language that is not his, and, most pointedly, it enables Derrida to muse/mourn the Ara-

bic that was never his. But, because it never came to be his, this language whose claim on him he ignored, resisted, could not countenance is what haunts him into writing *Le Monolinguisme*. That is what Derrida, writing in relation to Paul Celan, calls the *"Geheimnis der Bergegnung*, the secret of the encounter in Celan and the whole poetico-political problematic of *Unheimlich*, the *Abgrund*, the *Urgrund* and the *Abgrund"* (Jacques Derrida, *The Beast and the Sovereign*, vol. 1, translated by Geoffrey Bennington [Chicago: University of Chicago Press, 2009], 309). All of the *-grund* terms, in one way or another, turn on the issue of "ground," and *Unheimlich*, of course, signals the experience of being "unhomed"—*Abgrund* speaks of the "abyss/chasm" in Celan's work. Through Derrida's invocation of Celan, it becomes possible to understand the significance of thinking *Grund*—the "ground" of Derrida's *Denken*—to *Le Monolinguisme*. Importantly, Derrida insists that all and any "ground or a foundation, they too risk being deconstructible" so that we remain vigilant about attending to the possibility (the necessity, we might say) of undoing that very "concept"—land, territory, paradigm, and so on—from which we work, that on which we "ground" ourselves (Derrida, *Beast and the Sovereign*, 310). Saliently, in his extended work on Celan, Derrida writes of the *"But*: after a blank the mark of a long silence, the time [*le temps*] of a meditation through which the preceding question makes its way. It leaves the trace of an affirmation, against which arises, at least to complicate it, a second affirmation" (Jacques Derrida, *Sovereignties in Question: The Poetics of Paul Celan*, edited by Thomas Dutoit and Outi Pasanen [New York: Fordham University Press, 2005], 7). In his opening discussion about circumcision, which "takes place only one time [*une fois*]," Derrida argues that "dating calls for some form of return," another way in which the singularity—*une fois*—of Algeria must be accounted for, "returned to," by Derrida (Derrida, *Sovereignties in Question*, 2).

25. Derrida, *Monolingualism of the Other*, 19.

26. The issue of "relation," of what is "between" (various) figures, is one I take up in my forthcoming book, *Entre-nous: Between the World (Cup) and me* (Durham, NC: Duke University Press), a book that is in many ways a companion piece to *The Burden of Over-representation*.

27. Jacques Derrida, *Cinders*, translated by Ned Lukacher (Minneapolis: University of Minnesota Press, 2014).

28. W.E.B. Du Bois, *The Souls of Black Folk* (New York: Bedford Books, 1997), 102. Poetically, Du Bois goes on to intensify his immersion in modernity: "Across the color line I move arm in arm with Balzac and Dumas. . . . I summon Aristotle and Aurelius and what soul I will, and they come all graciously with no scorn or condescension" (ibid.).

29. Giorgio Agamben is a figure whom Derrida takes to task for his lack of intellectual assiduity in volume 1 of *The Beast and the Sovereign*. See "Lecture 12," in which Derrida is relentless in his critique, formulating that line so memorable for the scathing attack it inscribes: "poor Foucault! He never had such a cruel admirer" (33C).

30. Giorgio Agamben, *Homer Sacer: Sovereign Power and Bare Life*, translated by Daniel Heller-Zoaren (Stanford, CA: Stanford University Press, 1998), 29.

31. Derrida, *Monolingualism of the Other*, 30.

32. Ibid., 73.

33. Ibid., 2.

34. Ibid., 30.

35. Jacques Derrida, *Specters of Marx: The State of the Debt, the Work of Mourning, and the New International*, translated by Peggy Kamuf (New York: Routledge, 1994), 153. Derrida makes this claim in his discussion about the "visor effect" as part of a broader critique about capital and automation. "The automaton," in Derrida's view, "mimes the living" (ibid.).

36. In "The Apparition of the Inapparent: The Phenomenological 'Conjuring Trick,'" the final chapter in *Specters*, Derrida's meditation on the ghost, mourning, and Marx offers a series of insights that are evocative for this reflection on the "idiom" and the "life-death" that is at its core. Derrida, it would seem, is already, in his work on Marx, writing toward the ghost/s that are, that have long, been calling (to) him, ghosts that—of this we can be sure—already know, have long since known, his name. In *Specters* we can already "see" (sense) the extent to which the ghosts have taken hold of him, have taken over his thinking. To this end, Derrida muses (as if mourning comes from the future, as if we have always been mourning), "One then mourns for the ghosts in which one had already expropriated oneself" (Derrida, *Specters of Marx*, 131)—that is, as if the ghosts "had already" extracted that which is valuable, that which is of (political) worth, from the self. In this sense, "one mourns" for that which has been given to and taken by the ghosts. The key distinction between Derrida and Heidegger, as it relates to life and Being, is that for Heidegger all Being leads toward death, while Derrida asserts the power of life-in-death. Derrida invokes this inextricability of life and death but extends his argument by suggesting that life and death as such anteriorize life-death. Derrida writes, "And this question would be a question of life or death, the question of life-death, before being a question of Being, of essence, or of existence. It would open onto a dimension of irreducible *sur*-vival or *surviving* [survivance] and onto Being and some opposition between living and dying" (Derrida, *Specters of Marx*, 147). Derrida, however, does more than anteriorize life-death to Being. He asserts a distinction by calling for "some opposition between living and dying" (ibid.). We must no longer be bound by either Heidegger's "being toward death" or Derrida's "life-in-death" but must work toward explicating, as fully as we can, what the terms of the "opposition" might be and how they operate. What kind of work is it, finally, that Derrida's opposition makes possible? What kind of effects might it produce?

37. Jacques Derrida, *Learning to Live Finally: The Last Interview*, translated by Pascale-Anne Brault and Michael Naas (Hoboken, NJ: Melville House Publishing, 2007), 38.

38. Ibid., 47.

39. Jean Birnbaum, "Bearing Loss: Derrida as a Child," introduction to ibid., 13.

40. Ibid.

41. Derrida, *Specters of Marx*, 16.

42. Here it is helpful to think about the ways Derrida posits the secret, and how it functions as a technical apparatus, in *The Post Card: From Socrates to Freud and Beyond* (Jacques Derrida, *The Post Card: From Socrates to Freud and Beyond*, translated by Alan Bass [Chicago: University of Chicago Press, 1987]). The secret, to offer a working synopsis of Derrida's argument, is like the postcard in that it

reads like an "open letter" that anyone can read. However, the postcard as such is also a communiqué of the most intimate and personal nature, so that whatever is read, other than by the addressee, will, invariably, constitute only a partial explication of what is intended. The secret, then, is inherently open, and intensely not.

43. Derrida, *Monolingualism of the Other*, 73.

44. As we later see in relation to Robinson, the notion of "friend" and "enemy" are not only fluid but also inflected with a politics of sincerity, so to speak, as well as a politics that veers suspiciously in the direction of expedience. At the most crude and material level, we could ask: Was Branch Rickey, the Brooklyn Dodgers owner who signed Robinson, promoted him to Major League Baseball, and then sought to provide advice, as well as strictures, for how to negotiate his role as the pioneering black player, motivated as much by principle, that of equality and justice for all—as by expedience—his recognition that the Negro Leagues were ripe for the picking and that by signing Robinson he was getting a jump on other clubs in Major League Baseball (MLB)? It seems difficult, at least in the account of some critics, to detect Rickey's "true" motives, but as a result the distinction between "friend" and "enemy" becomes increasingly harder to sustain. As much, that is, as that in-distinction has historic consequences: the integration of MLB.

45. Racially cast, this is precisely the time of the African subject in modernity. Incarnate in that movement is often a brutal process of desubjectivization, the political attack on the subject, the violences done to the subject, and the thinking of a resubjectivization—the making of a subject that bears within itself the very history of its own overcoming, its own to come. Resubjectivization is founded on the imagining of a new political, so that contemporaneous with it is the trace of desubjectivization: the trace of something else, that which is left after the correspondence between these two modes of political being, home and the diaspora, colonialism and postcolonialism, has been disrupted, if not sundered.

46. Derrida, *Learning to Live Finally*, 36.

47. Arthur Nortje, "Dogsbody Half-Breed," in *Dead Roots* (London: Heinemann, 1973), 105.

48. Friedrich Nietzsche, *Twilight of the Idols*, edited by Michael Tanner, Translated by R. J. Hollingdale (Westminster: Penguin Classics, 1990).

49. Here I am, of course, referencing Du Bois's opening meditation in *The Souls of Black Folk* about what he calls the "real question: "How does it feel to be a problem?" (Du Bois, *Souls*, 37).

50. Ibid., 39. It is this strife that produces in the "Negro" (to remain felicitous to Du Bois's terms) his "twoness,—an American, a Negro; two souls, two thoughts, two unreconciled strivings; two warring ideals in one dark body, whose dogged strength alone keeps it from being torn asunder" (ibid., 38). These qualities, of which "dogged strength" might be the most important (the struggle to simply stay alive, to confront the demands of "double consciousness" while only rarely affording the Negro self the luxury of flinching, retaining a sense of self in the face of violence of both the physical and the psychological variety), speak to the condition that Derrida delineates in *Le Monolinguisme*: "two unreconciled strivings," "warring" in "one dark body." What "dogged strength" it must take for the philosopher from El Biar to give "equal" importance to these "two [competing] thoughts," to give, we might say, at least some "time" to Arabic, to not be overwhelmed—how

does one do this? How does one stand against this?—by the sheer force of French, this language that is not "his."

51. Derrida, *Specters of Marx,* 175.

52. In a word, this is precisely the project of *Ghostly Demarcations,* in which Derrida's *Specters* is taken up in a symposium by Jacques Derrida et al. (*Ghostly Demarcations: A Symposium on Jacques Derrida's* Specters of Marx, edited by Michael Sprinker [New York: Verso, 2008]).

53. Derrida, *Specters of Marx,* 176.

54. See *Webster's Unabridged Dictionary* (New York: Random House, 2001).

55. Ibid.

56. In *Webster's* the distinction between "conversation" and "talking" is by no means absolute. In fact, much as we routinely use "talking" and "conversing" (as well as "speaking," of course) interchangeably, *Webster's* definitions do not allow for an easy separation of one from the other. For the purposes of elucidating and intensifying the difference between these two practices, for the sake of animating the Derridean distinction, the focus in this discussion is on those definitions in *Webster's* where the difference is most stark.

57. Quoted in Derrida, *Specters of Marx,* 174; original emphasis.

58. Martin Heidegger, *Being and Time,* translated by Joan Stambaugh (New York: State University of New York Press, 1996), 34.

CHAPTER 1

1. Michel Foucault, *The Use of Pleasure,* vol. 2 of *The History of Sexuality,* translated by Robert Hurley (New York: Vintage Books, 1990), 6.

2. After a few short weeks, the Pirates players abandoned the helmets (which were cumbersome, resembling those used in the mining industry) while in the field, establishing a tradition of wearing helmets only while at bat, which has become standard in baseball.

3. The waiting period for eligibility into the Hall of Fame is five years, but the voters for the Hall (accredited journalists) decided not to enforce this statute because of the tragic circumstances surrounding Clemente's death. Clemente, who had a history of doing charity work in the off-season, died on December 31, 1972, flying on a mission to deliver aid to Managua, Nicaragua, after an earthquake had struck the city eight days earlier. Clemente, aboard a plane that was notorious for its history of safety and crew issues, died in a crash off the coast of his native Puerto Rico. Clemente was aboard because, as a result of corruption on the part of the Somoza regime, the three previous relief efforts had not seen aid delivered to the people affected.

4. There is a statue of Clemente at the entrance to the Pirate's PNC stadium.

5. Rickey tried to sign outfielder Monte Irvin of the Newark Eagles, but Eagles owner Effa Manley refused to let Irvin leave without compensation. Rickey duly curtailed his pursuit of Irvin, who would sign for the New York Giants (later the San Francisco Giants) in 1949 for $5,000.

6. Don Newcombe is one of only two baseball players to have won the Rookie of the Year, the Cy Young Award (for the best pitcher in either the American or the

National League; Newcombe won the 1956 National League Cy Young, the year the Cy Young was inaugurated), and the Most Valuable Player. (The other player who accomplished this feat was Detroit Tigers pitcher Justin Verlander.) Newcombe was also the first African American pitcher to win twenty games in a season. Also, among Newcombe's accomplishments was his prowess as a pinch hitter, a true rarity for a pitcher. Over his career, which began with the Dodgers in Brooklyn and then in Los Angeles, after which he played for the Cincinnati Reds and the Cleveland Indians, Newcombe batted .271, with fifteen home runs.

7. Roger Kahn, *The Boys of Summer* (New York: First Perennial Classics, 2000), 94.

8. In order to facilitate ("ease") Robinson's passage into the International League, Rickey also signed African American pitchers Roy Partlow and John Wright to the Royals. Neither lasted very long (a fate that has been the subject of some debate, including the contention that the Royals manager, Clay Hopper, a native of Mississippi, could have made more use of Wright or been more patient with Partlow); by mid-July 1946 Robinson was the only black player in the International League.

9. Paige is deemed by many to be the greatest pitcher that the game of baseball has ever known. Born in 1906, he pitched his last professional game in June 1966. He made the All-Star game for the St. Louis Browns in both 1952 and 1953.

10. In his autobiography, *Maybe I'll Pitch Forever*, "Satchel" Paige expresses a barely stifled resentment that it was Robinson instead of him who broke the "color barrier" (Satchel Paige and David Lipman, *Maybe I'll Pitch Forever: A Great Baseball Player Tells the Hilarious Story behind the Legend* [Lincoln: University of Nebraska Press, 1993]). Paige was, of course, in a difficult position, because he was Robinson's teammate in Kansas City and he harbored the ambition of pitching in the "Majors." In fact, some players in the Negro Leagues thought that Robinson had been chosen because he was a "lesser" player and if he had failed in the "Majors," the possibility of desegregating MLB fully would have been dealt a severe blow. Robinson's burden of representation, then, was borne with a measure of ill will, resentment, and jealousy from within his "own" ranks. He was, then, in more ways than one, entirely "on his own."

11. As quoted in Jules Tygiel, *Baseball's Great Experiment: Jackie Robinson and His Legacy* (New York: Oxford University Press, 1993), 137.

12. Rickey considered recruiting Irvin, who had been offered a football scholarship at the University of Michigan, which he could not accept because he could not afford the cost of relocating to Ann Arbor. Irvin attended Lincoln University, where he also played football. Rickey, however, did not think that Irvin was "ready" for the particular challenges that MLB would present to its first African American player.

13. Michael G. Long, ed., *Beyond Home Plate: Jackie Robinson on Life after Baseball* (Syracuse, NY: Syracuse University Press, 2013), xxv.

14. Kahn, *The Boys of Summer*, 44.

15. Jacques Derrida, *The Animal That Therefore I Am*, translated by David Wills (New York: Fordham University Press, 2008), 27.

16. Ibid.

17. Ibid., 27; original emphasis.

18. In *Was Heißt Denken?* Martin Heidegger reflects on the importance of "not-acting," so to speak, when he offers his critique of "thought." In remarking on the "course of events [that] demand that man should act," that "what is lacking, then, is action, not thought," Heidegger undoes this political propensity—this seemingly always operative political injunction, to act, to take action—by suggesting that "it could be that prevailing man has for centuries now acted too much and thought too little" (Martin Heidegger, *Was Heißt Denken?*, translated by Fred D. Wieck and J. Glenn Gray (New York: Harper and Row, 1968), 4.

19. Karl Marx, "The Eighteenth Brumaire of Louis Bonaparte," *The Marx-Engels Reader*, edited by Robert C. Tucker (New York: W. W. Norton, 1978), 595.

20. Jacques Derrida, *Cinders*, translated by Ned Lukacher (Minneapolis: University of Minnesota Press, 2014), 30; original emphasis.

21. Jackie Robinson, *I Never Had It Made: The Autobiography of Jackie Robinson* (Hopewell, NJ: Ecco Press, 1995), 78.

22. For a first, and what now feels like a preliminary, elucidation of the "burden of over-representation," see Grant Farred, *What's My Name? Black Vernacular Intellectuals* (Minneapolis: University of Minnesota Press, 2003), 177–179.

23. As quoted in Tygiel, *Baseball's Great Experiment*, 72.

24. The city of Boston has a notorious history in sport and race. The Red Sox passed on a number of black players, Robinson included, before signing Green. In fact, the city's National Hockey League (NHL) franchise, the Bruins, signed a black player, Willie O'Ree, a year before the Red Sox signed Green. The NHL is hardly renowned as a sport either hospitable to or popular with the black population in the United States. The Bruins' signing of O'Ree is an even greater indictment of the Red Sox, in no small measure because O'Ree was the first black player signed to an NHL team, earning him the sobriquet the "Jackie Robinson" of the NHL. In April 1945, Robinson, Sam Jethroe (outfielder, Cleveland Buckeyes), and Marvin (infielder, Philadelphia Stars) were given a summary tryout with the Red Sox. The three Negro League players never heard from the Red Sox again. The black players the Red Sox passed up, after having scouted them, includes an array of stars. In addition to Robinson, the team declined to pursue "Satchel" Paige, Ernie Banks, Willie Mays, Don Newcombe, Hank Aaron, and Frank Robinson. In October 1974, Frank Robinson became the first black manager in MLB, when the Cleveland Indians appointed him as their skipper.

25. As quoted in Tygiel, *Baseball's Great Experiment*, 72.

26. Judith Butler, *Giving an Account of Oneself* (New York: Fordham University Press, 2005), 17, 8. In *Zami: A New Spelling of My Name* (Watertown, MA: Sheba Feminist Publishers, 1982), Audre Lorde posits the notion of a "biomythography," a concept that insists that there can be an account of the individual subject without including an entire community.

27. In *What's My Name?* I discuss Ali and, to a lesser extent, Johnson as figures of transgression in this regard. In fact, part of Ali's allure derived from his conversion to the Nation of Islam (a highly controversial decision); his refusal to subscribe to the political terms of the civil rights campaign, where a certain Du Boisian discourse of black bourgeois respectability obtained; and, as a matter of socio-political comparison, his complete disregard for the model of black athletic humility for which Joe Louis was held in high esteem by the dominant media.

28. See Michel Foucault, "Part 5: Right of Death and Power over Life," in *Introduction*, vol. 1 of *The History of Sexuality*, translated by Robert Hurley (New York: Vintage Books, 1990).

29. Butler, *Giving an Account of Oneself*, 85.

30. Kahn, *The Boys of Summer*, 44.

31. Arnold Rampersad, *Jackie Robinson: A Biography* (New York: Alfred A. Knopf, 1997), 164. Rampersad also notes that there were three white southerners, including, most famously, Pee Wee Reese (a Louisville, Kentucky, native), who did not sign the petition to bar Robinson from the Dodgers. The other two were Eddie Stanky (who was born in Philadelphia but attended college in Alabama) and Pete Reiser (Missouri). For a brief explanation of the three southern players' reasons for refusing to sign the petition, see ibid., 164. Harold Henry Reese, the Dodgers' captain, was the first player to publicly show his friendship to Robinson, in a 1947 game against the Cincinnati Reds. When Robinson faced horrendous racist attacks from spectators in the stands of the Reds' Crosley Park stadium, Reese, in a show of defiance and solidarity with his teammate, famously walked over to Robinson during pregame drills and draped his arms around him. Stanky later came on board in a game against Philadelphia, when he responded to the racist taunting by the Philadelphia manager, Ben Chapman, a man whose racial antipathy was widely known.

32. And, as we now know, though it has long been forgotten by history, before there was Jackie Robinson, and more than a century before Parks, the black schoolteacher Elizabeth Jennings caused consternation when she claimed her right to ride a New York streetcar on July 16, 1854. Like Parks, Jennings was a respectable, church-going member of her community. In fact, she was an organist in her church; Jennings and her family were part of the New York black bourgeoisie, a family that included abolitionist preachers and businesspeople. See http://www.nytimes.com/2005/11/13/nyregion/thecity/the-schoolteacher-on-the-streetcar.html.

33. Rampersad, *Jackie Robinson*, 99.

34. Ibid., 90.

35. Because of segregation in the army, Robinson was not allowed to play on the all-white Fort Riley baseball team. There was no black Fort Riley team. One of the players on that all-white team, Pete Reiser, would later be one of Robinson's Dodgers teammates.

36. Twelve years prior to the event, Blake had denied Parks entry onto the bus he was driving unless she used the back door. Parks had sworn that she would never again ride on a bus that Blake was driving.

37. I address the Parks event in greater detail in the first chapter (on Ron Artest) of Grant Farred, *In Motion, At Rest: The Event of the Black Athletic Body* (Minneapolis: University of Minnesota Press, 2013).

38. Rampersad, *Jackie Robinson*, 102.

39. Jules Tygiel, "The Court-Martial of Jackie Robinson," *American Heritage* 35, no. 5 (August/September 1984), available at http://www.americanheritage.com/articles/magazine/ah/1984/5/1984.

40. Rampersad's terms are even more stark: "Contrary to fact, the legend of Robinson as a violent man continued to grow" (Rampersad, *Jackie Robinson*, 109).

41. William Shakespeare, *Othello,* edited by Kim F. Hall (Boston: Bedford/St. Martin's, 2007), act 1, sc. 1.

42. Quoted in Kahn, *The Boys of Summer,* 108.

43. Shakespeare, *Othello,* act 3, sc. 3.

44. Foucault, *The Use of Pleasure,* 27; original emphasis.

45. In this regard, we might consider Martin Luther King Jr.'s invocation of St. Augustine in his "Letter from Birmingham Jail": "An unjust law is no law at all." In his "Letter," King makes his case for the "morality" of nonviolence as a political strategy against precisely such laws. See http://kingencyclopedia.stanford.edu/kingweb/popular_requests/frequentdocs/birmingham.pdf.

46. Friedrich Nietzsche, *On the Genealogy of Morals*, translated by Walter Kaufmann and R. J. Hollingdale (New York: Vintage, 1969), 88.

47. Ibid; original emphasis.

48. According to Marian Hobson, Derrida considers *Glas* a "'Menippean satire'" (Marian Hobson, *Jacques Derrida: Opening Lines* [New York: Routledge, 1998], 2). A "Menippean satire" generally assumes the structure of a novel, and its point of critique is a mental attitude. (In classical mythology, Menippe is the daughter of Orion. She and her sister Metiche offered themselves as sacrifices to end the plague in Boeotia.)

49. Jacques Derrida, *Glas*, translated by John P. Leavy Jr. and Richard Rand (Lincoln: University of Nebraska Press, 1990), 42.

50. Ibid., 3.

51. Nietzsche, *On the Genealogy of Morals.*

52. Ibid., 89.

53. Ibid., 65.

54. Derrida, *Glas,* 39.

55. Nietzsche, *On the Genealogy of Morals,* 65.

56. Ibid. Even, that is, if we assign a functional definition whereby "moral" signals a commitment to a code of conduct that is based on the distinction between right and wrong and also pledges fealty to truth, we cannot but think the "immoral" if relations between self and other begin from the premise of the "will to self-maltreatment."

57. Ibid., 57, 88; original emphasis.

58. Ibid., 65.

59. Ibid., 59; original emphasis.

60. Ibid.; original emphasis.

61. This term is borrowed from Fredric Jameson's *The Hegel Variations: On the Phenomenology of Spirit*. The Jameson term is preferred to, say, the more modern German *postulieren*, because Hegel's term, which, according to Jameson, is probably derived from Fichte, from his moment to ours (which leads through a figure such as Gadamer), is felicitous to thinking as such. In this regard, see Fredric Jameson, "Idealism," in *The Hegel Variations: On the Phenomenology of Spirit* (New York: Verso, 2010), chap. 3.

62. See, among other works, Rick Swaine's critique of the exclusion of black players in *The Integration of Major League Baseball: A Team by Team History* (Jefferson, NC: McFarland, 2009).

63. Kahn, *The Boys of Summer,* 302.

64. Nietzsche, *On the Genealogy of Morals*, 60.

65. Kahn, *The Boys of Summer*, 402.

66. Ibid., 396.

67. Nietzsche, *On the Genealogy of Morals*, 60.

68. Kahn, *The Boys of Summer*, 404.

69. Following Derrida's argument in *Rogues*, we say that all states—that is, all nation-states—act, in one instance or another, as "rogue states" (Jacques Derrida, *Rogues: Two Essays on Reason*, translated by Pascale-Anne Brault and Michael Naas [Stanford, CA: Stanford University Press, 2005]). That is, every state transgresses the norms of international law, every state, at some juncture, "goes rogue." Some states, of course, are more apt to act as "rogue states" than others. Derrida critiques the *état voyou* in the wake of the September 11 attacks, especially as a response to the ways in which the U.S. government designated its foes the "Axis of Evil." Entirely unaware, in that speaking, of its own multiple aggressions—military adventurism, Cold War intrigue, interference in the affairs of other sovereign states from Iran (overthrowing Mohammad Mossadegh in 1953) to Zaire (supporting the assassination of Patrice Lumumba). It's a long list, of course, but the main point is that the United States is by no means exceptional in its capacity to behave as an *état voyou*.

70. See, in this regard, Nancy's *Hegel: The Restlessness of the Negative*, translated by Jason Smith and Steven Miller (Minneapolis: University of Minnesota Press, 2002).

71. Nietzsche, *On the Genealogy of Morals*, 60.

72. Ibid.

73. Quoted in Kahn, *The Boys of Summer*, 106.

74. Ibid.

75. Ibid., 108.

76. Ibid., 107.

77. Ibid.

78. Shakespeare, *Othello,* act 3, sc. 3.

79. Abdelkebir Khatibi, *Love in Two Languages*, translated by Richard Howard (Minneapolis: University of Minnesota Press, 1990), 3.

80. King, "Letter from Birmingham Jail."

81. Jacques Derrida, *Without Alibi*, translated by Peggy Kamuf (Stanford, CA: Stanford University Press, 2002), 13.

82. King, "Letter from Birmingham Jail."

83. See, in this regard, Peggy Kamuf's critique of resistance in her introduction to Derrida's *Without Alibi*.

84. In *Politics of Friendship* (translated by George Collins [New York: Verso, 1997], 83), Jacques Derrida reminds us of this when he issues a warning about what might follow the "loss" of the enemy: "The loss of the enemy would not necessarily be progress, reconciliation or the opening of an era of peace and human fraternity. It could be worse: an unheard-of violence, the evil of a malice knowing neither measure nor ground, an unleashing incommensurable in its unprecedented—therefore monstrous—forms; a violence in the face of which what is called hostility, war, conflict, enmity, cruelty, even hatred, would regain reassuring and ultimately appeasing contours, because they would be *identifiable*." It is

impossible to read this indictment of what-might-be and not be moved to reflect on the violence, on the condition, that Derrida describes here and not be provoked to remark on how Derrida appears to have made, once again, once again to our regret, our shame, and our deep disillusionment, the postcolonial condition "identifiable." The postcolonial presents an ethical problem not because it has assumed, assumes, an "unprecedented form" but rather because it is wholly familiar. It has long since been "identified," for all the wrong historical and political reasons, as that which must be struggled against. This is, for its bleakness, once again a moment of Derridean politics because, as Derrida has long insisted, politics—no matter what is or what is *l'avenir*—must always be taken up, again, "as if for the first time."

85. Frantz Fanon, *The Wretched of the Earth*, translated by Richard Philcox (New York: Grove Press, 2004), 17.

86. Derrida, *Politics of Friendship*, 31.

87. Ibid., ix, original emphasis.

88. See https://www.azlyrics.com/lyrics/bettywright/tonightisthenight.html.

89. Kahn, *The Boys of Summer*, 394.

90. Fanon, *Wretched of the Earth*, 161.

91. This is a variation on Nietzsche's "Greek ideal of *agon*—aggressive competition contained within ultimately cooperative bounds," to borrow a phrase from Nietzsche biographer Julian Young (Julian Young, *Friedrich Nietzsche: A Philosophical Biography* [Cambridge: Cambridge University Press, 2010], 16). In order to work "cooperatively," to stake claims to Jackie Robinson, to make evident (reveal) Robinson the Nietzschean figure, the process must begin from—or it must in that critical moment submit to—the premise that a certain antagonism ("aggressive competition") between the black subject and the mode of critique he is being subjected to is constitutive of this undertaking. Etymologically, *agon* signals the prize awarded in athletics and the arts (music, poetry, drama, painting), and, as such, Jackie Robinson, the "Nietzschean figure," is the "prize" for engaging the figure of MLB integration in a mode entirely unanticipated by both philosopher and baseball player.

92. C.L.R. James, *Beyond a Boundary* (New York: Pantheon Books, 1983), 99.

93. Shakespeare, *Othello*, act 1, sc. 1.

94. Jacques Derrida, *The Politics of Friendship*, translated by George Collins (New York: Verso, 2005), ix.

95. Frantz Fanon, *Black Skin, White Masks*, translated by Charles Lam Markmann (New York: Grove Weidenfeld, 1982), 109.

96. Fanon, *Wretched of the Earth*, 158.

97. Jacques Derrida, *Of Hospitality*, translated by Rachel Bowlby (Stanford, CA: Stanford University Press, 2000), 40.

98. There is a Fanonian echo here. The very last line of *Black Skin, White Masks* is a memorable one because it seems of a philosophical piece with Derrida's call for the "question of the future," the question come from the future. At the end of his text, Fanon offers a plea that resonates, if only because of its address to the infinite future that can be made only as a question, that can take only the form of a question: "My final prayer: O my body, make of me always a man who questions!" (Fanon, *Black Skin, White Masks*, 232).

99. Eric Cheyfitz, personal communication. Printed with permission from the author.

100. Kahn, *The Boys of Summer,* 357. Robinson and Campanella's was not always, as Kahn points out in *The Boys of Summer,* a politically strained relationship. Neither were Robinson and Campanella unrelentingly critical of each other. Rather, they were different (black) men—men who had emerged from different situations, had different interests (Campanella liked to visit aquariums in cities such as Chicago; Robinson liked to play the horses), and had different groups of friends in the Dodgers' clubhouse (Robinson was close to Reese and Gil Hodges)—and, most importantly, they viewed the politics of race in distinct ways. They were also competitors, two black men at the forefront of the Dodgers' integration movement. In their own way, they were friends. And theirs bore the hallmark of what Deleuze and Guattari understand as friendship: "Friendship would then involve competitive distrust of the rival as much as amorous striving toward the object of desire" (Gilles Deleuze and Félix Guattari, *What Is Philosophy?*, translated by Hugh Tomlinson and Graham Burchell [New York: Columbia University Press, 1994], 4). Robinson and Campanella inclined as much toward one another as they diverged from one another. It was a dialectic of the most complicated variety, made all the more so because of the historic moment in which they found themselves, the historic movement they were spearheading. After all, the nature of friendship has long proved both an unending lure for philosophers and too elusive to be pinned down by them. See, for example, Derrida's sustained preoccupation with the remark that is attributed to Aristotle, "O my friend, there is no friend," nowhere taken up more rigorously than in, as is appropriate, *The Politics of Friendship.*

101. Cheyfitz, personal communication.

102. See http://tjrs.monticello.org/letter/100.

103. See Alexander Hamilton, *Federalist* No. 1, accessed at the Avalon Project, Lillian Goldman Law Library, Yale Law School, http://avalon.law.yale.edu/18th_century/fed01.asp.

104. It is, of course, precisely this discourse that is at the fundament of the reparations movement, a movement given new impetus by the "discovery" in 2016 of the sale of 272 slaves in 1838 to save Georgetown University from financial ruin. See "Coming to Terms with Georgetown's Legacy of Slavery," *Washington Post,* April 20, 2016, https://www.washingtonpost.com/opinions/coming-to-terms-with-georgetowns-legacy-of-slavery/2016/04/20/b0bc8b6a-066d-11e6-bdcb-0133da18418d_story.html?utm_term=.272688d8f852.

105. Shakespeare, *Othello,* act 3, sc. 3.

CHAPTER 2

1. Gilles Deleuze, *The Logic of Sense,* translated by Mark Lester with Charles Stivale (New York: Columbia University Press, 1990), 52. In addition to thinking the "singular" in the terms offered by Deleuze, in this project the singular is proposed as a singular moment of triumph, a moment of singular triumph; the singular, moreover, is properly understood as that moment or encounter that cannot be replicated or repeated that, nonetheless, contains within itself something other

than the singularity of the moment itself. The singular is utterly itself, belongs to only itself inasmuch as it can never fully belong to only itself. The singular as such, belongs to history, or, as Deleuze would rightly insist, the singular point in the "series" leads to an encounter with another "singular point," both (or however many of them) would—finally—cohere in the "Event," capitalized by Deleuze.

2. This is, of course, another of the monikers, the "Land of the silver fern," by which New Zealand is known.

3. John Carlin, "How Nelson Mandela Won the Rugby World Cup," *The Telegraph*, October 19, 2007.

4. A "scrum" takes place after a play stoppage, when one side has been penalized for a transgression. In the "scrum" the two packs of forwards line up against each other, with the scrumhalf of the "non-offending" side "putting" the ball into the scrum; the ball is, in general, worked back to the side that has "put" the ball into the scrum ("scrum," that is, as a moment of possession of the ball). A "loose scrum" develops when there is no transgression; it results from contact (often deliberately set up to retain possession and to force a territorial advantage—to advance the ball toward the opponents' goal line) between players. The "loose scrum" produces a series of drives also known, broadly speaking, as "rucks" and "mauls."

5. Martin Heidegger, *Was Heißt Denken?*, translated by Fred D. Wieck and J. Glenn Gray (New York: Harper and Row, 1968), 143.

6. It would be more accurate to say, in Afrikaans, "*Om te dink is te dank; om te dank is te dink*"—"To think is to thank; to thank is to think."

7. Heidegger, *Was Heißt Denken?*

8. Deleuze, *The Logic of Sense*, 74.

9. In Hegel's discussion about "experience" as a "retrospective effect," to coin a term, that is apropos of how we might understand the event of Pienaar and Mandela, "we learn by experience that we meant something other than what we meant to mean; and this correction to our meaning compels our knowing to go back to the proposition, and understand [*fassen*] it in some other way (Georg Wilhelm Friedrich Hegel, *Phenomenology of Spirit*, translated by A. V. Miller [Oxford: Oxford University Press, 1977], 39). To cast this in the terms of *The Burden of Over-representation*, the (original) "proposition" is (for Pienaar) the "experience" of apartheid, of being, to invoke this pun deliberately, on its "right" side. This is the "experience" that Pienaar's "No, Thank you" negates, making it necessary to produce a new "proposition." In this way negation is the proposition—the propagation—of that "experience" (the experience *l'avenir*) that makes the new proposition politically legible. The *Grund* of the new proposition is simultaneously hostile to and familiar with (and, as such, absolutely necessary to) the reason for the coming into being of the new proposition. The new proposition is at once the negation of and the inexorable fulfillment of the terms of the "original" proposition.

10. Fredric Jameson, *Representing Capital: A Reading of Volume One* (New York: Verso, 2011), 23.

11. In his well-known essay on apartheid, Derrida designates this South African term as "Racism's Last Word" (Jacques Derrida, "Racism's Last Word," translated by Peggy Kamuf, *Critical Inquiry* 12 [Autumn 1985]).

12. Fredric Jameson, *The Political Unconscious: Narrative as a Socially Symbolic Act* (Ithaca, NY: Cornell University Press, 1981), 9. Jameson's injunction, apropos of this discussion, takes up the project of the "historical origins of the things themselves and that more intangible historicity of the concepts and categories by which we attempt to understand those things" (ibid.). In its own way, this undertaking is extended in *Representing Capital* through the concept of "synchronicity through temporality": the intent is to make "tangible" the "historicity of the concepts and categories" by which, in this case, the predominant discourse, reconciliation, is understood.

13. Jameson, *Representing Capital,* 45.

14. Deleuze, *The Logic of Sense,* 89; original emphasis.

15. Jean-Luc Nancy, *Hegel: The Restlessness of the Negative*, translated by Jason E. Smith and Stephen Miller (Minneapolis: University of Minnesota Press, 2002).

16. Slavoj Žižek, *Tarrying with the Negative: Kant, Hegel and the Critique of Ideology* (Durham, NC: Duke University Press, 1993).

17. Jameson, *Representing Capital,* 45.

18. In *Postmodernism, or, the Cultural Logic of Late Capitalism*, Jameson—as part of a discussion of Andy Warhol's "Diamond Dust Shoes"—describes the "ideal schizophrenic" as that subject "easy enough to please provided only an eternal present is thrust before the eyes" (Frederic Jameson, *Postmodernism, or, the Cultural Logic of Late Capitalism* [Durham, NC: Duke University Press, 1991], 10). There is, in this regard, something of the "ideal schizophrenic" about the discourse—and the day-to-day politics, the everyday political articulations that held sway in post–February 1990 South Africa. It is not so much that the apartheid past was denied or refused, but rather that the euphoria of the moment, the lack of critique, elevated the moment to that which recalls the desire for an "eternal present," the "eternal present" of, that is, the moment after. The moment after, after apartheid, is knowable as postapartheid, but as such is a name that cannot fully—cannot even begin to—express the desire holding onto, with a historic fierceness, that moment after, the moment that must neither be lost to history nor succeeded, again, by history. This is, of course, a critique that demands further attention, an undertaking that is beyond the scope of this book.

19. Deleuze, *The Logic of Sense,* 54.

20. Ibid., 5.

21. Ibid.

22. Ibid., 8.

23. Jacques Derrida, *The Animal That Therefore I Am*, translated by David Wills (New York: Fordham University Press, 2008), 27; original emphasis.

24. Ibid.; original emphasis.

25. Jacques Derrida, *The Gift of Death*, translated by David Wills (Chicago: University of Chicago Press, 1996), 2.

26. Matthew 25:35, in *The New Oxford Annotated Bible,* edited by Michael D. Coogan (New York: Oxford University Press, 2010)

27. See Dire Straits performing live during the "Brothers in Arms" tour at Wembley Arena in London, available at https://www.youtube.com/watch?v=uUIrGp1H1pA.

28. John 3:16, *The New Oxford Annotated Bible.*

29. Derrida, *The Gift of Death*, 3.

30. Ibid., 86; the phrase is a composite term, summarizing Derrida's argument.

31. This national designation, the blues as "American," is, of course, misleading insofar as many British musicians, from the Rolling Stones (who borrowed openly from the blues when many of their rock contemporaries in the United States were chary of acknowledging their debt to the genre) to the Beatles and Eric Clapton, were equally influenced by the tradition.

32. In this regard, Derrida's notion of the "polylogue—many voices in conversation" is a useful way of thinking about the several registers of in/action, resistance/endurance (to pose them, for a moment, as dialectically related), "not-being-able"/"not-doing," that are in play in a critique of the burden of "passivity" (Derrida, *The Gift of Death*, 5).

33. Ibid., 28.

34. Žižek, *Tarrying with the Negative*.

35. See, for example, Hebrews 13:2 and Leviticus 25:45, *The New Oxford Annotated Bible*.

36. "Sense of the world" constitutes the title of Nancy's book (Jean-Luc Nancy, *The Sense of the World*, translated by Jeffrey S. Librett [Minneapolis: University of Minnesota Press, 1997]). Quote appears on page 3.

37. Ibid.

38. Jean-Luc Nancy, *The Speculative Remark: (One of Hegel's Bon Mots)*, translated by Céline Surprenant (Stanford, CA: Stanford University Press, 2002), 11.

39. The trophy awarded to the winning team was named after William Webb-Ellis, who invented the game of rugby football, as it is properly known, on the playing fields of the English boarding school of the same name, circa 1823.

40. Deleuze, it must be said, allows for the possibility—so constitutive of the event—that Pienaar's act might not entirely know itself. (It is, of course, impossible for the event to know itself as in the "present," as Deleuze insists.) And so, for Deleuze, "personal uncertainty is not a doubt foreign to what is happening, but rather an objective structure of the event itself insofar as it moves in two directions at once, and insofar as it fragments the subject following this double direction" (Deleuze, *The Logic of Sense*, 3). It is precisely Pienaar's not knowing, or not-yet knowing, that makes the event possible, so that his "uncertainty"—however much or little of it exists—is not an impediment to the event but already, a priori, "structured" into the event. The event, we might say, is that "happening" that emerges out of "uncertainty."

41. Ibid., 88.

42. In the invocation of the scriptural, it is in this regard that it is worth recalling Emmanuel Levinas's argument that religion provides the "ultimate structure" for thinking the relation between "same and other" (which demands the turn to "Whole" and, of course, "Infinity")—that is, for how we think the conditions that gird the relation to the world (Emmanuel Levinas, *Totality and Infinity*, translated by Alphonso Lingus [Pittsburgh, PA: Dusquesne University Press, 2005], 80).

43. Deleuze, *The Logic of Sense*, 53; original emphasis.

44. Ibid., 69; original emphasis.

45. Ibid., 49.

46. Ibid., 34.

47. Ibid., 8.

48. For further elaboration of the work that only a "minor literature" can do, see Gilles Deleuze, *Kafka: Toward a Minor Literature*, translated by Dana Polan (Minneapolis: University of Minnesota Press, 1986).

49. Nancy, *The Sense of the World*, 2.

50. Jacques Derrida, *Without Alibi*, translated by Peggy Kamuf (Stanford, CA: Stanford University Press, 2002), xxviii; original emphasis.

51. Ibid.

52. Ibid., xxvii.

53. There is always, in any declaration of (self-)worthiness as offered by Wayne, more than a smidgeon of the confessional. In fact, we might say that declaring the self to be "not worthy" is a way of ensuring that we do not arrive at the truth— at the truth of the matter, at the heart of the matter. Instead, and this does not apply (exactly) to Pienaar, what the confession privileges—and raises to the level of discourse—is the performative so that it is the act itself, the speaking (whether through rote intonation or not); the practice (in the sense that it is both "liturgical" and the outcome of repetition) is what matters, rather than, so to speak, the "substance" of the address. See, in this regard, Derrida's essays in his collection *Without Alibi*: "The History of the Lie," "Le Parjure, *Perhaps*," and "Typewriter Ribbon"—especially the essays on Augustine and Rousseau.

54. Derrida's exact phrasing, offered in a critique of the "un-naturalness" of "citizenship," is this: "The withdrawal of French citizenship from the Jews of Algeria, with everything that followed, was the deed of the French alone. They decided that all by themselves, in their heads; they must have been dreaming about it all along" (Jacques Derrida, *The Monolingualism of the Other; Or, the Prosthetics of Origin*, translated by Patrick Mensah [Stanford, CA: Stanford University Press, 1998], 16).

55. In her introduction to Derrida's *Without Alibi*, Peggy Kamuf raises the issue of "resistance" in a way that resonates with Pienaar's negation. "But why anticipate, why call up resistance?" Kamuf asks. "It's a familiar tactic[;] we've all used it many times—to respond in advance to imagined or anticipated objections, as if one could conquer the other's resistance before it has even had a chance to manifest itself" (Kamuf, "Introduction," 7). The effect of "resistance" so rendered seeks to foreclose critique—through "anticipation"—by preparing itself for that strand of thinking within it that is likely to raise "objections." Most important, however, is Kamuf's intimation that such "anticipation" serves the function of "conquering the other's resistance"—that is, ensuring that the other's word is either proscribed, from the beginning (thereby de-limiting what the other can give voice to, what the other can argue, how the other can argue), or denied outright (leaving the other without voice, speechless, as it were). There is, as the inevitable consequence of the combination of Pienaar's negation and the demands of propriety of the moment, a distinct element of "denying," so to speak, Mandela his right, the right, to the possibility of Kamufian "resistance."

56. Jacques Derrida, "Paul de Man's War," translated by Peggy Kamuf, *Critical Inquiry* 14 (1988): 594; original emphasis.

57. There is a tradition in *lettres de l'Afrikaner* that addresses the issue of a *volk* "at war" with itself. This tradition includes the writings of, among others, Eugène

Marais, N. P. van Wyk Louw, Ingrid Jonker, Beyers Naudé, Breyten Breytenbach, David Kramer, Menan du Plessis, and J. M. Coetzee.

58. Derrida, *The Gift of Death*, 27.

59. Ibid., 68.

60. Ibid., 44.

61. Ibid., 46; original emphasis.

62. Ibid., 43.

63. See Alain Badiou, *Ethics: An Essay on the Understanding of Evil*, translated by Peter Hallward (London: Verso, 2002).

64. Derrida, *The Gift of Death*, 66.

65. Ibid., 67.

66. Levinas, *Totality and Infinity*, 80.

67. The politics of forgiveness, what it means to forgive, who has the "power" and the right to forgive, and what is unforgivable, is a difficulty that haunts this book. I address the difficulty only schematically here, not out of an effort to avoid it, but (such is the nature of the writing project) in order to maintain something of the thread of an argument intact. I do so, regrettably, at the expense of treating forgiveness more fully. However, Derrida's work, again, is what most informs the haunting, especially an interview ("On Forgiveness: A Roundtable Discussion with Jacques Derrida," moderated by Richard Kearney) and an essay ("To Forgive: The Unforgivable and the Imprescriptible") in Jacques Derrida, *Questioning God*, edited by John D. Caputo, Mark Dooley, and Michael J. Scanlon (Bloomington: Indiana University Press, 2001). In his essay Derrida raises the issue of the death camps, animals, and, as it pertains to the "imprescriptible," the work of Vladimir Jankélévitch – for Derrida a thinker critical to understanding the infinite possibilities of forgiveness, or, the possibility of infinite forgiveness.

68. Friedrich Nietzsche, *Thus Spoke Zarathustra*, translated by Graham Parkes (New York: Oxford University Press, 2005), 41.

69. Galatians 6:7, *The New Oxford Annotated Bible*.

70. Isaiah 2:4, *The New Oxford Annotated Bible*.

71. Derrida, *The Gift of Death*, 41.

72. Quoted in John Carlin, "One Team, One Country," *Observer Sport Monthly*, October 5, 2003.

73. Ibid.

74. The New Zealand captain that day, Sean Fitzpatrick, recalls the feeling of being up against an entire, unified nation rather than just fifteen players: "To see him walking into the stadium with Francois' jersey on, and to hear 72,000 people start chanting Mandela, Mandela. . . . Then there's 15 of us there looking, thinking 'God, how are we ever going to beat these buggers!'" The late Joost van der Westhuizen, South African scrumhalf, remembers: "I think the best thing was to see him in a Springbok jersey[;] that was the best thing for us—it was a total surprise. Then we realised that the whole country is behind us, and for this man to wear a Springbok jersey was a sign, not just for us, but for the whole of South Africa, that we have to unite, and we have to unite today." Quoted in "From the Archives: History of Sport—South Africa Emerges from Its Dark Past," *SportsPro*, December 6, 2013, available at http://www.sportspromedia.com/notes_and_insights/ashes_hero_doliveira_and_the_battle_against_racism_in_cricket/.

75. Quoted in Carlin, "One Team, One Country."

76. Ibid.

77. Ibid.

78. Giovanna Borradori, ed., *Philosophy in a Time of Terror: Dialogues with Jürgen Habermas and Jacques Derrida* (Chicago: University of Chicago Press, 2003), 94.

79. Among a certain generation that came of age in the twenty-first century, the term "frenemy" is used to describe that odd relationship where the other is neither friend nor enemy but is, in an entirely irresolvable, dialectical way, both. There is something distinctly Nietzschean about the term, even if such philosophical *Grund* might be strenuously denied—or not.

80. Nietzsche, *Thus Spoke Zarathustra*, 36.

81. During apartheid, it was common for the disenfranchised to root against the Springboks. One of the key political decisions Mandela made early in his tenure as president was to oppose the proposal to drop the moniker "Springbok" in favor of the "Proteas" (a local flower unique to South Africa's Western Cape region). The reason was that Mandela both recognized the importance of the sobriquet to Afrikaners and, in the difficult moment of transition to black majority rule, wanted to offer the retention of the name as a gesture of goodwill to the new political minority.

82. Nietzsche, *Thus Spoke Zarathustra*, 32.

83. Derrida, *The Gift of Death*, 51.

84. Ibid., 26; original emphasis.

CHAPTER 3

1. Jacques Derrida, *Without Alibi*, translated by Peggy Kamuf (Stanford, CA: Stanford University Press, 2002), xxxiv.

2. Jacques Derrida, as quoted in Benoît Peeters, *Derrida: A Biography* (Malden, MA: Polity Press, 2013), 345.

3. Jacques Derrida, *Specters of Marx: The State of the Debt, the Work of Mourning, and the New International*, translated by Peggy Kamuf (New York: Routledge, 1994), xv.

4. Peeters, *Derrida*, 433.

5. Ibid., 93.

6. Ellis Park was transformed, temporarily, into a football ground for the duration of the 2010 World Cup, in part because of its centrality and its superior facilities. In Cape Town, the existing stadiums, Athlone and Green Point, were upgraded to host matches.

7. This essay was republished in *Critical Inquiry* 12 (1985).

8. Peeters, *Derrida*, 123.

9. See Jacques Derrida and Geoffrey Bennington, *Jacques Derrida*, translated by Geoffrey Bennington (Chicago: University of Chicago Press, 1995).

10. I posit Augustine as an African thinker in my essay "'Denn keener trägt das Leben allein': The Thought of St. Augustine," *South Atlantic Quarterly* 109, no. 2 (Spring 2010). See also Jacques Derrida, "Typewriter Ribbon: Limited Ink (2)," in *Without Alibi*, translated by Peggy Kamuf (Stanford, CA: Stanford University Press, 2002).

11. Jacques Derrida, *Of Spirit: Heidegger and the Question*, translated by Geoffrey Bennington and Rachel Bowlby (Chicago: University of Chicago Press, 1991), 1.

12. See Marin Heidegger, "The Self-Assertion of the German University," http://la.utexas.edu/users/hcleaver/330T/350kPEEHeideggerSelf-Assertion.pdf; Jacques Derrida, *Sovereignties in Question: The Poetics of Paul Celan*, translated by Thomas Dutoit (New York: Fordham University Press, 2005.)

13. In *Beyond a Boundary* (New York: Pantheon Books, 1983), C.L.R. James uses this phrase in relation to a black cricketer, Learie Constantine, and one of the white members of the West Indian cricket establishment, H.B.G. Austin, who was crucial to the promotion of young Learie's career. Constantine, James says, appreciated Austin's support, but, for all that, in James's wonderful phrase, "he saw him whole." (See the chapter "One Man in His Time: Prince and Pauper" in which James reflects on Constantine's career and the Trinidadian club, Shannon, that produced him.)

14. Victor Farías, *Heidegger and Nazism*, translated by Paul Burrell, with the advice of Dominic Di Bernardi (Philadelphia: Temple University Press, 1989). A chapter in *Derrida*, Peeters's biography, is dedicated to the "affairs" of Heidegger and de Man. Derrida was especially vulnerable to the charges in *Heidegger and Nazism* precisely because he turned so often, with such regularity, to Heidegger's work—so much so that much of the criticism that erupted in France after Farías's book was published was accompanied by sloganeering aimed at those French intellectuals who acknowledged the fundamental importance of Heidegger's work. Phrases such as "Heil Heidegger!" and "Heideggerians of Paris" gained, for a moment, a certain pejorative resonance (Peeters, *Derrida*, 380).

15. Peeters, *Derrida*, 382.

16. Ibid., 385; original emphasis.

17. Heidegger, *Was Heißt Denken?*, 15.

18. Derrida, *Specters of Marx*, xx.

19. Derrida, *Without Alibi*, xvii; original emphasis.

20. Ibid.

21. In his work *Ex Captivitate Salus*, Carl Schmitt is at pains to register his disagreements with Stirner, except for *The Ego and Its Own*. For Schmitt, Stirner's "verbal aphorisms are unbearable . . . his cigar-smoking, basement-bar bohemian lifestyle . . . is disgusting. But Max knows something important. He knows that the *I* is no object of thought" (Carl Schmitt, *Ex Captivitate Salus*, translated by Matthew Hannah [Cambridge, UK: Polity Press, 2017], 65). Carl Schmitt, then, as a philosopher who stands critically opposed to the self-indulgent "I."

22. Derrida, *Specters of Marx*, xv.

23. Ibid., xvii.

24. In this regard it seems worth recalling the way Henri Curiel, an Egyptian Jew who was a key figure in the founding of both the Egyptian and Sudanese Communist movements, found himself most politically effective, not on the streets of his beloved Paris but in his jail cell in Zaitoun, just outside of Cairo. "For many of his friends," his biographer Gilles Perault writes, "Henri Curiel was at his best in prison" (Gilles Perault, *A Man Apart: The Life of Henri Curiel*, translated by Bob Cumming [Atlantic Highlands, NJ: Zed Books, 1987], 84).

25. I am reminded here of a telling comment Stuart Hall once made. "I would rather," Hall remarked, "be politically right and theoretically wrong than be theoretically right and politically wrong." The thrust of Hall's argument was not to insist on a distinction between "politics" and "theory" but, I would insist, to recognize—although this would not have been the "theoretical" point girding Hall's argument—how politics is "subject to," at the mercy of, the event. See Stuart Hall, "The Great Moving Right Show," *Marxism Today* (January 1979): 14–20, http://banmarchive.org.uk/collections/mt/pdf/79_01_hall.pdf. See also Hall's *The Hard Road to Renewal: Thatcherism and the Crisis of the Left* (New York: Verso, 1988).

26. Derrida, *Specters of Marx*, xv.

27. See Leon Trotsky, *The Permanent Revolution and Results and Prospects* (New York: Pathfinder Press, 1978). In a series of essays dedicated to enshrining the proletariat as the dominant historical class, Trotsky's disappointment with the October Revolution is in itself a critique of the circumscription of the socialist project into a nationalist straitjacket: "The vicious baiting of the revolution serves, in turn, only to clear the ground for the theory of socialism in one country, that is, for the latest variety of nationalist socialism" (ibid., 159).

28. In thinking the in-exhaustibility of politics, it might be worth considering the notion of "generational bequest," the act of "handing over." This is distinct from the political abdication of political responsibility—which is, as Derrida insists, "infinite"—or a certain recusal from activism. It is, rather, to conduct politics in such a way as to at once embrace the responsibility of political "training"—to be inducted into activism and take on the work of inducting the next generation (where "generation" is understood not only chronologically but also in terms of political expertise and education) into politics—and be open to fulfilling a new and/or diminished role should the political conjuncture demand it.

29. Derrida, *Without Alibi*, xvi.

30. Heidegger, *Was Heißt Denken?*, 4.

31. Derrida, *Without Alibi*, xxxvi.

32. Ibid., xxi; original emphasis.

33. See the "Introduction" to Grant Farred, *In Motion, At Rest: The Event of the Athletic Body* (Minneapolis: University of Minnesota Press, 2013).

34. Derrida, *Specters of Marx*, 120.

35. Ibid., xv.

36. Ibid.

37. Ibid., 176.

38. In *Of Spirit: Heidegger and the Question*, we see Derrida extend his critique of Heidegger's privileging of that which comes from the self—we have focused on Heidegger's "impatience" with languages other than German and Greek—to what might be presumed, but not with any finality, to be a kind of "natural progression" of the dimension of language: an aversion to the other, to the other as foreigner. Derrida, unstinting in his critique, writes: "All of that, which accepts lie and destruction, is evil, the foreigner: foreign to spirit *in* spirit" (Jacques Derrida, *Of Spirit: Heidegger and the Question*, translated by Geoffrey Bennington and Rachel Bowlby [Chicago: University of Chicago Press, 1991], 63).

39. Inscribed in the very title of this text is the specter of death, a specter raised both through a play on technicality (through the art of photography) and

through the invocation of that other famous trope that is invoked here through "remains." "Still photography" captures, in the main, small, inanimate objects—as if, that is, to freeze them, to hold them in place—so that the "still" of Derrida's title evokes a kind of deathly, if beautiful, pose: life held in place, or kept alive, by technology. "Remains," of course, belongs very much to the language of death: that which is left over in the wake of cremation, what is "burnt"—or reduced—to its finest components, a figuring of death that Derrida takes up in *Cinders* (Jacques Derrida, *Cinders,* translated by Ned Lukacher [Minneapolis: University of Minnesota Press, 2014]); in *Cinders* Derrida thinks "cinders" in relation to, as intimately connected to, the trace.

40. Jacques Derrida, *Athens, Still Remains: The Photographs of Jean-François Bonhomme*, translated by Pascale-Anne Brault and Michael Naas (New York: Fordham University Press, 2010), 1.

41. Peeters, *Derrida,* 395.

42. Jacques Derrida, *The Gift of Death,* translated by David Wills (Chicago: Chicago University Press, 1996), 41.

43. In *The Gift of Death,* especially following the passage just quoted, Derrida engages in an extended critique of Heidegger's *Sein und Zeit,* turning on that memorable Heidegger phrase, "Keiner kann dem Anderen sein Sterben abnehmen" (No one can take the Other's dying away from him) (Derrida, *The Gift of Death,* 42). No one, in short, can die in the other's place. Our dying is, finally and irrefutably, ours.

44. William Shakespeare, *Hamlet,* edited by Harold Jenkins (New York: Methuen, 1982), act 1, sc. 1.

45. Ibid.

46. Ibid.

47. Ibid.

48. In this regard, see Derrida's *The Postcard: From Socrates to Freud and Beyond,* translated by Alan Bass (Chicago: University of Chicago Press, 1987).

49. Ibid.

50. Derrida, *Specters of Marx,* 8. This is an insight, of course, that is shared by Michel Foucault in his work on power—power's capacity to proliferate itself without presence, a mode of power that he introduces in Michel Foucault, *The Order of Things: An Archaeology of the Human Sciences* (New York: Vintage Books, 1973).

51. See Michel Foucault's *Discipline and Punish: the Birth of the Prison*, translated by Alan Sheridan (New York: Vintage Books, 1995).

52. Nowhere is the ubiquity of the sovereign more subjected to critique in the Foucault oeuvre than in *The Order of Things,* which turns on *Las Meninas,* a 1656 painting by Diego Velazquez, the leading painter of the Spanish Golden Age. In Foucault's rendering, the force of *Las Meninas* is that the king can, as represented in the painting, see everything, see everything from every angle.

53. Derrida, *Specters of Marx,* 8.

54. See Friedrich Engels and Karl Marx, *The Communist Manifesto* (New York: International Books, 2014).

55. Derrida, *Without Alibi,* xvii.

56. See Grant Farred, *What's My Name? Black Vernacular Intellectuals* (Minneapolis: University of Minnesota Press, 2003), in which I use Derrida's critique of

the *khora* to explicate "Clay's" adoption of "Ali." See also Jacques Derrida, *On the Name*, edited by Thomas Dutoit and translated by David Wood, John P. Levy Jr., and Ian McLeod (Stanford, CA: Stanford University Press, 1995).

57. "Applied Derrida: An Interview," August 12, 2002, available at www.hydra.umn.edu/derrida/applied.html.

58. Derrida, *Specters of Marx*, 126; original emphasis.

59. Ibid., 175.

60. Ibid., 164.

61. Ibid., 174.

62. Ibid.

63. Shakespeare, *Hamlet*, act 1., sc. 5.

64. In this regard see Derrida et al., *Ghostly Demarcations: A Symposium on Jacques Derrida's* Specters of Marx, edited by Michael Sprinker (New York: Verso, 2008), especially the essays by Antonio Negri ("The Specter's Smile") and Fredric Jameson (""Marx's Purloined Letter"). Neither Negri nor Jameson is convinced by Derrida's "appropriation" of Marx, but each offers his own insightful critique. In his response at the end of the Sprinker volume, "Marx and Sons," Derrida responds to both of them, although Derrida sympathizes more with Jameson's argument than with Negri's. Derrida's sharpest disagreements, however, might be said to be reserved for Aijaz Ahmad ("Reconciling Derrida") and Tom Lewis ("The Politics of 'Hauntology'"). (Derrida is also critical of Gayatri Spivak, who reflected on *Specters* in another venue. Derrida shows himself to have no patience with those who, like Spivak, are proprietary about Marx. "What will never cease to amaze me," Derrida writes, is the "jealous possessiveness of so many Marxists . . . the[ir] appropriation of an inheritance named 'Marx!'" (Derrida et al., *Ghostly Demarcations*, 222).

65. As pertains to this particular moment in Derrida's reflections on Marx, Derrida works very much in the spirit of Heidegger, especially Heidegger's essay "Bauen Wohnen Denken," "Building Dwelling Thinking" (Martin Heidegger, *Poetry, Language, Thought*, translated by Albert Hofstadter [New York: Harper and Row, 1971]). Derrida is most explicitly indebted to Heidegger when he invokes "earth and sky," which are famously part of the Heidegger "fourfold"—"earth, sky, man, gods" (Derrida, *Specters of Marx*, 174).

66. Here, of course, I am invoking Jameson from *Postmodernism, or, The Cultural Logic of Late Capitalism* (Durham, NC: Duke University Press, 1992).

67. In positing Marx as a "Marrano," Derrida is drawing on his comparison between Marx and Spinoza, the latter of whom was a Marrano. However, what is more striking in the Marx-Spinoza sequence is Derrida's acknowledgment of how he has both "secretly" and "openly presented" himself (openly) as a Marrano in works such as "*Aporias, Circumconfessions,* and *Archive Fever*—and, doubtless, elsewhere as well" and "less openly *everywhere*—for example, in *Le Monolinguisme de l'autre*" (Derrida, "Marx and Sons," 260).

68. Derrida, *Specters of Marx*, 105; original emphasis.

69. Derrida, *Without Alibi*, xv; original emphasis.

70. Derrida, "Marx and Sons," 213.

71. Derrida, *Specters of Marx*, 153.

72. Ibid., 175.

73. Ibid.

74. Shakespeare, *Hamlet*, act 1, sc. 5.

75. Matthew 26:39, in *The New Oxford Annotated Bible*, edited by Michael D. Coogan (New York: Oxford University Press, 2010).

76. Derrida, *Specters of Marx*, 3.

77. See ibid., 260nxvii. See also Peeters, *Derrida*, 503, which reiterates Derrida's argument for himself as a Marrano.

78. The relationship between psychoanalysis and Judaism occupies Derrida in several of his writings, from works such as *Forgiveness and Cosmpolitanism* to *Psyche: Inventions of the Other*, vol. 1, and many others. Nowhere, however, does Derrida think Freud, psychoanalysis, and Jewishness so deliberately as in *Archive Fever*, where the issue is addressed in a tone redolent with vulnerability. In an especially salient moment, Derrida tries to imagine how "radical evil can be of service," how "infinite destruction can be reinvested in a theodicy," and, in a tone that betrays an unmistakable pathos, how the "devil can also serve to *justify*— such is the destination of the Jew in the Aryan ideal" (Jacques Derrida, *Archive Fever*, translated by Eric Prenowitz, [Chicago: University of Chicago Press, 1996], 13; original emphasis).

79. Jacques Derrida, *The Other Heading: Reflections on Today's Europe*, translated by Pascale-Anne Brault and Michael Naas (Bloomington: Indiana University Press, 1992), 82.

80. I have in mind, of course, Frantz Fanon's critiques of colonization in *Les Damnés de la terre* (*The Wretched of the Earth*) and *Peau noire, masques blancs* (*Black Skin, White Masks*).

81. Derrida, *Specters of Marx*, xx; original emphasis.

82. "Belonging" as such is a question I take up in my forthcoming book, *Entre-nous: Between the World (Cup) and Me* (Durham, NC: Duke University Press).

83. Derrida, *Specters of Marx*, 83; original emphasis.

84. Derrida, *Specters of Marx*, 12.

85. Ibid., 5.

86. In *Cinders*, Derrida writes about the indestructibility of what remains. Derrida's phrase for this is *il y a là cendre*—"there are cinders there, cinders there are" (Derrida, *Cinders*, 3). In his rumination about death, that which remains, the trace, burning, among other things, Derrida writes, somewhat unexpectedly, about the "pyramids." "*The erection of the pyramid guards life—the dead—in order to give rise* [donner lieu] *to the for-(it)self of adoration*" (Derrida, *Cinders*, 28; original emphasis). Derrida, of course, is much occupied with death and dying, so that is not surprising that he raises this issue. However, what is salient is this brief reference to ancient Egyptian culture, a moment that by itself is hardly significant but that in light of this project, however truncated and seemingly out of place the moment is, serves to provoke yet one more thinking about the force of return—to Algeria, to North Africa, to the Maghreb—as a feature of Derrida late in his life.

87. See Grant Farred, "'Nostalgeria': Derrida, before and after Fanon," *South Atlantic Quarterly* 112, no. 1 (2013): 145–162.

88. Derrida, *Without Alibi*, xviii; original emphasis.

89. Ibid., xx; original emphasis.

90. In *On the Shores of Politics* (translated by Liz Heron [New York: Verso, 1995]), Jacques Rancière argues, very much in the spirit of Socrates, that all philosophy comes from the sea. As he puts it in the "Introduction," the "legend invariably has the political begin at one boundary or another, be it the Tiber or the Neva, and end up at another, be it Syracuse or the Kolyma: riverbanks of foundation, island shores of refoundation, abysses of horror or ruin" (Rancière, *On the Shores of Politics*, 1). It is because of this privileging of the sea that Rancière is so determined to situate philosophy "on land," as it were. He wants to argue against the preponderance of the sea.

91. Derrida, *Specters of Marx*, 112.

92. Ibid., 109.

93. Song of Solomon, 4:1–9, *The New Oxford Annotated Bible*.

94. Derrida, *Specters of Marx*, 75.

95. Ibid., 71.

96. Derrida, *Without Alibi*, xxii.

97. Chapter 3 of my *In Motion, At Rest* reads the event of (Zidane's) *coup de boule* through Derrida's philosophy.

98. Derrida, *Specters of Marx*, 110.

99. Derrida, *Without Alibi*, xvii.

Index

Grant Farred teaches at Cornell University. His most recent books include *Long Distance Love: A Passion for Football* (Temple); *Martin Heidegger Saved My Life*; and *In Motion, At Rest: The Event of the Athletic Body*.